Modern reality is a reality of decreation, in which our revelations are not the revelations of belief, but the precious portents of our own powers.

WALLACE STEVENS, *The Necessary Angel*

DICKINSON
the modern idiom

DAVID PORTER

HARVARD UNIVERSITY PRESS

CAMBRIDGE, MASSACHUSETTS, AND LONDON, ENGLAND 1981

Library of Congress Cataloging in Publication Data

Porter, David, 1928–
    Dickinson, the modern idiom.

    Includes bibliographical references and index.
    1. Dickinson, Emily, 1830–1886—Criticism and
interpretation. I. Title.
PS1541.Z5P626   811'.4   80-24322
ISBN 0-674-20444-1

To my sons
Tom, Dave, and Steve

Acknowledgments

Dickinson's poem "titles," that is, her first lines, appear here without identifying numbers since they can readily be found in my index of first lines and that in the variorum edition of the poems. Her idiosyncratic spelling and punctuation have been preserved, except in a few instances where they are excessively distracting.

For encouragement in the writing of this book and for criticism of the most rigorous kind, I am indebted to Richard Wilbur, R. W. B. Lewis, and Archibald MacLeish. Richard Sewall's splendid biography of the poet and equally splendid conversation aided me all along the way. My colleagues at the University of Massachusetts, Amherst, particularly Everett Emerson, Paul Mariani, and Jeremiah Allen, helped with wide-ranging counsel and administrative support. The conclusions drawn here, however, are entirely my own.

I benefited from professional and other kindnesses shown by the late Rebecca Patterson, Paul Kurt Ackermann and Ruth Lepson of *Boston University Journal,* the editors of *ESQ,* Dore Ashton, David Leeming, Randolph Parker and Nancy Newton, D. K. Adams, Brian Harding, Mark Bond-Webster, Ted Pearson, John Lindsay-Opie, Elémire Zolla, Cipriana Scelba, Luigi Filadoro, Franz H. Link, Vincent DiMarco, and Heinz Scheer.

My students at the University of Massachusetts and the dedicated guides at the Dickinson Homestead were willing listeners and critics of various parts of the manuscript, as were seminars and more general audiences at the universities of Connecticut, Massachusetts, Birmingham, Freiburg, Catania, Palermo, Genoa, and Rome; the David K. Bruce Center for American Studies at Keele; the King's School, Canterbury; and the International Dickinson Symposium convened in Amherst in 1980.

The staffs of the Library of the University of Massachusetts and the Robert Frost Library of Amherst College helped in every way possible. William B. Goodman encouraged the work from the beginning, and Joyce Backman applied, as usual, a keen and graceful editorial hand. Nonny Burack typed the manuscript drafts and read proof with her customary skill and learning.

It is a pleasure to acknowledge the 1977 Fellowship of the National Endowment for the Humanities which provided time for the major portion of the writing. A sabbatical leave from the University of Massachusetts and a grant-in-aid from its Research Council were also important forms of assistance. Teaching scholars are time-bound without such aid.

My wife Lee gave me the gift of time as well, and I am attempting to return that favor in kind.

Texts of Emily Dickinson's poems are reprinted by permission of the publishers and the Trustees of Amherst College from *The Poems of Emily Dickinson,* 3 vols., edited by Thomas H. Johnson, Cambridge, Mass.: The Belknap Press of Harvard University Press, Copyright 1951, © 1955, 1979 by the President and Fellows of Harvard College; from *The Complete Poems of Emily Dickinson,* edited by Thomas H. Johnson, Copyright 1914, 1929, 1935, 1942 by Martha Dickinson Bianchi, Copyright © 1957, 1963 by Mary L. Hampson, by permission of Little, Brown and Company in association with the Atlantic Monthly Press; from *Emily Dickinson Face to Face* by Martha Dickinson Bianchi, published by Houghton Mifflin Company, Copyright 1932 by Martha Dickinson Bianchi, reprinted by permission of the publisher; from *The Life and Letters of Emily Dickinson* by Martha Dickinson Bianchi, published by Houghton Mifflin Company, Copyright 1924 by Martha Dickinson Bianchi, reprinted by permission of the publisher.

Chapter 1 appears here revised from an earlier version published in *ESQ: A Journal of the American Renaissance,* volume 20, 1974. Chapter 2 is included in revised form by permission of *Boston University Journal* where it first appeared in volume 23, 1975.

Lines from Hart Crane's poem "To Emily Dickinson" are reprinted from *The Complete Poems and Selected Letters and Prose of*

Acknowledgments

Hart Crane, edited by Brom Weber, by permission of Liveright Publishing Corporation, Copyright 1933, © 1958, 1966 by Liveright Publishing Corporation; reprinted also by permission of Laurence Pollinger, Ltd.

Lines from Donald Davie's poem "July, 1964" are reprinted from *Collected Poems, 1950–1970* by permission of Oxford University Press, and from *Essex Poems*, by permission of Routledge and Kegan Paul Ltd.

Lines from T. S. Eliot's *Ash-Wednesday* are reprinted from *The Complete Poems and Plays, 1909–1950*, by permission of Harcourt Brace Jovanovich, Inc., and by Faber and Faber Ltd., publishers of *Collected Poems, 1909–1962*.

Lines from "Epilogue" from *Day by Day* by Robert Lowell, Copyright © 1977 by Robert Lowell, are reprinted by permission of Farrar, Straus and Giroux, Inc., and by Faber and Faber Ltd.

Lines from Wallace Stevens' poems "Sunday Morning" and "The Man on the Dump" and from *The Necessary Angel* are reprinted from *The Collected Poems of Wallace Stevens*, Copyright 1954 by Wallace Stevens, and *The Necessary Angel*, Copyright 1951 by Wallace Stevens, by permission of Alfred A. Knopf, Inc., and Faber and Faber Ltd.

Lines from James Tate's poems "Heatstroke" and "The Human Eraser" are reprinted by permission of The Ecco Press, 1979, from *Riven Doggeries* by James Tate, Copyright 1973, 1975, 1976, 1977, 1978, 1979 by James Tate.

D. P.

Amherst, Massachusetts

Contents

Introduction:
A Swarm of Mysteries

This book extends the inquiry begun in my first work, *The Art of Emily Dickinson's Early Poetry*. It seeks to deepen prevailing views of our foremost woman poet and to establish the existence of an extreme, perhaps terminal, American modernism of which she is the first practitioner.

The Dickinson who emerges is of a startling identity that always awaited us in her words and mirrored our epoch without our knowing precisely why. I believe that the truth of her life and of one of the great poetic endowments in America breaks free here of the banalities that cling to her reputation.

My concern has been to discover and preserve her *otherness*. Her audacity required an inordinate freedom that needs still to be respected. Seamus Heaney, the Irish poet, marked this drama when, standing with me amid brilliant sunshine and May blossoms in Dickinson's garden, he hugged his arms about him in feigned chill and exclaimed with a pleasurably wild surmise, "She scares me!"

"My Life had stood – a Loaded Gun," Dickinson began a poem of her early thirties. That concentrated figure seems to me now to be a stunning emblem for her life and work which, otherwise, contain no shapely story; instead, explosive capacity without the enabling authority and direction the literary tradition offers. It is this Dickinson without the aid of a great exterior force whose line cuts through to the root modernism visible in American poetry of the last several years.

Her awareness of her apartness can be seen in the letters and poems. Indeed, she thought about suicide in a crucial cluster of powerful poems, well aware that it was given to her to be done with life. A reader can glimpse her character coming into being and sustaining itself in adversity. Life astonished her with its denials. They were one of the peculiar springs of vitality for her art. Once she had recognized the fact of deprivation, the possibility of her art opened out. The golden-thread metaphor of an important 1850 letter, brilliantly revealed by Richard Sewall in his biography of the poet, now gleams with significance. It marks the existential center where her art fed on her deprivation.

A new approach to her work is needed to show us how the peculiar features of Dickinson's writing outside the familiar anthology selections have a common denominator that throws light on all of the Dickinson mysteries. She withdrew twice over: from publishing and from a public life in the community. Her posthumously published poems have inevitably come to stand for her life so that in effect she is the creation of her writing. Yet the actual history of her art, its onset and its survival, in fact involves several real and formidable women beginning with Mary Lyon and Elizabeth Barrett Browning and extending to our own time.

Most of all, the new viewpoint involves a fresh look at the poet's worksheets, including the scraps of paper on which she sometimes wrote. There the single presence is Dickinson's writing, and whether in poems or letters it is writing that is not communicative in the usual sense but patently literary. To examine the scraps that fall out of the acid-free envelopes now protecting them from disintegration—corners of wrapping paper, slit-open envelopes, pieces pinned together, printed directions for operating an oil lamp, a cooking-chocolate wrapper—is to realize that printed versions of the poems necessarily recreate the figure of the artist. The originals make up a discontinuous collection of texts—scraps, sheets, packets—once stored in a dresser drawer. But it is in the printing that she exists for readers. Printing gives the impression of orderliness and continuity in the poet's work; the bound volumes imply a certain coherence and completion. But values associated with printed poetry—a tradition and a self-conscious artist—apply to her only in a special way.

Finding Dickinson requires an intricate going-back-through. A reader must penetrate the print that she did not authorize, with its straight lines and capitals, its even margins and spacing, the stanzaic regularity, the *visual definiteness;* go through the contorted syntax and beyond the unanchored tropes; back despite the absent tissue of her work and through her reclusion and her silence to the immediacy of the scraps and pencil. Formalist criticism, my own earlier studies included, worked from the book and the Dickinson who emerged was a formalist creation. Printing of necessity had done to her what camera and editing do to the live performance of an actor, and so formalism has missed the deepest and fullest identity. The critical convenience of seeing her poems as one long poem is a further distortion of the fact of the text.

What should hold our attention instead is the special experience of reading Dickinson's poetry. She made no pact with her readers, gave, them no plan of the whole. Her work lacks architectural dimension to direct the reader's activity within its space. In short, a reader emerges from the most empathetic and pleasurable immersion in the body of poetry quite unable to report its order of knowledge or perception.

The satisfying result of looking anew at the poet's life and the manuscripts, of going back through with consciousness of the many mysteries, is the discovery of what has always been true: Dickinson earnestly meant what she said. In particular, she was thoroughly sincere in her request when she sent her poems to Thomas Wentworth Higginson, the eminent man of letters, and asked, "Are you too deeply occupied to say if my Verse is alive?" She meant what she said, it is clear, when she advised him that the "Representative of the Verse" was not herself but "a supposed person." To discover that she was not being coy or condescending or ironic but simply candid is a breakthrough to the truth. The same holds true of the other letters, including her setting-out letter to John Graves when she was twenty-five.

What mysteries then are to be comprehended? To begin with, I have sought to provide a new understanding of her cryptic mannerisms. This has involved constructing a primer for reading Dickinson's problematic poems. One way was to restore the syntax that Dickinson habitually elided. This linguistic archeology leads to the hidden patterns of the poet's composing methods: her basic units of composition as the scraps of manuscript reveal them; her grammatical defects, lost referents, and dropped inflections; the tropological distance and abstraction; her habits of revision as they relate to her first lines and favored polysyllabic words. Dickinson's syntactical and lexical irregularities provide an opening into the essential precinct of her work. We discover the origins of some of the problems in her poems and the habits of her mental arrangement. The hymn form, for example, severely constrained her verse and what she was able to perceive with it even as she invested that narrow shape with intimate and unsurpassed power.

I have tried to increase our understanding as well of the problem of Dickinson's preoccupation with death as a subject, and of those most curious of all her works, the wife and bride poems. From a close view of her composing methods and the origins of difficulties in her language comes a clarification as to the limited validity of psychobiography based on poems in which style is more insistent than meaning. We find in these poems the radicals of *writing*, which releases language from its communicative function and allows many other linguistic effects to occur. An answer then presents itself to the essential question: Why did Dickinson write?

Her fateful meeting with Higginson when she was thirty-nine years old is an important part of my new employment of the evidence. That extraordinary interview leads to solutions of the vexing technical and conceptual mysteries that swarm about this poet: why the poems remained unpublished and even untitled during her lifetime; why the poems are brief and make a collection but no whole, everything connected by "and" and "and" as Elizabeth Bishop said in another context; why the poems rank alike, making the same claims on readers; why history and, yes, a social conscience remain largely outside the poems; why she is the only one of our major poets without an agenda for her art; and why, finally, her art at the end performed in the same ways it had at the beginning of her career. It is an uncommonly evasive performance in which she is rigorously excluded from the information but caught in the evasions and idiosyncrasies of style.

This study is by no means an indictment of Dickinson's poetry. The puzzles occupy the same stage as her artistic brilliance: the intense concentration, the surprise of her violations of selectional rules, the short aggressive lines that catch motion, the intimacy of the voice, the polysyllabic tours de force, the linguistic control over destructive emotions, the metonymic deftness, the capacity for psychological accuracy as great as any in the language, and the abrupt wisdom. There is no boredom in Dickinson because there is no prose. With the apprehension of the actual poet—the genius together with the enigmas—we see simultaneously the moment of one of the major divides in American poetry when the language changed.

My approach takes account of the central phenomenon: although Dickinson is a major poet, she provided almost none of the expected discourse that our great poets have furnished. Absences and omissions, in instances of striking artistic evasiveness, constitute Dickinson's deepest identity. Her freedom and her attitude reveal themselves in these customary acts not performed, conventions rejected, and discursive shapes unfulfilled.

So this is not a conventional study, but a way of finding the major self signaled by what she did not do. My approach is free from formalist assumptions, particularly from the belief that words are the sole meaning-conveying elements of her art. This gives us a fresh eye unclouded by the dense shades of disputation over meaning. In going beyond semantic analysis we locate the angle from which the anomalies of syntax, structure, and textual character become intelligible. By registering crucial meaning separate from the written utterance, Dickinson in fact constitutes an exemplary critique of formalism. The obstacles in Dickinson's poetry are essential revelations, a path to the solution of the riddles.

There is absence at every level: morpheme, word, phrase, poem, text, corpus, and the life as its matrix. The mysteries of what the poet and the poems do not do, as I have suggested, make a unique catalogue, headed surely by the fact that her art did not change over more than two decades of composition. She composed no *ars poetica* to characterize her work. There is little outside reference in her poems, no dialogue with her time. The poems simply do not look outward. They have no inherent order of priorities or perception.

"You start drawing conclusions from omissions," Hugh Kenner said of Joyce's portrait of Bloom. In Dickinson, uniquely, we come from a full reading of the poetic canon able not to convey its pattern of mind but instead its peculiar incohesion. This study is not a poem-by-poem interpretation, therefore, but a search for the location of primacy in the body of poems. In the end the issue becomes the relationship of her language to the reality of her life as an artist. In other words, absence and insubordination in Dickinson make sense; her fugitive identity is inseparable from her language. In that idiom where she exercises her renunciations, evasions, and defects and thus inserts her freedom in the resistant medium of language, the absences are where she commits herself. With appropriately altered vision we are able to see what we most want to see in her work: the place where she establishes her individuality within the inherited system of language.

In this freedom Dickinson founded a language. Her problematic idiom—word-centered, disorderly, unfinished, splendid—has effects on us as readers that we recognize as modern. The familiar becomes strange because the poems carry an agitation and troubled ignorance out of sight. They are, to use Dickinson's word, haunted. By the pitch of the words and the nature of the perception, her language activated new receptivities. With cramped syllabic form and short lines that crowd syntax, its idiosyncratic neglect of grammatical inflection and full rhyme, its constant need for motion and evanescence, her expression summoned particular realities: contradiction, surprise, deviance, mystery. This unyielding remystification of signs establishes Dickinson first of all as an early member of the modern movement of poetry.

The Dickinson strain of modernism, however, at its extreme is unprecedented. It inaugurates in American literature two main characteristics: the menacing ascendance of consciousness and the disappearance of an artistic goal. In Dickinson, metaphysical homelessness combines with genius; the links are lost between sensations and understanding; the moments of skepticism and dejection arrive. There emerges the quality of a new art, one that does not order experience but disperses it, overnourishes it by language, and creates not a stay against confusion but takes part in the confusion itself. Her art, as I say later on and not disparagingly, is the onset of Babel in American poetry. Dickinson's radical modernism thus is not a theme but a way of knowing, a way of art: it is an idiom of irrepressible consciousness and inescapable derangement come together.

Beyond this unique intensity without a theme, the idiom foreshadows an emerging tradition of women poets in America. Dickinson provided mutilating language by which women could see the concealed ironies and killing contradictions of their lives. She was, to use Adrienne Rich's marvelous metaphor, one of the first to dive into the wreck of a female life. She marked the territory in a letter in 1878 that speaks of the "depths in every consciousness from which we cannot rescue ourselves – to which none can go with us."

With Emerson, she was an innovator who opened the way for modernist voices and attitudes, naming new, sometimes psychologically profound, categories of existence. My concentration on her language performance thus rejects the familiar thematic studies that have found in American poetry continuities rather than fractures. In this regard, my study relates to the discussion in my book *Emerson and Literary Change*. Dickinson and Emerson were, in ways we need to understand more clearly, language makers, but contradictory ones, who prepared new eyes and new ears for the modernist era. At opposing extremes, they are the central poets of our literature. We have in Dickinson and in Emereson a rare demonstration of the proposition that the language of art can shape the grasp of our intelligence. This view of a radical epistemology, together with locating artistic shift and alteration, is also tied to my book on Emerson. Both are studies, finally, of the way a culture alters its perception.

Dickinson's is a separate, radical, cutting strain deep within the more orthodox modernism. In her work we see enacted the losing of the program for poetry. This explains in part why only Dickinson stands between Whitman and Edwin Arlington Robinson in that long, amazing end-of-the-century hiatus in American poetry.

We have in Dickinson not order but restlessness. The shiny, buzzing, stumbling fly is one of her emblems of this state. Hers is an idiom that is hyperconscious, a relentless performing of the artistic consciousness in an unintelligible world. Irregular in observation, the idiom is autogenous, turned inward, decomposing the world into piecemeal reflexions and aggressive words. Let us say it is an art of willful genius; it runs a line full of tension from Dickinson more than a century ago through early twentieth-century modernism to certain kinds of postmodernist poems that are being written today. Something terrifying in the writing operates apart from the commonly observed richness and ambiguity of high modernist art. This is its simultaneously incoherent and fierce imagination. It is the Dickinson mark of modernism: the mind explosive with signifying power but disinherited from transcendent knowledge. Unable to compose broad fields of ordinary experience, Dickinson's language produces a strange discourse that is full of gaps and shadows and brilliant glints of light. It pulled poetic art away from prose into a crisis. And in just this brilliant extremity, the idiom is a hazardous path for other poets, the way to what I call terminal modernism. These chapters, then, are a study of a special kind of restlessness and the significance of incoherence.

My attention to the relationship of language and identity and to the artistic self established outside grammatical norms proceeds in the following chapters from what is different and strange in Dickinson's language to the conceptual matrix behind the strangeness, and finally to Dickinson's unique force in modernism. She retreated from reality into words, and I have tried to trace that astonishing and proleptic event in the poetry.

Chapter 1, "The Crucial Experience," appears here substantially the same as when first published in 1974. This was an earlier attempt to find a pattern of coherence in the body of poetry. I see now that it locates a preoccupation, that of aftermath—"The After Mind," "That engulfing 'Since,'" as she called it in two poems—that is quintessentially modern: life after its vital meaning has climaxed. Chapter 2, "Strangely Abstracted Images," inaugurates a group of four chapters that isolate the most difficult, even indecipherable, elements of her work and then describe the problems of the hymnal form, how she wrote and revised, and how the problematic poems can be read. At the end of Chapter 5 the main stylistic mysteries are, I trust, solved.

Chapters 6 and 7 outline the poems' conceptual matrix, and here we find the surprising identity we have sought. The conceptual mysteries are clarified in its light. The problematic poems become intelligible, in particular Dickinson's vexing death preoccupation, the wife and bride poems, and the evasive gun poem. The three chapters that close the book deal with Dickinson's special protomodernism, opening an unfamiliar view into the destructive heart of modernist art.

The example of Dickinson provides a glimpse of why art has a history. My emphasis on the obscurities of her verse and the way her language disperses the world is intended to chart a previously unmapped territory in the realm of art and imagination in America. She wrote to the end. There has existed no stronger will *to say*. That will is narrow, but at its most powerful it is unsurpassed.

1   The Crucial Experience

A sure sense of coherence in Emily Dickinson's poetry evades readers of her piecemeal canon. She delighted in spareness, as William Carlos Williams once said, and had a distaste for lingering. Those habits of economy and fragmentation in her brief poems continually defeat our efforts to summarize her. In addition, the poems and letters teem with other problems and mysteries: the poet's life refuses to explain the poems; the canon is large (almost eighteen hundred poems and fragments and over a thousand letters); a chronology of composition has so far been impossible to establish; the poet never made a deliberate selection from her works for publication, she is inconsistent in her attitudes; and, finally, the quality of the poems is uneven. What, then, holds the poetry together?

Despite the biographers, the elementary experience has little to do with inaccessible lovers. The crucial affair for her, rather, is living after things happen. It is a preoccupation with afterknowledge, with living in the aftermath. The perspective of poem after poem is from afterward, from behind the "soft Eclipse." It is this back-looking view, for example, which, together with the wonderful synecdoche of the horses' heads, creates the shock in the closing lines of "Because I could not stop for Death." The vision repeatedly angles out of psychic voids that follow crisis, where in "larger – Darknesses – / Those Evenings of the Brain," as she says in poem 419, unfolds the frightful leisure in which to seek what will suffice.[1]

A poem that may stand as a paradigm of engrossment in the afterward begins with these familiar lines:

The Crucial Experience

> After great pain, a formal feeling comes –
> The Nerves sit ceremonious, like Tombs –
> The stiff Heart questions was it He, that bore,
> And Yesterday, or Centuries before?   (P-341)

Afterward is the condition of the best known poems of physical and psychic death: "Safe in their Alabaster Chambers," " 'Twas just this time, last year, I died," "I died for Beauty," "I heard a Fly buzz – when I died," "My life closed twice before its close." It is the condition in the poems that look back on crucial changes in status: "The Soul selects her own Society," "I'm 'wife' – I've finished that – / That other state," "I'm ceded – I've stopped being Theirs." Excruciating experience of the aftermath constitutes the subject of "I felt a Funeral, in my Brain" and "I got so I could take his name." Aftereffects pervade the poems of soft nostalgia over Indian Summer days that come after the "real" summer, the most familiar perhaps being "These are the days when Birds come back." Dozens of the rarely anthologized poems deal with afterward. One such that characteristically surveys the experience begins:

> There is a Languor of the Life
> More imminent than Pain –
> 'Tis Pain's Successor – When the Soul
> Has suffered all it can –   (P-396)

The stark poems of aftervision are counterbalanced in the canon by others with a similar perspective but a less grave tone. These include not only the poems of Indian Summer but all those that rehearse agreeable past experiences held in "Amethyst remembrance" or which, as in the famous hummingbird poem ("A Route of Evanescence"), describe ecstatic sensation so short-lived it exists only in its resonance.

Poems of the aftermath appear throughout Dickinson and, to the extent that Thomas Johnson's dating of fair copies is a rough approximation of periods of composition, they reflect a steady absorption across twenty years of writing. I want first to set up a conceptual position for seeing that obsession and then consider what is even more important to understanding Emily Dickinson as an artist: the poetic strategies her habit of afterness engendered. For they made possible the achievement of a poetry that keeps its sensibilities intact while taking as its ground the wastes of inward desolation. These concerns reach directly to a consideration of how psychic schema stand at the origin of poetic form.

In Dickinson's actualization of the post-crisis state, space opens to a bewildering size while time goes slack in a great "leisure of the Future" (P-856). Affliction "ranges Boundlessness" beyond "Contentment's quiet Suburb," as she says in poem 963. Consciousness performs on a barren tract, a condition expressed characteristically by Dickinson's yoking of disparate word groups, as in "miles of Stare" (P-243), or where seasons are "indifferent" and existence is presided over by a "God of Width" (P-1231). In one carefully unflinching poem, the speaker sees mirrored in the looking glass the very image of these expanses of negation.

> Like Eyes that looked on Wastes –
> Incredulous of Ought
> But Blank – and steady Wilderness –
> Diversified by Night –
>
> Just Infinites of Nought –
> As far as it could see –
> So looked the face I looked upon –
> So looked itself – on Me –   (P-458)

Life in the aftermath is a profound void. Even the solitude of death seems crowded society compared with "that profounder site / That polar privacy / A soul admitted to itself" (P-1695). Dickinson scanned these dark holes in psychic space with various canny metaphors, but death was the allegory always at hand, for death killed time and introduced the terrifyingly drained interval between experience and the "most profound experiment appointed unto Men" (P-822). In these plunges out of time, the prospect opens upon "Vast Prairies of Air / Unbroken by a Settler" (P-564), "Seas / Unvisited of Shores" (P-695), and "Chaos – Stopless – cool" (P-510).

By such stunning dislocations the plots of human lives break down. Frank Kermode identifies these breaches by his parable of the clock. All agree, he writes, that the clock says *tick-tock*. "*Tick* is our word for a physical beginning, *tock* our word for an end ... The clock's *tick-tock* I take to be a model of what we call a plot, an organization that humanizes time by giving it form; and the interval between *tock* and *tick* represents purely successive disorganized time of the sort that we need to humanize."[2] In the aftermath of the climactic *tock*, a season without form opened up for Dickinson. She called it "like Midnight, some – / When everything that ticked – has stopped" (P-510). She summoned language to name it and to make experience there visible. It was a profound exercise of humanizing. Methodically she defined that psychic dead spot by its negatives, the mind circling the experience with homely instruments of perception. It was not death or night or frost or fire, yet tasted like them all.

> It was not Death, for I stood up,
> And all the Dead, lie down –
> It was not Night, for all the Bells
> Put out their Tongues, for Noon.
>
> It was not Frost, for on my Flesh
> I felt Siroccos – crawl –
> Nor Fire – for just my Marble feet
> Could keep a Chancel, cool –
>
> And yet, it tasted, like them all,
> The Figures I have seen
> Set orderly, for Burial,
> Reminded me, of mine –
>
> As if my life were shaven,
> And fitted to a frame,
> And could not breathe without a key,
> And 'twas like Midnight, some –
>
> When everything that ticked – has stopped –
> And Space stares all around –
> Or Grisly frosts – first Autumn morns,
> Repeal the Beating Ground –
>
> But, most, like Chaos – Stopless – cool –
> Without a Chance, or Spar –
> Or even a Report of Land –
> To justify – Despair   (P-510)

The opening phrase of poem upon poem unhesitatingly visits the place of aftermath: "I saw no Way – The Heavens were stitched," " 'Twas like a Maelstrom, with a notch," "I am alive – I guess," "There is a pain – so utter," "Behind Me – dips Eternity," "From Blank to Blank," "Time feels so vast that were it not," "There is a finished feeling," "A nearness to Tremendousness," "Somewhere upon the general Earth," "I've dropped my Brain – My Soul is numb."

Dickinson drew part of her peculiar power from precisely this habitual backward-looking perspective, which Yvor Winters called fraudulent. In his essay entitled "Emily Dickinson and The Limits of Judgment," he says of the poem "Because I could not stop for Death": "In so far as it concentrates on the life that is being left behind, it is wholly successful; in so far as it attempts to experience the death to come, it is fraudulent, however exquisitely."[3] He argued with characteristically stiff reasonableness for absolute observance of the boundaries that Dickinson, for her part, habitually crossed. She repeatedly took the most extreme of tragic positionings, electing circumstances where the consciousness stands at the limits of its sovereignty. The perspective from beyond death seems not a morbid contortion of her viewpoint but a choice that cleared her sight. She worked it out deliberately in a single poem of the middle years.

> The Admirations – and Contempts – of time –
> Show justest – through an Open Tomb –
> The Dying – as it were a Hight
> Reorganizes Estimate
> And what We saw not
> We distinguish clear –
> And mostly – see not
> What We saw before –
>
> 'Tis Compound Vision –
> Light – enabling Light –   (P-906)

Thus death was a capital allegory rather than a pathological morbidity. It made the ultimate alteration in status and provided the inevitable metaphoric entry to the realm beyond *tock*. It was enormously valuable to a poetic consciousness bartering for release. She drew up the balance sheet:

> Things that Death will buy
> Are Room –
> Escape from Circumstances –
> And a Name –   (P-382)

Psychic death, "To die – without the Dying" (P-1017), also forced crucial removals beyond boundaries into the wilderness. They filled a profound need for metaphysical anxiety, which she labeled "Lapland's necessity."

> an awe
> That men, must slake in Wilderness –
> And in the Desert – cloy –
> An instinct for the Hoar, the Bald –
> Lapland's – necessity.   (P-525)

So obsessive was the need, like Hart Crane's, to return to the world with words that she joked about it in a marvelous quip (P-182) in which she said her tombstone would be her "Granite lip."

This contemplation of the darkness beyond night's darkness is the naked poetic act that evokes feelings of the universe experienced as a presence. It is a handling of sensation, rudimentarily organized by the allegory of death, which articulates, to use Marcel Raymond's phrase, a primitive feeling of existence in which the sense of the self and the sense of the whole can no longer be distinguished.[4] Dickinson's poems repeatedly perform incantations to call up the absent, seeking a fugitive spiritual reality. Indeed, that total openness to the sensations of existence seems to be the meaning of her declaration that she dwelt "in Possibility" (P-657). It is a statement of the creative resources of the void, of a constant presentiment, to borrow words from Raymond again, of the nebulous, irrational opacity that subsists beyond knowledge. Dickinson seems in fact to have sought this shamanic goal by the cryptic slogan of her poetics: "Nature is a Haunted House – but Art – a House that tries to be haunted" (L-459a).[5]

Visitations are the metaphorical openings to her special field of experience. They hold, as the poet wrote, "The possibility – to pass / Without a Moment's Bell – / Into Conjecture's presence" (P-286). Visitations thus inaugurate the period of afterward. The sensation is signaled in the most familiar poems of all, those that perceive faint terrors no farther away than the doorstep or the garden: "There's a certain Slant of light" and "Presentiment – is that long Shadow – on the Lawn." Springtime light "waits upon the Lawn" and "almost speaks to you," she writes elsewhere, and then "It passes and we stay,"

> A quality of loss
> Affecting our Content

As Trade had suddenly encroached
Upon a Sacrament.   (P-812)

Explicit concentration on such intrusions is commonplace, as in poem 1581, which ends:

The Thought is quiet as a Flake –
A Crash without a Sound,
How Life's reverberation
It's Explanation found –

Because they are a metaphorical precondition of her understanding of climactic emotion, visitations constitute a structural element in the poetry. They take the form not only of gently transmitted premonitions but also of assaults and crises. They are "Eternity / . . . presenting – Here" (P-889), gates to final realities, visits from the cosmos.

A Vastness, as a Neighbor, came,
A Wisdom, without Face, or Name,
A Peace . . .   (P-1104)

Several familiar poems will now appear to us clearly linked because of their famous visitors: the hummingbirds, the bees, and the snakes for example; the certain slant of light and the long shadow in the grass; the wind, the rain storms, and the frost; and preeminently Death, the country squire who kindly stops in his carriage. Their visitations range from ecstatic moments, as with the hummingbird, that leave only their aftersensation ("The Moments of Dominion / That happen on the Soul / And leave it with a Discontent / Too exquisite – to tell," P-627), to grave meetings that usher in finalities. Dickinson's comment on the psychological impact is wonderfully definitive.

The awful moment is
And takes it's fundamental place
Among the certainties –   (P-1106)

Crucial arrivals are far more frequent than one imagined. Even so, the poems form, sometimes simultaneously, only three or four basic tonal focuses: moments of exquisite pleasure, most often in nature; fleeting visitations that brush only in an oblique and momentary way the willful strangeness of existence; terrifying assaults that freeze the nerves; and, finally, visitations merely weird, vaguely premonitory, suggestive of vaster opacities. The bee poems, for example, disarmingly search exquisite moments in nature when encounters are laden with unsuspected consequence, as in "The Murmur of a Bee / A Witchcraft – yieldeth me." "A Route of Evanescence" is the best-known poem of the type, but other versions of the visit open potentially more frightful power, as in "The Wind – tapped like a tired Man." The spectral quality of the wind depends upon the same bird image.

> No Bone had He to bind Him –
> His Speech was like the Push
> Of numerous Humming Birds at once
> From a superior Bush –   (P-436)

The grisliest version of the visit to the bush chronicles with cold understatement the casual murder that accompanies the frost's soundless arrival: "Apparently with no surprise / To any happy Flower / The Frost beheads it at its play." Sunsets, on the other hand, are exquisitely gaudy visitors, like carnivals and trading ships, and at the same time literal visualizations of the day's aftermath, their appearance both exciting and paining the viewer with "harrowing Iodine" (P-673). Indian Summer, similarly, is the season's brilliant aftermath, offering "Summer's Recollection" (P-302) or for a moment typifying immortality, as in "These are the days when Birds come back."

A great many visitation poems play fleetingly at the rim of the void. The most famous is "A narrow Fellow in the Grass" where the snake's sudden notice induces instantaneous "Zero at the Bone." Snakes (she also used mushrooms) made for Dickinson supremely appropriate actors in the shocking visitation. They trailed strangeness out of the magical realm of "guile" and "awe" beyond the boundaries of the familiar world ("Sweet is the swamp with its secrets, / Until we meet a snake"). The metaphysical terror which the snake's trespass triggers is caught metaphorically by "Doom's electric Moccasin." The paradigmatic poem concerns a storm's arrival. Its eye is on what survives into the aftermath of the onslaught.

> There came a Wind like a Bugle –
> It quivered through the Grass
> And a Green Chill upon the Heat
> So ominous did pass

We barred the Windows and the Doors
As from an Emerald Ghost –
The Doom's electric Moccasin
That very instant passed –
On a strange Mob of panting Trees
And Fences fled away
And Rivers where the Houses ran
Those looked that lived – that Day –
The Bell within the steeple wild
The flying tidings told –
How much can come
And much can go,
And yet abide the World!   (P-1593)

Dickinson sought allegories of visitation that wrench one's perception. She courted this experience because it led to those stretches of aftermath where the consciousness, because estranged, is totally alert. She even courted it with indecent glee. A poem anthologists always overlook and to which a reader or two have attached solemn scholarly meditation chronicles, in fact, the visit of a spider to a privy and particularly to an unmentionable part of the occupant's anatomy. The victim flees without her clothes.

Alone and in a Circumstance
Reluctant to be told
A spider on my reticence
Assiduously crawled

And so much more at Home than I
Immediately grew
I felt myself a visitor
And hurriedly withdrew.   (P-1167)

Other poems of assault monitor responses that range from paralysis to coiled terror. One of her arrivals is a neat psychological bomb: "Remorse – is Memory – awake ... It's Past – set down before the Soul / And lighted with a Match." Another visitor is a molester ("He fumbles at your Soul") and, of course, Death, who comes for his victim as implacably as frost on the window pane and "easy as the narrow Snake" (P-1136). Images of the intruder grow increasingly stark until there stands before us her famous mask of death, "a Face of Steel – / That suddenly looks into our's / With a metallic grin" (P-

286). Perhaps no visitor stops life colder because of his victim's excruciating mixture of duty and terror than the faceless deflowerer in
"A Wife – at Daybreak I shall be," a poem I shall return to in a new
light. His wordless ascent to the bridal chamber precedes a frightful
initiation into adulthood.

> Softly my Future climbs the Stair,
> I fumble at my Childhood's prayer
> So soon to be a Child no more –
> Eternity, I'm coming – Sir

Inevitably speculation stirs on the causes of this invasion-aftermath
obsession. Possibly no more can be said than that Dickinson's inclina-
tion toward afterward was simply an unexplained but persistent
leaning. It was most certainly a peculiar prephilosophy, tragic at its
core, which sought situations on the heath where existence is fear-
fully unaccommodated. Her religious orientation made meditation on
the afterlife a natural activity. The dramatic structure of spiritual visitation followed by eternal life, whether of damnation or ecstasy, is
the basic Christian metaphor. Emily Dickinson grew up with it, and
at Mount Holyoke Seminary she wrestled with the angel himself.
Later, in her poetry, she transformed the issue into the problem of
consciousness traversing the interval of death and surviving into a
mysterious aftermath. The passage she described as

> Adventure most unto itself
> The Soul condemned to be –
> Attended by a single Hound
> It's own identity.   (P-822)

Her psychological difficulties no doubt also contributed to the
habit of afterreckoning. Sometime in the early 1860s, when she was
in her early thirties, an emotional crisis formed, perhaps accompanied
by a breakdown in health, that made death a palpable presence. In a
letter as late as mid-1863 she told her cousins she had "a snarl in the
brain which don't unravel yet, and that old nail in my breast" (L-
281). A similar experience of breakdown and survival into the aftermath compels in certain poems intense attention to the routine of
trivia as it organizes the time of postcrisis blankness (for example,
P-443). Remaining singular in such plural circumstances was a need

to which she turned repeatedly for subject matter. Whatever actuality her mental disorder had, its externalized form was the visitation-aftermath pattern. It is possible indeed to draw parallels, as the English poet Ted Hughes has done, between psychotic plunges and the primary poetic act of descent, shaman-like, to realms beneath rational mind. Psychosis, according to the psychiatrist and Dickinson scholar John Cody, may involve "an uneasy and potentially disorganizing openness to unconscious processes."[6]

The emotional fragility mirrored Dickinson's acute sense of differentness, which in turn produced all sorts of writing mannerisms, not least the contorted prose of the letters. She was serious when she observed that "All men say 'What' to me" and when she described herself to Thomas Wentworth Higginson as "the only Kangaroo among the Beauty" (L-271, 268). Her singularity showed itself in the way she examined the homely clichés of love, hope, and fulfillment, and drained the myths of easy religious faith. Thus she seemed to live constantly in a state of dislocation from her prosaic contemporaries. Moreover, when she started writing in earnest, producing a flood of poems in the early 1860s, she was past thirty. By then, conceivably, expectations of marriage, of a family, and of a settled identity were over, and the condition of afterward inevitably set the arrangement of interior time.

Whatever the reasons for her predisposition toward time-after, the obsession created specific elements of Dickinson's style. Her art of the aftermath was an intense setting of language in search of the feel of dead things. We see her studying the matter here:

> I tried to think a lonelier Thing
> Than any I had seen –
> Some Polar Expiation – An Omen in the Bone
> Of Death's tremendous nearness –
>
> I probed Retrieveless things
> My Duplicate – to borrow –
> A Haggard Comfort springs
>
> From the belief that Somewhere –
> Within the Clutch of Thought –
> There dwells one other Creature
> Of Heavenly Love – forgot –   (P-532)

The Crucial Experience

The subject of time-after is filled with the pitfalls of melodrama and self-pity, with the ponderosities of awe, and with emotional slither and the crutches of cliché, but Dickinson, except in moments of unwary facility, evaded many of them. She sent unexpected words into the space of aftermath where they sounded with an alien vitality: "Quartz contentment," "a Funeral in my Brain," cavalry "in the bosom," "A Dimple in the tomb." By such quick ventures, she forced extensions of the life that can be apprehended by language, demonstrating how the minutest circuits function on minimal power. Readers go back to her frugal poems with incessant surprise at the language. Other poetry seems hesitant and slack in comparison.

Her oxymorons transmit with exceptional economy a perception of the unexpected intricacies of catastrophe. The figures assert how orderly are the processes of devastation and the possibility of calibrating the immensities if we have fine enough resolution to our devices. The off-beat habit shows in the adjective in "Geometric Joy" (P-652), in the verb in "regulate belief" (P-1100), or in the modifiers in "dazzle gradually" (P-1129), and "stun by degrees" (P-315). By this atomizing perception she spies the hidden formalities of ruin.

> Crumbling is not an instant's Act
> A fundamental pause
> Delapidation's processes
> Are organized Decays.
>   . . . .
> Ruin is formal – Devils work
> Consecutive and slow –   (P-997)

Such contradictory yokings disclose the microlife beneath great boulders of abstraction. She seemed to loathe the unapproachable. Cold town matrons induced in her a devilish imagining of how it would be to "assault a Plush" or "violate a Star" (P-401).

Another of her strategies for grasping this inward life of an experience is the wry synecdoche. It enabled her poems to be precisely attentive where monotony was the condition; it induced linguistic vitality out of wasted experience. Of boundless depression she wrote: "I've dropped by Brain . . . / Vitality is Carved and cool," comparing yesterday's "Instincts for Dance – a caper part – / An Aptitude for Bird" (P-1046). She isolated by this selective device the trivialities people clutch to keep from coming apart, the times "we do life's labor – / ... With scrupulous exactness – / To hold our Senses – on" (P-443). She selected the telling gesture.

> I put new Blossoms in the Glass –
> And throw the old – away –
> I push a petal from my Gown
> That anchored there

All the definition poems—of hope, remorse, anguish, death—inspect the conventional labels. She discovers in terminal states surprising intensities of consciousness. The poems of the great void thus keep from puffing into formless exclamation because they are ballasted by her synecdochic exactitudes.

Passage from convention into the unfamiliar is also accomplished by her made-up words. The fulcrum word in the line "Suspense – is Hostiler than Death" (P-705), though grammatically admissible as a comparative, tips the line by its strangeness into a realm where neither suspense nor death possesses its familiar meaning. It is a transaction of the sort she accomplishes in a line inspecting the process of resignation, which she calls the "slow exchange of Hope for something passiver" (P-652). These words begin the tilt into an alien world where old meanings do not apply and where the old consciousness must be super alert. The constant possibility of slipping off the ledge of the familiar also depends upon a basic habit of structural shift.[7] The exemplary poems "Safe in their Alabaster Chambers," "I died for Beauty," "I heard a Fly buzz – when I died," "I started Early – Took my Dog," and several others begin with disarming serenity and assurance, but by their ends and by extraordinary linguistic stealth they have exposed the dark ground beneath the plain surfaces. Readers unwittingly get taken to the edge and must look over. The experience is Dickinson's characteristic passage beyond *tock*. The disparate lexical references, the freakishly precise images, the made-up and willfully grammatical comparatives, the structural instability: each of these activities opens interstices through which appears the void of afterward. Each interstice also opens the prospect of the passage from comprehension to stunned ignorance.

These moments of dislocation converge to concentrated effect in the single poem "Further in Summer than the Birds." It is a masterpiece in the art of the aftermath. In 1883, seventeen years after she first mailed it to Higginson, she dug it out to post to Thomas Niles, editor of a Boston publishing house. It seeks characteristically to feel the turn, so gradual as to be imperceptible, from high summer to its afterseason, the subtle change that insect sounds convey.

> Further in Summer than the Birds
> Pathetic from the Grass
> A minor Nation celebrates
> It's unobtrusive Mass.
>
> No Ordinance be seen
> So gradual the Grace
> A pensive Custom it becomes
> Enlarging Loneliness
>
> Antiquest felt at Noon
> When August burning low
> Arise this spectral Canticle
> Repose to typify
>
> Remit as yet no Grace
> No Furrow on the Glow
> Yet a Druidic Difference
> Enhances Nature now   (P-1068)

The habitual stages of visit, aftermath, and void join here transmuted but still wonderfully transparent. Time is dying into fall from the climactic days of summer when the birds held sway. The sun declines with faint anticipations of the wintry aftermath to come; the visitation of the cicadas (Dickinson used the common term cricket) is apparent from their drone, inducing the strange instinctual sensation into which the poem works itself.

The opening line ushers the reader directly into the aftermath, beyond the birds, beyond the high season, beyond normal associations. In this way the poet invites fugitive aspects of commonplace events, as if, for example, she sought the feel of a stage when the performance is over. The stress pattern of the line itself is off-beat and so faintly cadenced that it holds to the common meter form mainly by its eight-syllable count. The chirring of the insects sounds four distinct times in this first line by identical phonemes and then echoes in the third line. (The earliest editors changed "Further" to "Farther," not hearing the subtle violence it did to the onomatopoetic drone.)

Into this poetic field of aftertime and chirring sound, Dickinson inserted various lexical groups in unstable relationships, thus creating sensation more complicated than the lexical meanings alone. The adjectives progressively drain the atmosphere until substance is shot through with spectral feeling. Each adjective is reductive, quieting, dissolving: Pathetic, minor, unobtrusive, gradual, pensive, Antiquest, spectral, Druidic. The adverbs—Further, low, now—along with three *no*'s insistently promote the insubstantiating process. The oxymoronic junctures begin to disconcert: minor Nation, unobtrusive Mass, gradual . . . Grace, low / Arise.

At a more basic level, two distinct sets of substantives act upon each other to create a third province which is the fugitive state the poem is after. The nouns of nature—Summer, birds, grass—impel against the nouns of social ceremony and ritual—nation, mass, ordinance, custom, canticle—issuing into a third cluster of feeling—loneliness, noon, repose, grace, glow—which in its contrasting strangeness conveys the intimate feel of "Druidic Difference." That trancelike state sounds in the open vowels that whoo-whoo toward the close, in the line "No Furrow on the Glow" and in the echoes all around: Noon, low, no, now. The verbs contribute to the estrangement because they denote acts of conjuring and transmutation: celebrate, see, become, enlarge, call forth, remit, enhance.

Winters' gloss on this poem clarifies the cryptic lines that begin the poem's last stanza by his paraphrase: "There is as yet no diminution of beauty, no mark of change on the brightness."[8] Yet the change is in the poem because it is at work in many ways. "Druidic Difference" is just this felt nextness of a magical universe where aftertime is the mother of beauty and where the sense of the self and the sense of the earth's processes can no longer be distinguished. The visitation of the insects has opened into the interval after *tock*. Ordinance and man's legislated life have given way to instinct, preparing us for that Druidic pause in time. The inherent persuasion in the poem comes emphatically to view if we compare it with a superficial attempt of Dickinson's to gather a similar moment of passage:

The Crickets sang
And set the Sun
And Workmen finished one by one
Their Seam the Day upon.

The Crucial Experience

> The low Grass loaded with the Dew
> The Twilight stood, as Strangers do
> With Hat in Hand, polite and new
> To stay as if, or go.
>
> A Vastness, as a Neighbor, came,
> A Wisdom, without Face, or Name,
> A Peace, as Hemispheres at Home
> And so the Night became. (P-1104)

The crucial experience of visitation and aftermath is all here. Variously transformed in numerous poems, it is the experience around which an essential portion of the canon coheres. Emily Dickinson claimed the aftermath as her special territory. It was as much her fecund ground as Manhattan was Whitman's or Paterson was Williams'. In that realm of least promise she found the performing imagination.

2 *Strangely Abstracted Images*

Abstraction, we are told repeatedly, is inimical to poetry. Yet in images that are so abstract they have given up their sensuous immediacy to pure meaning, Dickinson asserted her poetic individuality. Featureless, inconsistently successful, these peculiar figures with no light-catching body perform in her poems on occasion so audaciously as to reveal the interior moment when for her events became apprehended by language.

The paradigmatic image of this abstract sort is also one of Dickinson's most familiar. It appears in a simile at the end of "Safe in their Alabaster Chambers" and signifies in that terminal position the unarguable proposition that mighty Doges, even as the meek of the earth, shall fall to death in cold silence.

> Diadems – drop – and Doges – surrender –
> Soundless as dots – on a Disc of Snow –

The problem with the image "dots – on a Disc of Snow" takes the form of a paradox: while no exact image will form in the mind's eye (what sort of dots? what sort of disc?), the figure works superbly as poetry. The poem as a whole is an elegy for the senses that death extinguishes, but the poem does not console. The assured doctrinal belief posited by the opening word "Safe" is stealthily dislodged by negatives as the lines proceed one by one and is resolutely nullified by the contrived inanimation of the final image. It is a marvelous endgame.

> Safe in their Alabaster Chambers –
> Untouched by Morning –

And untouched by Noon –
Lie the meek members of the Resurrection –
Rafter of Satin – and Roof of Stone!

Grand go the Years – in the Crescent – above them –
Worlds scoop their Arcs –
And Firmaments – row –
Diadems – drop – and Doges – surrender –
Soundless as dots – on a Disc of Snow –   (P-216)

Dickinson tried out a large assortment of variant images of deadness for the second stanza: silence, echoes, frost, a "numb" door, eclipse, marble, icicles, and polar caverns, but she settled for "dots – on a Disc of Snow." It is difficult to imagine another figure that does so much so well as this bleak endscape. The sweep and grandeur of the cosmic visions of Crescent, Worlds, Arcs, and Firmaments which begin the second stanza are shrunk and contained by the small geometry of the dots and disc and then quietly obliterated by the snow. In addition, the falling motion of the dots (they trail the verbs "drop" and "surrender") reverses the lofty connotations and pomposities of Resurrection and Firmaments. The six single syllables of the dots-and-disc image neutralize the splendid polysyllables Alabaster and Diadems. Snow inexorably deprives "Safe" of its coziness, and "Soundless," the lefthand term of the final simile, rests appropriately opposite and linked to the substanceless image. Not identifiably visual, but rigorously composed of clipped consonants and repeated sibilants, the image "dots – on a Disc of Snow" expresses in phonetic preciseness and geometric abstraction the qualities of slight matter, minuscule size, and the feel of *cold inert insignificance*. It is a dead image that constitutes a ghostly knowledge.

Archibald MacLeish has attended to Dickinson's drained images most ably of all her readers. Some of the images, he writes, are "so strangely abstracted as to be almost transparent." Of the illogical coupling of her images "either in metaphor or out of it," he says, "it takes more than a second reading or even a third to demonstrate that there are images at work at all." He gives examples:

"Amethyst remembrance," "Polar expiation." Neither of these exists upon the retina. Neither can be brought into focus by the muscles of the eye. The "blue and gold mistake" of Indian summer seems to exist somewhere in the visible — or would if one could only get rid of that "mistake." And so too does "The Distance / On the look of Death" and "Dying – is a different way – / A Kind behind the door." But who can describe the graphic shape of "that white sustenance / Despair"? And yet all of these present themselves as images, do they not? — *act* as images? Where can remembrance be amethyst? Where but in the eye?[1]

Of Dickinson's customary use of abstractions like Grace and Bliss and Balm and Circumference, MacLeish says with delightful conviction: "The poems of almost any other poet would go down, founder, if they put to sea in generalizations as leaky as these." He inspects as an example Dickinson's poem about the early morning songbird's disappearance, which ends with these lines:

> At Half past Seven, Element
> Nor Implement, be seen –
> And Place was where the Presence was
> Circumference between.   (P-1084)

What saves Emily Dickinson's abstractions from shipping water? MacLeish says it is the Dickinson *voice* in the poems, its "extraordinary mastery of tone," the "laconic restraint" appropriate to New England, the "wholly spontaneous tone," the "liveness in the voice." Universal words, he writes, "generalizations, abstractions, made particular in a particular voice, can be poetry. As Emily Dickinson proved once for all."

But when she fails in the launching of her abstractions, they sink lifeless and undecipherable. Or, as in her slogan "My business is Circumference," they drift, inaccessibly subjective, cryptic, and opaque. A model of these faceless blocks to understanding is the subject phrase "Contemplation for / Cotemporaneous Nought" in poem 982.

> No Other can reduce
> Our mortal Consequence
> Like the remembering it be nought
> A Period from hence
> But Contemplation for
> Cotemporaneous Nought
> Our Single Competition
> Jehovah's Estimate.

Extant versions indicate that Emily Dickinson struggled for as long as three years in the mid-1860s with this curiously impacted poem. It is an impossible object, transfixing readers with a sphinx's stony gaze. I shall return later to its difficulties.

Dickinson achieved varying degrees of success with figures made of abstractions: "Brooks of Plush – in Banks of Satin," for example, to suggest the sound of the satisfied laughter of the happy dead in their coffins (P-457); "Great Streets of silence" and "Neighborhoods of Pause" for the expanse of timelessness (P-1159); "a maritime conviction" for the feel of the sea in the air (P-1302); "the obligation / To Electricity" for the debt owed revelation (P-1581). For the most part, they *mean* but do not *be*. Such resort to disembodied conceptual figures presents itself whenever we look for it in Dickinson. Two further examples, small successes of a comparable sort, though derived from different grammatical structures: "No Goblin – on the Bloom" from poem 646 and "no film on noon" from letter 235. Only by great transfusions of implication from their contexts does it become clear that each means there is no diminution of beauty, no apprehension, no alteration of the perfect.

The exemplar of this particular form of abstraction, now doubly deobjectified by its negative, is the image "No Furrow on the Glow" in the spendid poem of the cicada's hum introduced earlier, "Further in Summer than the Birds" (P-1068). The last eight lines seek the instinctual sensation of seasonal change.

> Antiquest felt at Noon
> When August burning low
> Arise this spectral Canticle
> Repose to typify
>
> Remit as yet no Grace
> No Furrow on the Glow
> Yet a Druidic Difference
> Enhances Nature now

The image "No Furrow on the Glow" succeeds for a reader after he has known this poem a long time. Like the examples cited just previously, it similarly means there is no decline from the ideal. Specifically in this poem of high summer it means there is no evident break in summer's full brilliance (though there is simultaneously the felt turn of the season toward fall, winter, and death — which is what the poem is *about*). It is an idea image (what sort of furrow? what sort of glow?), Dickinson having floated out this figure as an unattached trope in free linguistic orbit.

Ezra Pound, in an essay on Cavalcanti, described a realm beyond the plastic where the poet's aesthetic requires something more than simple visual mass, not limiting itself to "the impact of light on the eye." He characterized this lost domain of Cavalcanti's as a "radiant world where one thought cuts through another with clean edge, a world of moving energies *'mezzo oscuro rade,' 'risplende in se perpetuale effecto,'* magnetisms that take form, that are seen, or that border the visible, the matter of Dante's *paradiso*, the glass under water, the form that seems a form seen in a mirror, these realities perceptible to the sense, interacting."[2]

Dickinson's plunge into such obscurity, which Yvor Winters cited as the source of her "nonsense," produced her drained images. To the extent they were habitual, they are radical signs of her peculiar stance before reality. A reader thus would gain valuable insight by perceiving the motion of her mind in that crucial engagement. Is it possible to be present at the making of one of those impalpable images, to locate ourselves, as Roland Barthes says, "at that very fragile and rather obscure moment when the relation of a real event is about to be apprehended by literary meaning"?[3] There, perhaps, the hidden coupling of sensation and language would be revealed. It would take us closer to the elemental act of bonding language to discrete experiences that are both inescapable and unutterable.

Dickinson's worksheet trials for a poem dated about 1861 enable us to go behind one of her opaque figures, to pierce the text to the situation that is the image's raw material. Poem 291, beginning "How the old Mountains drip with Sunset," is copied on two sides of a single sheet that the poet threaded into one of her dresser-drawer packets when she was about thirty-one. It is a popular anthology piece because the imagery of sunset and night coming on is exquisitely various and evocative ("Mountains drip with Sunset / . . . the Hemlocks burn"), the metaphors are fresh and offbeat ("the Houses blot"), and the sounds exotic and syncopated ("How the Dun Brake is draped in Cinder"). But at its core, the poem is the old artful dodge, the speaker protesting she can never do justice in words to the scene facing her ("Have I the lip of the Flamingo / That I dare to tell?") even as she proceeds to do just that. Virtuoso performance is the poem's reason for being. In this respect, of course, it is an honorable descendant in a line that includes *The Divine Comedy* ("my vision was greater than our speech, which fails at such a sight"—*il mio veder fu maggio / che 'l parlar nostro ch'a tal vista cede*) and a fit sibling to "When Lilacs Last in the Dooryard Bloom'd" ("How shall I deck my song for the large sweet soul that has gone?")

Dickinson's language in the poem explores with sensuous abundance the sunset and the coming of night (her constant analogue of death), "visions" that the voice says "paralyzed" the great painters.

> How the old Mountains drip with Sunset
> How the Hemlocks burn –
> How the Dun Brake is draped in Cinder
> By the Wizard Sun –
>
> How the old Steeples hand the Scarlet
> Till the Ball is full –
> Have I the lip of the Flamingo
> That I dare to tell?
>
> Then, how the Fire ebbs like Billows –
> Touching all the Grass
> With a departing – Sapphire – feature –
> As a Duchess passed –
>
> How a small Dusk crawls on the Village
> Till the Houses blot
> And the odd Flambeau, no men carry
> Glimmer on the Street –
>
> How it is Night – in Nest and Kennel –
> And where was the Wood –
> Just a Dome of Abyss is Bowing
> Into Solitude –
>
> These are the Visions flitted Guido –
> Titian – never told –
> Domenichino dropped his pencil –
> Paralyzed, with Gold –

The image that occupies the crucial last position—after the mountains, the hemlocks, the village, and the yard—represents the severest test of the artist's skills. Just at this point, in this preferred position, we encounter the image that stops us cold.

> And where was the Wood –
> Just a Dome of Abyss is Bowing
> Into Solitude –

Eye muscles will not bring into focus a "Dome of Abyss," much less its "Bowing into Solitude." Such apparent humbug sends a diligent reader to the worksheets in search of an editor's transcription error or signs of some acute word block in the face of which the poet let the effort collapse. The search yields the poet's variants, and they in turn lead through the "Dome of Abyss" to the literal occasion behind the image. A more recognizable landscape begins to emerge from the fairly pedestrian metaphor she rejected: "Acres of Masts are standing / back of Solitude." By rectifying the inverted syntax in line 18 we see that the complete variant sentence visualizes, in fact, woods being swallowed up in night.

> where the Wood was[,]
> Acres of Masts are standing
> back of Solitude

Her use of "Masts" in place of "trees" begins the habitual motion of abstracting away from perceived reality that culminated in the impossibly abstract "Dome of Abyss" image. "Dome," we discover from a poem that she attached to a cocoon and sent to her nephew Ned about 1864 (P-893), holds an extraordinary cluster of associations for the poet. Not only is it intended to suggest the otherness of natural creation—she called the cocoon "Dome of Worm"—but the figure also stands in apposition to "Drab Habitation," "Tabernacle," "Tomb," "Porch of Gnome," and "Elf's catacomb," thus for her combining with alienness (were there domes in Amherst?) qualities of miracle, mystery, and death. "Abyss," we know from other Dickinson poems, signifies a feeling.

> There is a pain – so utter –
> It swallows substance up –
> Then covers the Abyss with Trance –
> So Memory can step
> Around – across – upon it –   (P-599)

Bonded together then in the new anatomy of "Dome of Abyss" is Dickinson's *feeling* of deep darkness within an enclosure that itself is wrapped in obscurity. "It is Night – in Nest and Kennel." It is darkness folded within night. We are near the realm of Milton's famous *palpable obscure* or what our contemporary Ted Hughes in his poem "Pike" calls the *darkness beneath night's darkness*. Emily Dickinson, moreover, attempted to perceive the very process that produces the complicated experience of a felt world beyond the visible world just disengaging itself from our sensory receptors.

The raw material, then, of the "Dome of Abyss" image is not only a preverbal but a preconscious sensation: the feel of woods unseen that one yet knows are there. What shall we compare to this habitual Dickinson moment of a presence conceived as an absence? An impalpable thickness? Perfume, fog, a window pane? It is the felt presence of the invisible, a sensuous absence, or, indeed, as in the "Dome of Abyss" poem, *an absence felt as a presence*. What linguistic shell games one must engage in to suggest what Dickinson, in her art of saying where a thing had been, distilled in such phrases as "Miles of Stare"! The death of the gods is an inflated but comparable thing. Place was where the Presence was.

Abstract expressionist artists since Kandinsky have sought representations of this sort of experience that unknowably *is*. Materialization of incipient abstract forms occurs in Jackson Pollock's poured paintings, where he abandoned the brush (especially in *Blue Poles*, 1952), and in the motifless shapes of Robert Motherwell, Franz Kline, and Mark Rothko. The closest parallel in recent sculptural art to Dickinson's abstractions is the glass and steel construction of Christopher Wilmarth called "Nine Clearings for a Standing Man." It is abstraction made strikingly expressive without a trace of figurative quality. With Dickinson's "Dome of Abyss" we stand at a comparable threshold of both verbal and figurative consciousness. The variant readings show us the poet attempting to haul instinctual feelings into language and thus into consciousness. In those trial words of hers for poem 291 we witness the stages by which she labored to grasp a sense of her own existence.

Dickinson's conceptual attempt at this threshold moment is discernible in variant expressions on a worksheet from about 1870. In this least finished draft of poem 1165, written perhaps as long as nine years after "Dome of Abyss," Dickinson labored to speak the idea of apogean experiences the senses are unequipped to handle. The completed version of the poem has eight lines.

Contained in this short Life
Are magical extents
The soul returning soft at night
To steal securer thence
As Children strictest kept
Turn soonest to the sea
Whose nameless Fathoms slink away
Beside infinity

In the least finished worksheet, the poet applied herself to defining
that stunning moment referred to in line two. She tried terms of in-
visibility, power, and vast distance. The trip metaphor had already
lodged in the ninth line of the worksheet version.

Contained in this short Life
Were wonderful extents
Discernible to not a friend
Except Omnipotence
A friend too straight to stoop
Too distant to be seen
Come unto me enacted how
With Firmaments between
The soul came home from trips
That would to sense have dazzled

Variants for "wonderful extents" in line two of this worksheet indicate how she sought repeatedly to name the moment's full and contradictory impact. Besides "wonderful" and "magical," she sorted
through "terrible," "miraculous," "tenderest," and "exquisite." In
the final line of the worksheet, however, she is reduced to making a
literal statement of the problem we as readers have wrestled with: experience that will not link up with language or sense. Those "wonderful extents" are "trips that would have dazzled sense" (*to* is an
awkwardness left over from the syntax of variant experiments). The
variants for the lines explicitly define for us as they did for the poet
the limits of sense-linked images. The revelations not only fatigue response (producing "the tired sense," another variant), but they are
trips "Unmanifest to sense" and "Unwitnessed of the sense."

In these literal assertions and amid all the trials and rejections is the
chronicle of Dickinson's attempts, as in "Dome of Abyss," to ambush
experience outside cognitive capacities and beyond linguistic grasp.

Those terribly abstract images that puzzle us, to her mind possessed these experiences.

Hart Crane celebrated this seeking beyond new thresholds into new anatomies. He admired in her, as in Melville, a resurfacing in cryptic embassies from submerged mute territories. It was a bringing back of the sensately indistinct vision. For Crane as for Dickinson, the art was not merely to experience these shamanlike soundings. The poet had to undertake the risky business of deep salvage and in the end to link us by language lines to those remote experiences.

Example after example documents Dickinson's resort to abstractions to summon what no word had labeled. In poem 532 she concocted the term "Retrieveless things," one of them being "An Omen in the Bone / Of Death's tremendous nearness." In the mock-solemn poem of the spider's assault in the privy, she called the invasion "an offense nor here nor there" (P-1167). In the heavily revised poems from around 1874 about the miraculous overnight appearance of the mushroom ("Vegetation's Juggler"), she finally proposed for that fungoid upstart another vexatious image without body: "The Germ of Alibi" (P-1298). Her cousin Fanny Norcross, baffled by this impossible invention, transcribed it for Higginson as "The *Joy* of Alibi." What the poet wanted spoken, of course, was the unprecedented surprise of a minuscule invasion from *elsewhere*. Her snake in poem 1740 similarly comes from the place she called "guile" and "awe," precincts that stand outside the familiar world.

Her impossibly abstract metaphor for the strange peace during the suspended moment at dusk before night has begun reads "Hemispheres at Home" (P-1104). The metaphor tilts into the absurd because it strains to render inward experience by an image the eye simply cannot construct. The poem begins "The Crickets Sang / And set the Sun." It ends with this ballet of imponderables:

> A Vastness, as a Neighbor, came,
> A Wisdom, without Face, or Name,
> A Peace, as Hemispheres at Home
> And so the Night became.

Existentialist criticism can help us to realize Dickinson's nonfigurative images at the poem's surface and to conceive in a theortetical way the critical moment at the deep threshold where language grips phenomenological experience. Thus we glimpsed in variant trials how the new anatomy of "Dome of Abyss" sought to feel darkness being formed inside night. We stood there at the emergence of the figure from preconscious into conscious existence. The process seems to indicate the first moment of literary creation when a word string is deliberately formed to hold a human experience. In the variants behind the abstract images, we see the creative movement by which, to use the terms of Georges Poulet, "the work of art passes from a shapeless and momentary state to a formal and lasting state."[4] This passage he calls the "time of the work of art" as it proceeds from the moment to coherence, from the ephemeral to the eternal. We have observed the process by which the writer both apprehends and creates herself. Piercing the layers of variants that lead to the abstract images gives us, then, a perception of mind becoming incarnate in form.

That instinctual and most evasive of Dickinson's perceptions is what the existentialist critic Marcel Raymond means by fugitive spiritual reality and a presentiment of the nebulous, irrational opacity that subsists beyond knowledge. The raising of that experience to consciousness, so audaciously undertaken by Dickinson, is one of the chief elements that produces repeated surprise in the reading of her poetry. This encounter of Dickinson's with presentiment was her sphinx, demanding to be possessed, verbalized, solved, created. It was a vision of final reality and she presumed to give it a name. The abstract images, then, by which she meant to name the experiences are a basic act of self-discovery. They are what the instincts can be *said* to feel.

Characteristically, it is specific unnameable experience she attempts to name: a light in spring "That Science cannot overtake / But Human Nature feels" (P-812), or the famous slant of light on winter afternoons:

> Heavenly Hurt, it gives us –
> We can find no scar,
> But internal difference,
> Where the Meanings are –   (P-258)

"My business is Circumference," Dickinson said. Apparently her attempt to colonize realms beyond the boundary of the senses has something to do with the vexing word "Circumference" that so exercises Dickinson readers. If circumference was the limit of experience, then circumference contained these instincts too.

Strangely Abstracted Images

Her unformulated poetics of abstraction is now discernible: the abstract images, daring gestures intent upon enormous intake, are meant to incarnate that feeling of immanent reality. When they succeed Dickinson's secret ecstasies surface in their strange nonobjective spaces. They were to her the verbal signs of a shadowy existence.

If there is an implicit rationale presiding over her habit, it is this: she rejected finite figures, the old anatomies, so as to enable a fuller reconciliation of language with far-off phenomenological states. Thus a reader begins to understand that the abstractness, problematic for him, for Emily Dickinson was a way to *say it all* about an experience. She dreaded falsifying the reality of an experience by the habits of tangibility. To be particular sometimes was to limit falsely. She believed that objectifying was death for the instinctual state. She evidently avoided a more palpable naming in order to hold onto the unnameable merger with irrational existence. The experience was thus kept to a degree "secret," and by this secrecy it retained for her its actual, full, and mystical feeling.

Each of her attempts was an original birth. In among the variants, we trace the moment when figures crucial to individual poems are created from phenomenological experience. They are high-risk performances in defiance of the drag of familiar language patterns. In this engagement we come close to the hidden precinct where, as Ernst Gombrich has said of the creative act, the angel stands guard with the flaming sword.

By isolating the abstracting gesture that troubles us so much, retracing it wherever possible, we spy a movement in the irreducible part of the poet's consciousness. There we identify that urgent grasping for presentiment that constitutes Dickinson in her profound solitude.

3　The Puzzling Idiom

Dickinson wrote with a concentration of mind and language so extreme that barely a handful of poems exists without some measure of impenetrability. Although relatively few worksheets survive, those that do demonstrate her strenuous engagement with language inside the narrow hymnal form. This pressure shows most plainly in the way her famous first lines impatiently engage and sometimes assault the reader.

After Sunday visiting and pruning honeysuckle in the garden, she wrote in 1854 to her brother Austin, who was nearing the end of his law studies at Harvard, "I'm so tired now, that I write just as it happens, so you must'nt expect any style. This is truly extempore, Austin – I have no notes in my pocket" (L-165). Her habit, as these remarks when she was twenty-three indicate, was to draft incessantly and to concentrate. Dickinson late in her life even made drafts of notes she sent to her sister-in-law Sue next door. The urgency of her expression, visible sometimes in the appearance of a quick, penciled hand on scraps of used paper, makes all the more astonishing one of the unique aspects of her poetry, the fact that while she did not stop writing to the end, the poetry never changed. Its form, its concerns, its style over three decades did not in any essential way alter or evolve. Partly because of this single-minded application, as we shall see, her poetry achieved its characteristic and at the same time most inimitable quality, its compactness. That drastic elimination of discursive space resulted often in individual poems of three or four dozen words at a threshold state of organization that can just barely be called a poetic event. It is this concentration, signaling the end of anecdotal poetry, that creates many of the problems in the poems.

Dickinson rejected the cumulative capability of prose together with the need of actual experience in a proximate world to which the language could refer. In the place of narrative and reference that would systematically direct, a reader encounters language distorted by defects in syntax and grammar, unreasonable transpositions, extreme ellipsis and lost connectives, and many other types of contortions or excisions. Because these problems create indefiniteness, readers going back to familiar poems thought to be perfectly intelligible often find instead confusion not seen before. This is one of the special experiences of reading Dickinson. In poems made indistinct by such problems, a careful reading will take a willing reader to significance in Dickinson's work which is not only new and startling but which indicates about her work the greatest consequence of all, her role as a language founder.

The problems in Dickinson's habitual technique are, in fact, those conspicuous places where she exercised her freedom within the language order and thus are moments when she committed herself. These defects are the nodes of meaning where her personal identity is most intense. The impersonal part of poetry, the impersonal conventions of language, are in these instances charged with personal meaning. Through these difficulties a reader can glimpse the inward character of this poet that lies out of sight. Her idiosyncratic diction and deviant constructions begin to reveal Dickinson in the act of taking an attitude. The resistances in her poems, then, while they prevent definitive meaning, reveal most forcefully the Dickinson that counts, the disruptive and prefiguring force. Difficulty, as Yeats said, forces one down under, like a plow, to original matter, and for us the difficulty reveals Dickinson in her absolute originality.

One more observation needs to be made at the outset. Dickinson's poems make strong claims as intimate, personal disclosure and are most often read this way as autobiography, but the poems, we must note well, have a patent literariness, a heightened rhetoricity, that establishes their status as texts. We should regard them so. This means that as readers we must, in a way, construct the grammar of the language of Dickinson poems. To read her work is, as with any strongly deviating poet, to learn a personal dialect imbedded inside our received language.

Language is formed along two planes, the lexical plane where word selection is made and the intersecting positional plane where the words contract relations with other signs. In the intersection of these planes we have the linguistic event of the poem. Dickinson's problems exist on both planes, but mainly on the horizontal. On the vertical axis she skillfully violates normal selectional rules, but on the combinatorial axis she compacts so severely as to force ellipsis bordering on code. The result is that she increases the density of her style, at the same time extending the distance of her texts from a verifiable subject matter, willingly letting style dominate discourse. The excitement exists not in the reality signified but in the verbal actions of the poems.

We can recompose and accurately read Dickinson's poems once we have separated them along the linguistic planes and pursued her figurative excursions. We are not after meaning but, rather, the way in which the poems function, make or refuse to make their meaning. Where does Dickinson create her particular language with its particular way of seeing and not seeing? The difficulties for us as readers of Dickinson's poems are in fact the places where her special reality is inserted into the otherwise familiar ground of our shared language. We seek that reality, and it is startling.

Word Order

No other poet consistently practiced such extreme reduction and still managed a poetic complexity. "I only said the Syntax – / And left the Verb and the pronoun out," she said cryptically in one poem. Her severe revision of normal transformational rules by which sentences are formed either challenges or baffles readers. It is a highly deviant language that risks everything, for in the extreme ellipsis and transpositioning she has pared away the very armature of meaning, the syntax of the utterance. Although a considerable amount of modern poetry, especially American, has forsaken syntactical precision for psychological process, sometimes set along a vague course of impatiently clustered imagery, a literature that aspires to *meaning* must possess a definable syntactical core. This, then, is my reason for spending time at the outset unpacking the closed-in forms of Dickinson's writing. Editorial intrusions in her work from the beginning in 1890 are evidence of the felt need to construct normal sentence forms out of her compressed mannerisms. Misreadings point up the constant risk she ran by such distillation, by encoding expression not only short of meaning but short even of an adequately suggestive withholding of meaning.

Dickinson wrote at the extremes of linguistic tolerance, and seemingly without a discernible reason for doing so. When Helen Hunt Jackson, a friend and energetic traveler, broke her leg in 1884, the poet wrote a consolatory note of great and clear charm in which she spoke of the captivity of convalescence, but then added some baffling lines that lead to the fine punning metaphor of the prism:

> Pursuing you in your transitions,
> In other Motes –
> Of other Myths
> Your requisition be.
> The Prism never held the Hues,
> It only heard them play –   (P-1602, L-937)

The meaning in the first four lines can be derived of course, but why such strained compaction in a simple get-well note? What Dickinson meant, of course, is that pursuing Helen in all her travels and occupations is like pursuing a mote in a sunbeam and that she is really capturable only in fantasy ("other Myths"). That is, simply, "Helen, you inhabit a world unknown to me!"

When the poet needed exactly coupled syntax, as in the satirically breathless train poem, "I like to see it lap the Miles," she could write it, seventeen lines in a single careful sentence. Letters exist in direct and elemental prose, the more powerful for this simplicity, as in her description of how the news of her father's death arrived. She was writing to her cousins the Norcrosses: "We were eating our supper the fifteenth of June, and Austin came in. He had a despatch in his hand, and I saw by his face we were all lost, though I didn't know how. He said that father was very sick, and he and Vinnie must go. The train had already gone. While horses were dressing, news came he was dead"(L-414). Similarly, Dickinson could write a poem so undemanding that any newspaper would have published it, for example her conventional celebration of a soldier hero. With an apparent and rare reference to the Civil War, eschewing the mystery and encoding we are used to, it begins "He fought like those Who've nought to lose," tells how he "Invited Death – with bold attempt," and declares that he is left alive at the end of the battle "Because / Of Greediness to die."

Transpositioning, sometimes twice doubled over, is one of the habitual ways Dickinson revised the rules of normal sentence formation. We will see later why this and other sudden extinguishings, as in the Helen Hunt letter, occur so often in her poetry. For the moment it presents us with one more difficulty to impede a serious reader. Poems of the sort occur across the three decades of her writing years. In poem 574, for example, the apparently autobiographical speaker "I," ill through the bright days of summer, finally is well enough to go out in the fall to see "the things in Pod" that were "A'blossom" when she "strove" with pain. The summer colors have deepened in harvest time, fall seeming to try "To cheat Herself," to distract herself with redder colors from the approaching seasonal death. The stanza that pursues this point of self-delusion is painfully shuffled about:

> To cheat Herself, it seemed she tried –
> As if before a child
> To fade – Tomorrow – Rainbows held
> The Sepulchre, could hide.

What is meant is very simple by contrast to the difficult language placement: Summer seemed to have tried to delude herself as if rainbows held before a child about to die tomorrow could hide the sepulchre. Readers concerned to give Dickinson's poems a full performance are obliged to do the sort of syntactical restoration I have done here before discarding the reconstruction for Dickinson's own expression, however tortured. Poem after poem blanks out meaning with such problematical transpositions. Another case of subtler intention but comparable contortion occurs in the last two stanzas of the well-known poem beginning "What care the Dead, for Chanticleer":

> What care the Dead for Winter?
> Themselves as easy freeze –
> June Noon – as January Night –
> As soon the South – her Breeze
>
> Of Sycamore – or Cinnamon –
> Deposit in a Stone
> And put a Stone to keep it Warm –
> Give Spices – unto Men –   (P-592)

The final line has no clear attachment to previous lines. As we look for that connection, the difficulty of the final five lines and the analogy that the meaning rests upon grows. The dead are as untouched by the heat of June noons (a thematic echo from "Safe in their Alabaster Chambers" a year or so earlier and from several other poems) as men would be by a southern breeze kept in a stone jar. More fully: life can as easily be given to the dead as the South can give spices to men by depositing her breeze with its scent of sycamore and cinnamon in a stone jar and putting another stone on top to keep the warmth in.

As a final example, we can regard that most impacted of all Dickinson poems, one she labored over as the worksheets show. She seems to have been satisfied with the version below because it is a fair copy and signed. Its syntactical closure of the opening comparative "No Other" is at such an awkward distance that a reader is hard put to trace the parallel structure of the single-(or perhaps two-)sentence poem.

> No Other can reduce
> Our mortal Consequence
> Like the remembering it be nought
> A Period from hence
> But Contemplation for
> Cotemporaneous Nought
> Our Single Competition
> Jehovah's Estimate.   (P-982)

It is in fact a bitterly wrought commentary on the Calvinist view of man as unworthy. But that sense is got only with great difficulty by sorting out syntax and finding the *no other . . . but* construction. It comes down to a spare notion, showing how even this most frugal of all poets could be periphrastic in the space of twenty-seven words. She means: nothing so diminishes our life's importance as the thought that it will be over in a short time, unless it is God's estimate even now of our lives themselves as nought. The grim force, concealed as it is by the impaction, is enhanced, I suppose, only if readers persevere. There are whole areas of charged attitudes and intense intelligence lying concealed beneath Dickinson's cramped syntax.

Sometime in 1884 she wrote to young Samuel Bowles a simple remembrance of his father, who had died in 1878. Two lines of the eight-line poem she included in the brief note are a startling contortion in word order and metaphor. She wrote in strained obliqueness of the elder Bowles who had departed life ("who abdicated Ambush") that he was immortal ("now against his subtle Name / There stands an Asterisk") and then adds:

> As confident of him as we –
> Impregnable we are –   (L-935)

What she means is that we are as confident of his immortality as if we were infallible ("impregnable"). It is a curious knot to put in her reader's way, but it is characteristic and we want to know why.

Ellipsis so radical that it halts the reading of certain poems is another of the most noticeable of Dickinson's mannerisms. Her deletions occur so often that almost no poem is without a sudden absence of connective language. The difficulty presents itself in varying degrees. How, for example, could she think to get away with a stanza opening with the line "A Wonderful – to feel the Sun"? The answer is that the missing predicate nominative must be reconstituted by the reader from a parallel construction in the poem: "A Solemn thing within the Soul / To feel itself get ripe." Dickinson deleted the entire phrase "thing within the Soul," putting the burden of its restoration on a willing reader. The presumptuous line then carries in six words the meaning of twelve: It is a wonderful thing within the Soul to feel the Sun. The habit is apparent from the earliest poems. Two words, for instance, linked by a dash in poem 7 (1858 or earlier) carry the freight of at least eight or nine words that must be supplied silently. She leads into this amputated line with a properly complete syntactical chain, then deletes the verb and the clausal connective for which there is actually no place:

> Pearls are the Diver's farthings
> Extorted from the Sea –
> Pinions – the Seraph's wagon
> Pedestrian once – as we –
> Night is the morning's Canvas
> Larceny – legacy –
> Death, but our rapt attention
> To Immortality.   (P-7)

"Larceny – legacy" then holds the entire weight of a presumed phrase such as this: Loss is the necessary condition preceding reward or fulfillment. The idea is one of Dickinson's constant beliefs, that whatever is given involves the price of its denial. Here it is lodged in two words and a dash and depends upon the reader's obliging pause to recover, in his mind and not in the poem itself, the absent sense.

Her single line "To lack – enamor Thee" in poem 355 draws from lines extending back to the beginning of the poem " 'Tis Opposites – entice" so that the four words actually have the sense of something much longer: To be absent from you makes me love you. Dickinson is able, by a curious pretense of presence and intensity, aided by varying amounts of contextual help such as parallel constructions, to create sufficient pressure that the assiduous reader supplies the poem's details and, indeed, adequate meaning. Helen Hunt Jackson preserved what seems to be Dickinson's shortest stanza-length poem in a canon characterized by brevity, remarking to Higginson, "Wonderful twelve words!" Thirteen words long, in fact, it obliges the reader to supply much of the connective tissue.

> Spurn the temerity –
> Rashness of Calvary –
> Gay were Gethsemane
> Knew we of Thee –   (P-1432)

It is the familiar Dickinson knowledge that present agony is little enough compared to the pain that is possible and perhaps to come. This minimal poem, pendant on the single, fine alliterative paradox of the third line, cannot be satisfactorily paraphrased because it barely provides enough to work on, but the sense is something like this: Let us not rush to the promised judgment, for the trials of doubt are happiness compared to the final wager of annihilation.

Dickinson also habitually deleted auxiliary verbs so that a reader, to comprehend her words as a sensible chain and not simply verbal flashes, must once again go about restoring the absent. For a single example, a line on her cherished subject of sunset turning to night in poem 469 figures the evening sky in "Miles of Sparks" and the day as "The Territory Argent – that / Never yet – consumed." She means that day's sky was never yet consumed by its own burning from dawn to sundown. For all such examples of problematic elisions, we must recognize what intensity, if not coherence, of purpose was involved. We know that the poet was extremely upset after the *Springfield Daily Republican* published the poem beginning "A Narrow Fellow in the Grass" with a comma inserted which destroyed the necessary enjambment of the third and fourth lines and thus the syntactic sense. "The third and fourth were one," she wrote plaintively to Higginson, whom she had informed earlier that she "did not print"; the poem "was robbed of me."

I have called her habit of ellipsis drastic elimination. No other poet in English has carried the manner to such extremes. Her minute elegy for her father, "Lay this Laurel on the one," continues to baffle even her ardent readers, as do the well-known lines on her deeply held belief in the virtue of renouncing present pleasures for anticipated bliss. It is the admired but often skimmed and misunderstood "Renunciation – is a piercing Virtue."

> Renunciation – is a piercing Virtue –
> The letting go
> A Presence – for an Expectation –
> Not now –
> The putting out of Eyes –
> Just Sunrise –
> Lest Day –
> Day's Great Progenitor –
> Outvie
> Renunciation – is the Choosing
> Against itself –
> Itself to justify
> Unto itself –
> When larger function –
> Make that appear –
> Smaller – that Covered Vision – Here –   (P-745)

What makes a reader stumble here are radical deletion and transposition that obscure clauses, confuse subjects and objects, and generally knot the syntax chain. The poem is composed of three sentences that, reconstituted, read well enough but very abstractly:

> Renunciation is a piercing virtue, the letting go a presence for an expectation not fulfillable now.
> Renunciation is like the putting out of one's eyes just at sunrise lest day itself outvie God, day's great progenitor.

Renunciation is the choosing against one's present welfare since it will be justified later when a greater reward will make what filled one's vision here appear smaller by comparison.

With this we begin to feel how much concentration of consciousness Dickinson's compactions effect, for my paraphrase is flabby and banal as it stands. The compression in the original creates the urgency, the emotional tautness, and the intensity of half-articulated but fully conscious intentions. As readers, unless we first open out the syntax to let in all the meaning, then close the poem back up and let the aura surround it, we only skim these events of high specific gravity as if the verbal play were the entire poem.

A similar loss of adequate response may occur in a four-line poem on her father, the most distilled elegy she ever composed. The diction is skewed ("little Fate") and the syntax at one point is abruptly discontinuous, but the sense lies in mysterious seclusion behind the crowded words. We can open up this marvelous elegy of fifteen words that she sent to Higginson a year and a half after her father's death:

> To his simplicity
> To die – was little Fate –
> If Duty live – contented
> But her Confederate. (P-1352)

It is constituted of two sentences, and we can reverse the poet's process of distillation to reach the full expression before dispensing with paraphrases and simply holding the poem's fifteen words before us in the aura of unsaid language.

To his simple nature, death was no momentous event.
If Duty were a person, he would be contented just to be her ally.

To clarify it even more by making the crossing from "little Fate" to "Duty": To his simple nature, dying was a duty.

Perhaps Dickinson was verbose in her fifteen words! But as Dickinson readers we become capable of a kind of extraordinary compaction ourselves. What comes out of this poem is a simple consolatory belief that carries the day, consoles deeply. The poem demonstrates again that, no matter how simple the thought, her expression richly complicates the reading experience by making us arrange the meaning, finding in the impediments of the language the submerged force that explicitness will not provide. Problematic and intense, the poems will not release us too easily from the words' embrace, the ancient mariner's stare.

Examples abound, and it is tempting to go poem by poem through the unreleased significance on the pages of the variorum. But only one more example is needed to show how the habit of clotted expression breaks down meaning almost beyond recovery. This poem from about 1865, sent to Sue in a fair copy, was composed perhaps two years earlier.

> We miss Her, not because We see –
> The Absence of an Eye –
> Except it's Mind accompany
> Abridge Society
>
> As slightly as the Routes of Stars –
> Ourselves – asleep below –
> We know that their superior Eyes
> Include Us – as they go –   (P-993)

The meaning of the last stanza is clear enough and thoroughly Dickinsonian in its quiet belief in the dead's remembrance of the living. She assumed, in almost all she wrote, the existence of consciousness after death. What stumps us are the deletions that have left lines three and four high and dry, unconnected, blankly staring at us, their independent and stubborn existence complicated by the unattached pronoun *it's* (even allowing for the erroneous apostrophe Dickinson always used). The poem, I have come to believe, is composed basically of three sentences. The first five lines, however, are under great strain to say a fairly complicated thing in a total of only thirty-six syllables. To do this, in fact, the first two sentences share the same two phrases that constitute lines two and three, line two doing syntactical duty first as the object of the verb "see" and second as the subject of the verb "abridge." Here, if I am correct, is the way the three sentences, two of them overlapping, read:

1. We miss her (the dead, the absent) not because we cannot see her physically or she cannot see us ("The Absence of an Eye") but only if her mind (her consciousness of us) is also absent ("Except it's Mind accompany").

2. The physical absence ("The Absence of an Eye"), unless the consciousness of us is also absent ("Except it's Mind accompany"), abridges society (Dickinson also wrote the variants "impair," "debar," "deprive") as slightly as the journeys of the stars at night as we sleep.
3. We, asleep below, know that, like the stars, she still takes account of us ("their superior Eyes / Include us – as they go").

It is not possible to dismiss the poem as simply a variation on a Sunday school slogan—the dead do not depart but only reside above—for Dickinson by her garbled language has turned it so strange, to the point of unintelligibility, that a deeper significance is suggested. Some heretofore unrecognized need of the poet's mind has, by its intensity, forced language into functional disorder.

Cumulative weirdness of this sort impedes habitualization, as the Russian formalists knew, preventing us from sliding off poems with easy gratificatiion. There isn't the *transparency* of the familiar. This disjunction by way of impacted language, accomplished by ellipsis and transposition primarily, but not, I believe, by a sophisticated conscious design, is what makes her a better poet than her cherished Elizabeth Barrett Browning who, in a powerful but undefined transformative way and perhaps more than any other poet, inspired this American primitive. It is worth studying the obscurities in this Browningesque poem:

> "Why do I love" You, Sir?
> Because –
> The Wind does not require the Grass
> To answer – Wherefore when He pass
> She cannot keep Her place.
>
> Because He knows – and
> Do not You –
> And We know not –
> Enough for Us
> The Wisdom it be so –
>
> The Lightning – never asked an Eye
> Wherefore it shut – when He was by –
> Because He knows it cannot speak –
> And reasons not contained –
> – Of Talk –
> There be – preferred by Daintier Folk –

The Sunrise – Sir – compelleth Me –
Because He's Sunrise – and I see –
Therefore – Then –
I love Thee –   (P-480)

Although Dickinson bound this poem into one of her packets, it is by
no means a finished product. It troubles itself all the way through to
find its eight- and six-syllable lines, succeeding in an irregular way
with the eights dominant. The "defects" include a willful assigning of
gender to wind and grass, lightning and sunrise, but not to the eye.
They include a confusion of address and reference (I, You, He, She,
We), a gratuitous archaicism or two, and the analogies of wind-grass,
lightning-eye, and sunrise-seeing, which are parallel in conception
but disorderly in presentation. The syntactic reasoning of the poem is
rudimentary but chartable: Why—Because—Because—Because—
Therefore. When we have with difficulty sorted out the analogical
assertions of the poem, we have a version of love that is instinctive
and unsayable but declared in roughly coupled words that are themselves inordinately compelling. Here is an interposed paraphrase followed by the essential statement the poem makes.

"Why do I love" You, Sir?   question
Because
  The Wind does not require the Grass   analogy
  To answer – (why) when He pass(es)
  She cannot keep Her place.
(He does not require an answer)   reasoning
Because He knows
And (You do not)   reasoning
And We (do not) know –
(It is) Enough for Us
(To know that it is so).
  The Lightning – never asked an Eye   analogy
  (Why) it shut – when He (appeared) –
Because He knows (that the eye) cannot speak –   reasoning
There (are) reasons not contained (by language)
(That are) preferred by (the lesser) Folk
(i.e., the grass, the eye, me)
  The Sunrise – Sir – compel(s) Me –   analogy
Because (He is the Sunrise) – and I see (because of Him)
(For these reasons) – Then   reasoning
I love Thee –

The essential paraphrase is this: Why do I love you, Sir? Because, like the blown grass and the blinking eye, I cannot help myself. My love is as natural and unspoken as when grass is moved by the wind or the eye snaps shut from lightning or when seeing is made possible by the sunrise. What the poem says then is intelligible only if we are willing to unpack the syntax, lay the lines out, and then recompose the poem. It is fair to ask what is accomplished by this wedged style of Dickinson's with its apparent carelessness and unfinishedness. If we put some lines of the precursive poem alongside it, we see that Barrett Browning's are, by contrast, marshaled in the systemic reasonableness of the language and therefore sound prearranged if not indeed public and predictable.

> I love thee to the level of everyday's
> Most quiet need, by sun and candle-light.
> I love thee freely, as men strive for Right,
> I love thee purely, as they turn from Praise.

Dickinson's lines in comparison demonstrate the intimate, affective result of the unfamiliar forced by crowded syntax, ambiguous connectives, and thus uncertain sentence arrangements. The power of the strange emerges from the well-known. Thus compaction and impediment, when they do not suffocate meaning, can increase specific gravity. The tension of the strangeness concentrates in her poem in the strenuously simple point that the unstable word grouping makes: I love you because I have no choice. Now that is an intensely wrought simplicity that Browning's transparent language cannot accomplish.

Dickinson's syntax displacement and ellipsis create opaque moments in poem after poem, requiring careful naturalization. Yet they are worth our effort, for quite aside from the dozens of familiar poems, each with its own moments of shadow, those poems that are little read and never anthologized contain in more concentrated form Dickinson's occluded language and thus the mysterious vision behind them. Difficult, sometimes unyielding, they are a window into her unique self as an artist and the site of her strange freedom. Almost all are poems published in the twentieth century—because of their difficulty they were culled from the verse published in the 1890s. It was an inevitable process of selection by which the problematic poems were withheld from publication until our time.

The most important effect of this radical linguistic insubordination is the estranging vision by which beauty can be discovered in unexpected places. It was a complicated creative act of which Dickinson seems to have been less than fully conscious. She sought intuitively the rewards in the stubbornly alien, "delight as difficult as stalactite" as she pointed out in one severely reduced poem.

> Must be a Wo –
> A loss or so –
> To bend the eye
> Best Beauty's way –
>
> But – once aslant
> It notes Delight
> As difficult
> As Stalactite –   (P-571)

Because her compressed lines, themselves within compressed stanzas, cannot accumulate meaning or develop situations, the lines hammer quickly, as in the poem above, with a few sharp blows of highly concentrated signification. Together with the jammed syntax, the effect in the end, sometimes willy-nilly, is to complicate signification and thus to deepen meaning. This difficult language of extreme reduction thus holds powerful compulsions that are conveyed extralinguistically: an impatient need to speak, and the willful irregularity everywhere manifesting intense consciousness.

Word Choice

Breaches of rules on the semantic plane vex readers of Dickinson's poems, as do the defects of syntax. Sometimes the mannerisms that stand out so prominently are results of the unfinished state of her stanzas when she did not make final selections from among parallel jottings and suggested changes, even though she copied out the texts for her packets. All critics of Dickinson have drawn attention to these evasions of standard usage. Such deviations were the principal elements that her earliest editors were careful to repair for the first edition. The most willfully deviant of the poems had to wait until the twentieth century to be published in their unedited versions. What her contemporaries considered irregular and idiosyncratic, even obscurely crazy, this century was ready to regard as a virtue, liberation from conventional language.

The Puzzling Idiom

Taken together, these violations along the selectional axis contribute to the identifying voice of this poet. They are the chief activating strength of an otherwise conventional vocabulary. They are among the points where she exercised her freedom, separated her voice from others of the age, and inaugurated the audacious attitude we have come to see as postmodernist. It is necessary to distinguish valuable linguistic adventures from the highly mannered but weak stylistic devices that constitute her occasional pose as a child or the Druidic, gnomic Queen. This language shows Dickinson consciously altering her expression to a cloying oddness that draws attention to itself, parading a strained novelty that achieves only a false profundity. It is excessively deliberate, just off-center to no satisfactory purpose. When Samuel Bowles was in Europe in 1862, for example, she chose to convey to him the most conventional of sentiments in language of childish artlessness, as if language were conscious of itself for the first time. "We hope," she wrote, "you are more well than when you lived in America" (L-266). In another letter she said: "I don't know how many will be glad to see you, because I never saw your whole friends, but I have heard, that in large Cities – noted persons chose you" (L-272). At about the same time she was satisfied to write lines of verse such as these: "I can murmur broken" (P-151); "To scan a Ghost, is faint" (P-281); "The Daily Own – of Love" (P-580). The queenly habit appears in an 1873 letter to her cousin Perez Cowan: "It is long since I knew of you, Peter . . . I hope that you have Power" (L-386).

Hardly a poem is free of such deviations, which pull her language into a foreign area separate from the commonplace world of verbal intercourse. Her language becomes dense, giving up its communicative transparency. Against the background of the norms of usage, these Dickinsonian features are prominent because of their abnormality. She made choices that were not, as her editors knew, permissible actions in the accepted code. What resulted were highly unpredictable combinations of idiosyncrasies.

Dickinson's verbs persistently have their normal inflections lopped off. Critics have explained that the uninflected form is acceptable subjunctive mood, and this in some cases is right. The habit was so strong that when, for instance, she copied out William Ellery Channing's famous line "If my bark sinks, 'tis to another sea," she characteristically divided it so as to get a six-syllable line and put in her own capitals: "If my Bark sink / 'Tis to another sea" (P-1234). She had thus made the line her own with these personal devices. Her liberties with verb inflection extended more widely yet. She eliminated the distinction between active and passive voice and used them interchangeably. "Great Clouds – like Ushers – leaning" she wrote in poem 524 with that characteristic need to provide an audience for death (like the "Gazing Grain"). In the variant, however, as if there were no verb distinction, she made the line read "Great Clouds – like Ushers – placing." She means that Great Clouds *were placed.* This makes an image of "Creation – looking on," as she says in the next line. But how can we make sense of this slip except by ascribing it to carelessness or to the first quick drafting of lines later to be repaired? Significantly, however, she copied such seemingly careless usages into packets, indicating that she was satisfied with them in that state. She wrote in this same packet poem "The Flesh – surrendered – Cancelled" to mean that the flesh surrendered and *was canceled.* From the intransitive verb *surrendered* she changed instantaneously to a transitive form with no notice to the reader, who then must supply the absent auxiliary verb and make the meaning himself. She does it often as not, as here in poem 594 where, speaking of the Soul's secret battle with an unidentified "No Man," perhaps extinction or God, she wrote the lines: "Its bodiless Campaign / Establishes, and terminates." She means to say that the Soul's struggle is undertaken ("establishes") and reaches, still invisibly, its resolution ("terminates"). Grammatically the lines should read "Its Bodiless Campaign / *Is* established and terminates." Confusions such as this halt our passage through the poem, attention distracted by the mannerisms. Poem 515 is filled with this disconcerting (an appropriate word) pared-down verb form in defiance of what grammar calls for in the way of tense or number. The first two stanzas demonstrate:

> No Crowd that has occurred
> Exhibit – I suppose
> That General Attendance
> That Resurrection – does –
>
> Circumference be full –
> The long restricted Grave
> Assert her Vital Privilege –
> The Dust – connect – and live –

All together there are nine instances of uninflected verbs in the poem, which was not published until 1929. Higginson twice repaired the same grammatical defect in poem 619 when he published it in an article in 1890, altering the line "When Winter shake the Door." She dropped the auxiliary verb completely in poem 642, evidently to make her three-syllable line:

> And since We're mutual Monarch
> How this be
> Except by Abdication –
> Me – of Me?

We shall see later how such deviation leads beyond questions of style to qualities of mind. For the moment we observe that Dickinson's habitually uninflected verbs, though some indeed function properly as subjunctives, for the most part have no warrant in grammar.[1]

What does this liberty, which no college freshman would be allowed, accomplish? It can be interpreted as a way, barely conscious on the poet's part I believe, of denying time or transcending it, of taking an utterance out of time by using only the verb root and assiduously refusing any inflection that signifies restriction of tense or number. The deviance sounds to our ears gnomic, calling attention to the language, and simultaneously removing the language further from the referential reality outside the words. Within the poem, for reasons we must seek, the root word itself sufficed for her. For the reader, these deviations create a stubborn expressiveness that is beyond tense but, most especially, outside automatic perception. Her language becomes the center of our attention because it is the center of our problems.

Dickinson's lost referents are another problem for readers. These omissions contribute to the larger absence of an identifiable world visible through her language. Pronouns without apparent referents occur in several poems. The habit is fundamental, as one can see from the long list of works that begin with an unassigned "It," poems whose language then goes on to grasp this absent referent. In puerile passages, Dickinson used "it" as an awkward intimacy. "Would it teach me now?" she asked Higginson in an 1868 verse note (P-815). Elsewhere she evidently meant an unassigned "it" as a dehumanized term for a man soon to be a corpse (P-614). But these local cases of irrelation foreshadow whole poems without an evident subject.

The problem of the absent subject involves single pronouns that float unattached and metaphors sailing free of a solid reality outside the language, as in this poem where the subject is eternally obscured.

> It knew no lapse, nor Diminution –
> But large – serene –
> Burned on – until through Dissolution –
> It failed from Men –
>
> I could not deem these Planetary forces
> Annulled –
> But suffered an Exchange of Territory –
> Or World –   (P-560)

She used the closing lines in a letter to Higginson in 1863 when she discovered in a newspaper that he had gone to command a regiment in the Civil War. The lines there, by strenuous interpretation, seem to apply to this fact of Higginson's absence for which she had had no explanation. But the poem itself, copied into a packet, sits on the page without a subject. It may be about love or friendship or, indeed, about the sun burning until it is extinguished, an image in the poet's mind, but never mentioned, associated with human relationships severed by time. These problems of reference in Dickinson are elements of the poems that speak but do not name. There is no final reality, and the loss of that reality is a function of a language intent on saying itself and not on signifying a specific world. Dickinson's mannerisms and defects accelerate this withdrawal of language from its function of observation. Her punctuation, inconsistent and novel and much discussed by her critics, contributes in a visual way to denaturalizing the language and removing her expression even further from its function as a mimetic medium.

The crucial stylistic constant is Dickinson's violation of normal selectional rules on the lexical plane. This distortion, combined with her transpositions and omissions along the compositional plane, creates a complication of language sometimes so unusual as to conceal meaning and to separate words from things. It conveys powerfully a sense of estrangement that begins to suggest a rare and even alarming poetic mind. Poetry, of course, relies on the breaking of selectional rules, but a reader expects the context to indicate the way the breaches are to be read. Dickinson was acutely conscious of the way she violated the rules. She wrote to Mrs. Holland at one point referring to her nephew: "Ned tells that the Clock purrs and the Kitten ticks. He inherits his Uncle Emily's ardor for the lie" (L-315). The list of her deviations would be the recitation of the body of her poetry, for it was her principal lexical habit as it is one of the recurring sources of our problem of reading.

She changed codes by changing classes of words, substituting parts of speech, violating equivalences.

> Did you ever stand in a Cavern's Mouth –
>
> . . . .
>
> In such a place, what horror,
> How Goblin it would be –
> And fly, as 'twere pursuing you?   (P-590)

"Goblin" and "fly" as adjectives here make the dazzling gaiety of her language that we cherish. The lines are not significant for their definition of fright and loneliness—it is a definition poem of sorts—but for what they demonstrate about the graftings and transplants the language can undergo.

There is a catalogue, as well, of Dickinson's adjectival selections that create instant contradiction, the more powerful, as in all good poetry, for the surprise of their insight. It is a risky, open playfulness that one does not encounter in the sober work of her contemporaries. She copied two words from Emerson's poem "The Snow-Storm" that fit exactly her own selectional ploy: "tumultuous privacy." Dickinson's comparable effects strike us immediately as her familiar voice: "broken mathematics" and "Penurious eyes" (P-88), "a sudden sky" (P-282), "delirious hem" (P-414), "stumbling buzz" (P-465). "Sumptuous destitution" explodes with meaning, as Richard Wilbur showed us, and labels in an instant one of this poet's abiding angles of vision. She wrote "sumptuous despair" elsewhere (P-505), for the adjective was richly useful as she gripped the polar extremities of fullness and frugality, overwhelming amplitude and paralyzing sterility. "Outer wine" she wrote in poem 383, in a combination barely within the limits of intelligibility, to mean any exterior exhilarant compared to "that diviner Brand / The Soul achieves – Herself."

But this freedom of selection carried her toward an absolutely private lexicon. We can read then only with the help of the entire canon where, in many cases, she has done similar things. When she writes "I helped his Film – with Hymn" in poem 616, an allegory vaguely about giving sustenance to someone in the extremity of dying, we are at a loss to know what she is up to, even with interpretive help from the rest of the poem. Her speaker means that she sustained someone in his dying, his lessening of sight, with the assurances of faith; that is, "I helped his Film – with Hymn." When she writes in poem 925 "Robbed – was I – intact to Bandit – / All my Mansion torn," we know from variants that "intact to Bandit" means, in her private dialect, that she was robbed, but not by a bandit. Her loss came in another never-named way. Her secretive modes are in view in poem 523, where she seems to equate unlikely, always elastic, categories: "sum" with love, "Decay of you" with forgetfulness or rejection or death, "Barefoot Vision" with the joy of extravagant expense of love. In poem 786 "Vacuum" is her metaphor for loss, but she substitutes the word "longitude" for it in a variant so that "To fill the awful Vacuum" is, in her usage, the same as "To fill the awful Longitude."

A final example of a variant indicates how the Dickinson idiolect slips from the just marginally intelligible into a sealed territory. When she wrote in poem 284 "She knows herself an incense small," she meant "an offering small," as the variant shows, but the reader is ignorant of such metonymic transfers of terms except where variants show Dickinson's mind making its subjective equations.

When she is successful, she is marvelously inventive and suggestive. Her performance serves always to display the language. In the snake poem (986) she shows us less the way a snake looks than how ingenuity can reanimate language and put it up to saying new things, make us see afresh the life within language itself apart from an exterior reality. "A narrow fellow in the grass" centers our attention on the single word "narrow" because it is an unlikely quantification, almost mathematical. With the application of "narrow" to snake (the same occurs with "rides" in the next line), the text suddenly opens before us not a faithful picture of a snake, but a word performance violating the rules again, holding up to our view the dissociation of words and things. Her word looks in a new way at a snake, in the end not making the snake more snaky, but the language itself presumptuous, autonomous.

This separation is furthered by another characteristic of the verse: its instability caused by a speaker who is unlocated and unidentified.

As an instance, in poem 1277 Dickinson changes, in her variant, evidently without care for precise reference, from the personal "I" to what sounds like a more or less philosophical "We." In a poem about a spider, her habitual merging of identities occurs, once again blurring reference. In this poem, beginning "The Spider as an Artist," the possible significations beside an actual spider are an artist, a vaguely Christlike miracle worker, and the poet herself. The result, in a problematic way, is to run all these possibilities in together. The reader confronts persistent indefiniteness as these self-regarding texts withdraw from clarity into a verbal gaming, sometimes systematic playfulness of great intensity, and the felt hyperactivity of a poetic consciousness in which words lose touch with palpable things.

Metaphor and Metonym

The characteristic act of Dickinson's mind on the axis of semantic reference is metaphorical. Reality recedes in varying degrees behind her figures, and where they are most arbitrary, where her impatience to get at the few essential human experiences is strongest, and where the context supplied by the brief poems is not adequate to establish the metaphorical referents, the mystery of the poems is deepest. Certain poems lose sight of their subjects by their metaphorical extravagance. While "that White Sustenance Despair" is a stunning figurative close to the long poem beginning "I cannot live with You," because the context prepares the meaning, a metaphor such as "peninsula" ranges in and out of intelligibility depending on the adequacy of the context. In the tangled worksheet of the poem beginning "Two Butterflies went out at Noon" peninsula means both a solid place and fulfillment. The surreal metaphor "My Blue Peninsula" in poem 405 (Italy may be its distant origin) signifies the state of delight as hope is fulfilled. But in poem 1775, the "unknown peninsula" is evidently a bleak place without beauty that exists nowhere in nature but only in the mind. Finally, "Her unsown Peninsula" in poem 474 stubbornly resists definite meaning. Dickinson's troping habit oscillates between these poles of effective metaphorical meaning at one extreme and metonymic indefiniteness and lost reality at the other.

Tropic distance is so extended at times that Dickinson's own mental connection between figure and reality is lost or, at best, made partly intelligible only by translation. When she read in the *Spring-field Daily Republican* that Colonel Higginson had taken command of a regiment in South Carolina, she began her letter to him, as I noted earlier, with a declaration so abstract it defies clarification. "Dear Friend," she began, "I did not deem that Planetary forces annulled – but suffered an Exchange of Territory, or World" (L-280). Translated from its cosmic grandeur the line evidently was intended to say: I did not believe you had suddenly disappeared by some accident of celestial physics, but that you had moved or died. The letter is one of the most curious she ever wrote, contorted with mannerisms, strained with dense and at the same time oblique locutions such as this: "I found you were gone, by accident, as I find Systems are, or Seasons of the year, and obtain no cause – but suppose it a treason of Progress – that dissolves as it goes." In the end the letter concerns itself quite simply with Higginson's possible death in the war and, in Dickinson's unabashed if concealed way, wishes him life first, then, if necessary, immortality.

The same oblique habit obtains in the poems. "Her effacing fathom," a phrase in four lines of poetry that she sent to Higginson in mid-February 1876 (L-450), may mean Ecstasy's deepest mystery. Sometimes she was being, through metonymy, only childishly coy, as when she wrote to Mrs. Bowles who was in New York City (L-244): "You must come back – now – and bring the Blanket to Massachusetts." She meant bring her new baby. She wrote that she had spoken to Bowles once of his "Gem chapter," meaning his life after death (L-536). There is much more of this curious impalpability: "distant as an Order done / And doubtful as Report upon / Multitudes of Noon," she wrote, referring to how bees disappear in the evening; or "The Magic passive but extant" that exists "Somewhere upon the general Earth," meaning some inspiring love "That consecrated me" (P-1231); or "magic Planks" for, of all things, flying insects in the summer air (P-1198); or "A Freckled shrine" to mean a human heart (P-1311); or a "British sky" because bluebirds are its ships (P-1213); or "mellow – murmuring thread" to mean a pinetree (P-161); or "the bewildering thread" to refer to the mysterious makeup of human character (P-278).

When Dickinson is most hermetic in her metaphorical calculus, she is most baffling because she has withdrawn from the specific world her readers inhabit. There are exceptions of note, as we shall see with a little archaeological digging. But one of the problematics that introduces opaqueness into the poetry is the holophrastic tendency, which language systems abet, of trying to express a complex idea by a single term.[2] "Circumference" is her best-known catchall word. But in individual poems these sudden lurches into closed symbolism or into code words results in erecting the words themselves impassably between the language and the meaning. Each is an instance of communication blackout that is characteristic of Dickinson and will lead us eventually to a primary aspect of her radical modernism. As an example, in a superb poem about the wind that preceeds a rainstorm and at its onset is indistinguishable in sound from the rain ("Like Rain it sounded till it curved"), she writes of the rain's effect, and in the process we watch her accelerating images into metaphors and then beyond that into a private phrase seemingly packed with meaning but in fact unintelligible.

> A coming as of Hosts was heard
> That was indeed the Rain –
> It filled the Wells, it pleased the Pools
> It warbled in the Road –
> It pulled the spigot from the Hills
> And let the Floods abroad –
> It loosened acres, lifted seas
> The sites of Centres stirred
> Then like Elijah rode away
> Upon a Wheel of Cloud   (P-1235)

What is meant by "sites of Centres"? Probably that the storm loosens everything and seems to shake the very center-pin of things. The phrase works if we can locate the references behind this intangible metaphor. Elsewhere, but not characteristically, she has spelled out the metaphors in her mind, as she did in poem 575. " 'Heaven' has different Signs – to me," it begins, and the list of figures that signify heaven to her is specific and we recognize them all: Noon, Dawn, the orchard in the sun ("when the Sun is on"), birds in song, "Carnivals of Clouds," and sunset ("The Rapture of a finished Day"). Alternatively, the reader is hard put to understand, unless he investigates Dickinson's variant readings, the phrase "yawning Consciousness" from poem 1323. It means the consciousness of both "the chance of life" and the fact of annihilation.

When referential clarity fades out and cancels meaning, the reader is forced into a labor of decipherment. To use Dickinson's term, the reader attempts, if the promise seems great enough, to "fulfill the pantomime contained in the words." This is the constant endeavor. When the effort is applied to an already effective metaphor such as the "Gazing Grain" in the best known of all her poems, "Because I could not stop for Death," we experience the enormous power of her expression. Consideration alone will not disclose the source of its effect. It is a spot of curiously dark, indefinite knowledge that comes through the intense, unclear language. The figure is a measure of her troping distance as well as an instance where the power of the original sensation is preserved. The third stanza has the speaker in her carriage-hearse moving toward the graveyard:

> We passed the School, where Children strove
> At Recess – in the Ring –
> We passed the Fields of Gazing Grain –
> We passed the Setting Sun –   (P-712)

We feel that "Gazing Grain" is precisely right, quite aside from the pleasing alliteration, but we don't know why. Our search discovers that Dickinson, in a lyric about summer ripeness, inserted a single line that brings the reader up short by the leap of association it demands. She refers first to the nuts the squirrel hunts and then to the ripe berries.

> Oh, when the Squirrel fills His Pockets
> And the Berries stare
> How can I bear their jocund Faces
> Thou from Here, so far?   (P-956)

We surmise that fruit and grains are to be seen as eyes. This link is all we have needed. We may remember that Dickinson herself was shy of being looked at and so made a point to arrive at church early. In the pantomime behind the adjective *gazing*, we now see the full tableau: the ripe grains, tall and heavy-headed, humanlike, bend in unison suggesting a single object of their focus. There is a remarkable density of action within this metaphorical risk. We know that Dickinson, in her frugal poems, loaded other expressions with a weight of esoteric significance. In this, we see the way some of her better metaphors function. We see the poet's mind, that is, making its leaps with words, attempting to concentrate the reality within the words instead of directing our attention outside. *See what I am able to say,* the poems assert time and again. It is a word-centered and exclusive art in which the world itself grows indefinite and distanced. Example after example of the specific gravity of individual words and their mysterious removal from specific reality occurs in Dickinson's poems.

Her control over this recurrent figurative movement of mind is not precise, however, and the problem of elastic semantics sets in. She substituted meanings for words, as if the language existed for its own inherent bonding. The meaning waits to be assigned as it will. For example, when she writes of dwelling with Immortality, as in poem 679 or 680, the reference may be to spiritual expectation or to fame as a poet or to some other aspiration. Most likely it is only a partly conscious merging of two or three vague reachings of the self. When, elsewhere, she substitutes in her variants "Faith" for "Love" (P-491) or "transports" and "Treasures" and "aspects" for "Persons" (P-1404), we not only struggle to visualize the metaphorical figure but must accommodate still further to the flexibility of meaning in what seems a random substitution of terms. At the least, a reader becomes aware that such substitutions suggest the anteriority of her language to any specific occasion, the style before the meaning. This observation will serve us later when we consider at a deeper level the significance of this word-centered disregard for a precise referent. Dickinson throughout her life was in the habit of extracting stanzas from poems to put into letters where they refer to a theme or occasion quite different from the one that provided their original subject. She does this with a stanza from 1297, a poem about preparing to meet the lover in heaven: "Go slow, my soul" to face "his final eye." In a letter to the Norcross cousins the same lines refer to the season: "Go slow, my soul" to meet March. It was a characteristic switch for this poet, as it was when she sent out a reworked stanza of the splendid love poem beginning "There came a Day at Summer's full" as consolation for a death in her pastor's family.

The casualness of her focus is evident in "Going to Him! Happy letter!" where she was content to substitute feminine pronouns for masculine ones. Even love's language in the end was easily, innocently transferable. On one occasion she substituted the word "Herself" for "Dawn" so that the poem (P-1619) would refer to Helen Hunt Jackson. She substituted "Susan" for "Nature" in the line readers have made much of in discussing Dickinson's relationship to nature: "But Nature is a stranger yet." All of these transfers indicate the primacy of the language as against the contingency of the reality that presents itself as subject. She used a poem on autumn, beginning "As Summer into Autumn slips," to serve as a "portrait," as she said in a letter to Bowles in 1875, of her father. Nor did she hesitate to take a quatrain out of the intently focused poem beginning "Each Life Converges to some Centre" and send it with a note to stand for something quite trivial — Sue's missing a trip to Springfield from her Amherst home.

Dickinson acknowledged on at least one occasion the problem of her farfetched metaphors when she explicitly interpreted some of her lines for a friend. It was an extraordinary disclosure, for her characteristic response to a reader's bafflement was, as in the first "Master" letter in 1858, to compound the mystery. There she wrote, replying to an expression of perplexity from him and referring to poems she had sent: "You ask me what my flowers said – then they were disobedient – I gave them messages. They said what the lips in the West, say, when the Sun goes down, and so says the Dawn" (L-187). But years later, on a worksheet draft of the poem beginning "I shall not murmur if at last," she showed exactly what she wanted her short lines to bear. The poem, eight lines together with three lines of a new attempt, apparently has to do with Dickinson's refusal to meet face to face with the oldest of friends. The lines, evidently intended for her childhood friend Kate Anthon, who visited Amherst in 1877, contain the words "Treason" and "sight's ineffable disgrace," which Dickinson translates in a rare acknowledgment of the obscurity. Her paraphrase resembles Hart Crane's dutiful interpretation of his line "Frosted eyes there were that lifted altars" for Harriet Monroe. "My not being able to see you," Dickinson explained to her friend, "is not because I don't care ('Treason') – but because I should be speechless. I prefer to keep my dream of you rather than see the reality which might mar that dream ('sight's ineffable disgrace')" (L-1410). The three cryptic lines the poet penciled on the worksheet demonstrate how much she wanted to pack into a single phrase:

> We shun because we prize her Face
> Lest sight's ineffable disgrace
> Our Adoration stain

"Sight's ineffable disgrace," we learn from the paraphrase, is intended to say a great deal: Actually seeing you would stain-mar-flaw (variants) my adoration because it would make me speechless. The burden on twenty-two syllables is typical of the simultaneous density and vagueness of her metaphorical intention.

Of great consequence to the evolution of poetry in America, the poems establish a new and divisive relationship to reality. The language pulls back from clarity, from specificity, and from discernible referential links to an outside reality. So remote are her poetic episodes that we inevitably conclude that the basic movement of her mind is allegorical. In discussing Dickinson's "partiality for nonrepresentational poetry," Roland Hagenbüchle asserts correctly that the real difficulties in Emily Dickinson's poetry stem not so much from metaphorical but from metonymical references, where qualities are detached from objects. With metonomy, origins must be inferred from their parts or effects.[3] The further problem is that we sometimes do not find even an interior coherence in the allegories. What we find are allegories that slip in and out of focus. As a consequence we are caught in the bright but indefinite lights of a highly figural style.

Veiled poems with their meaning hidden and the circumstances figurative and unclear are most tempting for readers when the shadows hint at autobiographical disclosure. "I cautious scanned my little life" is a good example. Something of value is stored away only to disappear. Most likely, from the context, it is love or faith or both, that is, loved ones including Christ who have forgotten her or departed. She calls them "my priceless Hay." Similar figurative elusiveness occurs again and again, as in the well-known poem beginning "I held a Jewel in my fingers," where the significance of the jewel is unassigned but could be artistic apprenticeship or friendship or love. Equally evasive in its figuration is the poem readers vaguely associate with Dickinson's commitment to her poetic craft. Meaning is simply not sure, nor does the context suggest a focus upon which all readers might agree.

> Myself was formed – a Carpenter –
> An unpretending time
> My Plane – and I, together wrought
> Before a Builder came –
>
> To measure our attainments –   (P-488)

The free-wheeling emblematic character of Dickinson's chief mode is one of the main causes of our exclusion. The allegorical drama of sunrise and noon, light in the east and north, night and midnight, the northern lights and a mysterious "Two" who "Both lie," one upon a feminine bosom and one upon "Her Hem" (P-710), excludes our definite understanding even while it gives us pleasure. What holds us is the intensity of the metaphorical rush and the brilliant single figures that capture specifics, as this for the aurora borealis: "The North – Her blazing Sign / Erects in Iodine." Hundreds of poems exist in which the essential human passages of love and death contend in vague choreography with the sun and the sky—her Planetary Forces—and the sweep of days as if their ensemble somehow established meaning. It is dramatic arrangement cut loose from a specific program of meaning. This exemplary allegory vaguely reflects Dickinson's habitual regard for the career of the soul. The truth of the matter lies under the vexing unassigned pronouns.

> This is a Blossom of the Brain –
> A small – italic Seed
> Lodged by Design or Happening
> The Spirit fructified –
>
> Shy as the Wind of his Chambers
> Swift as a Freshet's Tongue
> So of the Flower of the Soul
> It's process is unknown.
>
> When it is found, a few rejoice
> The Wise convey it Home
> Carefully cherishing the spot
> If other Flower become
>
> When it is lost, that Day shall be
> The Funeral of God,
> Upon his Breast, a closing Soul
> The Flower of our Lord.   (P-945)

Intense, the lines carefully measured out, obviously of enormous significance to the poet since the loss of *it* is connected to "The Funeral of God," the poem still hides its meaning. It is pure choreography, where the visualization is partial and dreamlike, the words pseudo-signs, and the central matter deceptively out of sight. Dickinson begins poems of this sort a long way down the line of allegorical

thinking, that is *after* the emblems have let go their initial attachment
to a circumstance that a reader can visualize. We can watch that allegorical unhitching in the poems.

> The Flake the Wind exasperate
> More eloquently lie
> Than if escorted to it's Down
> By Arm of Chivalry.   (P-1361)

This is a demonstration in brief compass of the Dickinsonian parabolic motion. All that applies to the snowflake in this minute morality
play is in human terms—exasperation, eloquence, escort—and therefore the career of the snowflake has something to illustrate about a
deceased person whose life was troubled. The hidden metaphor appealed immensely to Dickinson and helps readers to tolerance and
then to investigation of her abstract allegories. The poem beginning
"I think the longest Hour of all" is apparently about the long moment
at the end of the funeral service when the hearse is due (or is one
waiting for a train?). At the end, however, meaning goes straight out
of sight. Readers suddenly don't know who the speaker is; the allegory does not close but leads to the anticlimactic drama of the childlike speaker's own departure for a yet bleaker location. We are not
sure of the setting or the occasion or why the speaker is there or what
her removal "further North" portends. The lines are tense with
pseudo-significance, the consequences crucial and yet we can't say
what they are or why they have come about. The poem "The Soul
selects her own Society" has great appeal for readers and would appear in any anthology of Dickinson's best works. Yet it characteristically drifts off to end with a kneeling Emperor (is it God? a lover?)
and a chariot at the gate. The most crucial act of all is concealed behind an unidentified, generic one. The poem ends with decisive
sound that belies its utter indefiniteness.

> I've known her – from an ample nation –
> Choose One –
> Then – close the Valves of her attention –
> Like Stone –   (P-303)

We have now become conscious of the peculiar ability of Dickinson to speak of vague things with absolute conviction, to remove the
world from our sight even as she enlists our attention to her shadow

drama. In thirty-nine words, with the apparent precision of a chemical equation, using the most elemental diction, she presents with total assurance, it seems, the law of the conservation of matter, the unalterable state of natural law, absolute being. That is, in thirty-nine words she has attempted nothing less than an allegory of fate.

> Banish Air from Air –
> Divide Light if you dare –
> They'll meet
> While Cubes in a Drop
> Or Pellets of Shape
> Fit.
> Films cannot annul
> Odors return whole
> Force Flame
> And with a Blonde push
> Over your impotence
> Flits Steam.   (P-854)

It is a poem about what cannot be destroyed or even altered, an attempt to get at the gray slate of the unchangeable. Yet she has introduced such impalpability into the poem that it torments us with its indefiniteness, especially in two blind but daring spots. The basic opposition in the poem is between what cannot be sundered or quantified—air, light, films (which often stand for fright or death), odors—all elements outside anyone's ability to manipulate or contain, and the opposed phenomena of things that "fit," that is, in her shorthand, things that have a shape and can be placed. What "Cubes in a Drop" signifies, like "dots on a disc of snow," escapes definitive meaning. But even this momentary opaqueness does not prepare us for the leap beyond meaning that comes with the metaphor of flame. Is it that if you "Force Flame," attempt to contain it, the element will gather elsewhere in its own form?

For all its compactness and conviction, the poem is a mystery of cryptic metaphors of cubes in a drop and forced flame. But even then a reader is not through, for the final movement of the poem into blindness occurs with the introduction of a "Blonde push." This is a phenomenon that can exist only in words. Conspicuously, we see that withdrawal of words away from a discernible reality. As readers before the pale traces of the literal sense, we end up in the web of words, and like siren-struck sailors we are not wholly troubled by the receding of an actual world before this other strange and estranging world made out of words—cubes in a drop, unannulled films, whole odors, and a blonde push. Such is Dickinson's allegory of fate: compressed, seemingly confident in its procedure, employing single words of unarguable meaning but joined in a chain that curves in and out of the intelligible and loops, finally, out of the real world into the autonomous system of language.

An equally vexed crossing into alien metaphors occurs boldly in the poem that begins "Her Sweet turn to leave the Homestead." The unsettling effect anticipates such deliberate postsymbolist impertinences as Ransom's "Bells for John Whiteside's Daughter" or, more spectacularly, Stevens' "The Emperor of Ice-Cream." In Dickinson's poem, death is presented alongside the terms of marriage until in a startling interpenetration of ritual imagery there is an ebb and flow of clarity. Opaqueness is also caused by the insertion into this split scheme of other powerful but indefinite images, producing the mystery of unconsummated symbols. That mystery gathers most emphatically in the elusive metaphors of "Darker Way," "Loaded Sea," "Art of Snow," "Trick of Lily" (all tropes for death), "the Palm – that serve the Desert," and finally the vague, liminal image of "the Crystal Angle." The poem opens in a typically disarming way with simple diction and conversational tone. But by the end, the perspective has slipped away from the dead woman to a conjectural suitor, thus carrying the poem into wildly necrophilic fantasy, inhuman remoteness ("pass the Crystal Angle") and then, by the artifice of the five-syllable conviction of "Equal Paradise" to a locution in the absence of knowledge.

> Her Sweet turn to leave the Homestead
> Came the Darker Way –
> Carriages – Be sure – and Guests – true –
> But for Holiday
>
> 'Tis more pitiful Endeavor
> Than did Loaded Sea
> O'er the Curls attempt to caper
> It had cast away –
>
> Never Bride had such Assembling –
> Never kinsmen kneeled
> To salute so fair a Forehead –
> Garland be indeed –

Fitter Feet – of Her before us –
Than whatever Brow
Art of Snow – or Trick of Lily
Possibly bestow

Of Her Father – Whoso ask Her –
He shall seek as high
As the Palm – that serve the Desert –
To obtain the Sky –

Distance – be Her only Motion –
If 'tis Nay – or Yes –
Acquiescence – or Demurral –
Whosoever guess –

He – must pass the Crystal Angle
That obscure Her face –
He – must have achieved in person
Equal Paradise –   (P-649)

Constructing normal sentences for the peculiarly evasive second, fourth, and fifth stanzas helps us to follow the weird metaphor crossings. The second reads: As a holiday, her leave-taking was a celebration more pitiful than if the sea attempted to cavort over the woman ("Curls") it had drown. The fourth: Despite the fair forehead of the corpse, the garland would more fittingly be put upon her feet, which are carrying her to heaven, than upon the brow that death has artfully frozen. The fifth stanza: Whoever asks her hand in marriage now of her Father will come only as close to Him and to her as the palm comes close to the sky above the desert. And so we are left with the "Distance" and the "guess." But what we see from the reading and the paraphrases is that the idea is very simple: The woman who should have been celebrating her marriage is instead the center of the dark holiday of her funeral. It is stock mid-nineteenth century graveyard fare, but what Dickinson's stark, cursory metaphors have done is to reinvest it with both strength and mystery by excursions into surreal territory, usurping reality in a powerful density of language. Like Blake's metaphoric poems, hers project as far as the edges of human contemplation, but where his are coherent allegories, hers are impeded, defamiliarizing, strangely contorted, labyrinthine in ways more daring than Ransom's offbeat irony in "Bells" and Stevens' extravagantly imperial philosophy of "Let be be finale of seem" in the shabby fact of tenement-house death.

 If there is a Puritan background to Dickinson's poetry, it is not in her upbringing, which was rural but social, upright but flexible and affectionate, conservative but secular, and ultimately materially prosperous. The Puritanism enters in the rhetoric and particularly in the troping habit that continually carries her away from specific reality to realms of metaphor and suggestions of transcendent visions. To her, as to the Puritan divines, reality impinged mainly in the figural imagination. Incidents in life became parables; the implications, revelatory. Even Dickinson's skillful use of colloquial language together with biblical metaphors had Puritan origins. That combined colloquial and metaphorical habit is described this way by Sacvan Bercovitch in *The Puritan Origins of the American Self*:

> To speak plainly was not primarily to speak simply, and not at all to speak artlessly. It meant speaking the Word—making language itself, as self-expression, an *imitatio Christi* because it conformed to scripture. The too well-known admonition that introduces the *Bay Psalm Book*, "God's altar needs not our polishings," far from curbing the use of image and metaphor, opens the full linguistic richness of the Old Testament to preacher and layman alike. Read the Bible, rhapsodized John Donne, and you will see that ours is "a *figurative*, a *metaphorical* God . . . a *God* in whose words there is such a height of *figures*, such *voyages*, such *peregrinations* to fetch remote and precious *metaphors*.[4]

The millennium, ever the star of hope in the eyes of the early New England clergy, made them metaphorically, as Dickinson did later, turn their faces toward the East and the Dawn. As Harriet Beecher Stowe said of them, "They were the children of the morning." Parables grew out of actual experience, as when colonial ministers substituted the crossing of the sea to America—with its shipwrecks, tempests, and safe arrivals at shore—for conversion as the crucial Christian event. It doubled as well for a homemade version of Moses crossing the Red Sea.

 But Dickinson adopted this New England rhetorical habit, which came to her mainly through the Bible and the hymns, to make her own brand of figuralism. And it was this private imagining, dependent on biblical figures, by which her language set itself against the meaning of existence and otherwise organized the basic problems of the spirit that had occupied her long-distant precursors in New England. It was a private typology that to our eyes in the late twentieth century makes problems of interpretation. Her mode, even to her contemporaries, invested reality always with strangeness, indefinite meanings, and above all surprise. By her figuralism, a transcendent, invisible world haunted the quick stanzas she turned out in such quantity. Life for her language was a various figural display or conglomeration of signs. It was thus the typology of her own affairs.

Dickinson's secular leap to meaning by way of tropes that are not biblical but local takes place before our eyes in poem after poem. It happens when her brief lines assume the metaphorical link without actually giving it. We as readers are inserted into the poetic environment by an image that is far along the line of figural interpretation. Take Dickinson's poems using a rat, a cat, sledding after an ice storm, and a stagnant pool. In each case, these homely images, quickly drawn with marvelous economy of line, change before our eyes into something else. Engaging in their own right, their real function for Dickinson, as each poem makes apparent by its end, is metonymic, that is, in their long link back as figural examples to an original but lost interpretive identification.

> The Rat is the concisest Tenant.
> He pays no Rent.
> Repudiates the Obligation –
> On Schemes intent
>
> Balking our Wit
> To sound or circumvent –
> Hate cannot harm
> A Foe so reticent –
> Neither Decree prohibit him –
> Lawful as Equilibrium.   (P-1356)

This is another poem, we see, about fate and our powerlessness before it, about things that *are*, like the inseparability of air and light. The rat is as fundamental as gravity itself. Dickinson's lines make a palaver, a silly ode to this lowly creature who stands for the law of the universe. The grand, characteristic, final pronouncement sums up the overstatements used from the beginning. The poem finally is about one of Dickinson's cosmic concerns, with the wit inherent. As a result of her figural transfer from rodent to unalterable fate, we keep this metonymic value of the rat in mind when we encounter it in other poems, for Dickinson had assigned her meaning to it as surely as if she had been a Puritan divine.

The cat poem similarly shows the troping distance opening up. The poem begins with a precise description on the order of William Carlos Williams' cat in the jam closet and ends in an allegory of denial, bliss fled. "Ah, Pussy, of the Sand" is no real cat at all, but rather the figure of man himself put in the way of disappearing hope.

> She sights a Bird – she chuckles –
> She flattens – then she crawls –
> She runs without the look of feet –
> Her eyes increase to Balls –
>
> Her Jaws stir – twitching – hungry –
> Her Teeth can hardly stand –
> She leaps, but Robin leaped the first –
> Ah, Pussy, of the Sand,
>
> The Hopes so juicy ripening –
> You almost bathed your Tongue –
> When Bliss disclosed a hundred Toes –
> And fled with every one –   (P-507)

In some other poems that we find abstract, impalpable, even impervious, Dickinson has concentrated on a half trope without its other completing half. In the ice-sledding poem, the crossing from image to figural significance is so abrupt that a reader is hard put to make the connection. When the crossover is finally made, we see with stunning clarity the saltatory quality of Dickinson's mind. In this late poem jotted down in pencil on the back of a torn-open telegram envelope, we have evidently, despite our difficulties, a poem that for her was complete, the movement and meaning sufficiently set. It did, that is, as much as she wanted it to do. Our difficulties as readers are located in two crossings where the poem suddenly turns opaque. The principal disjunction is at line seven where a peremptory shift occurs from image to figural interpretation. In other words, we ask by what leap of analogy we get from the ice sledding to a homily about the past.

> Glass was the Street – in tinsel Peril
> Tree and Traveller stood –

Filled was the Air with merry venture
Hearty with Boys the Road –

Shot the lithe Sleds like shod vibrations
Emphasized and gone
It is the Past's supreme italic
Makes the Present mean –   (P-1498)

Our first difficulty comes with the word "emphasized." What indeed is its subject? In what sense is anything here made emphatic? There is, in fact, a whole complex of occasions that will come into view. They center on the single word "italic," which makes all the associations visible. It is an arresting word, selected in violation of expectations, a word from the printing lexicon that makes a link between the icy day and a judgment on how the past seems to the memory. Again, Dickinson has summoned a surprising word aptly and made it function in a manifold way. What is italicized? The peril and the glass venture (note the inversions before the last two lines) are themselves a singular occasion when the land is iced-over. The sound of steel runners is italicized by the ice coating on the road. Like Dickinson's hummingbird, the sleds disappear in their metonymical vibrations. Ice emphasizes the sleds' speed, the sleds by their vibrations have emphasized the ice cover. This is perilous sledding. And it is here we observe the metaphoric leap, how the poet arcs from the ice-covered road and the extraordinary sledding to the past's special intensity with its crystal aura for the rememberer. The excitement of ice sledding compared to ordinary snow sledding is like the past compared to the present.

In that figural jump lies the opaqueness of the poem. Out of the withdrawn clarity and covert progression of meaning comes the complexity of response. The text forces the effort of a new consideration of yesterday that is not automatic but instead faithful to the mystery of remembrance itself, reproducing it in ordinary words but set slantwise in a Dickinsonian association.

The pool poem signals its complex human significance at the outset, first in the paradox of "stagnant pleasure" and in the implication of "pleasure" itself that emotional experience is involved. The obscurity has to do with the lost linkage between the pictorial envelope (to use Paul Ricoeur's term)—that is, the clogged pool—and the conceptual import: a human consciousness in comfortable stagnation but with the expectation that there will come moments of emotional torrent. We are helped in the mystery when we discover that shadows, though a possible trope, are in fact more literal, referring to ripples in motion. What the text assumes but does not bring to its surface is the conceptual half that completes the metaphor: a human stagnation, perhaps catatonic, impeding emotion. The verb "is" should be understood in the first line; otherwise the syntax does not close.

> A stagnant pleasure [is] like a Pool
> That lets it's Rushes grow
> Until they heedless tumble in
> And make the Water slow
>
> Impeding navigation bright
> Of Shadows going down
> Yet even this shall rouse itself
> When freshets come along.   (P-1281)

What exactly are the mind's rushes, allowed to grow so abundantly that they impede motion? Typically, Dickinson has not reached explicitness and so her text does not insist on an ideal reading. What she gives is *figure* and not concept. The reader must supply experience to it. Where we crave exactness and metaphysical closure, she gives us mystery and indefiniteness in a verbal display that yearns for meaning but effectively keeps it absent. What in a mind are the equivalences of bright shadows moving along? What, indeed, is the "bright navigation of Shadows"? What precisely is a freshet in the mind? The text is almost pure figure with the solution of references to be brought to it. Whereas she assigned fractional meanings in the rat and cat and ice-sledding poems, here she withheld even that explicitness. The reader is drawn into this mystery of the mind's language. This, one can say, is a modern poem because it gives enough to engage but withholds all the rest, leaving the reader resignedly in a quandary of urgent words and incomplete disclosure.

Reading the Poems

More than the meanings of words, including definitions to be found in Webster's 1844 dictionary that the poet used, is involved in apprehending Dickinson's poems. Almost none is a perfect poem, but rather each exists in some state of unfinishedness with variants in suspension around it. On top of this incompleteness of texts are the syntax and grammar distortions, the lost referents, the extreme ellipsis, and the distant and unanchored tropes. We have indeed, coexistent with the magnificent achievement, a catalogue of stubborn difficulties.

This Dickinson idiom of defects is not a grammar of assent. The idiom pulls away from reality by its eccentricity, refusing to mirror that reality in a straightforward, unambiguous way. It retires into its characteristic indefiniteness of reference. The effects of this divorce of language from the phenomenally experienced world creates powerful effects characteristic of the extreme modernist sensibility. The interstice between the self-regarding language and the lived-in world is a space of estrangement which produces excitement and a heightened sense of both anxiety and observation. Beyond this, the sporadic extinguishings of meaning that occur as a result of these difficulties restore the pleasurable imperviousness of experience, without an easy assent to or implication of an intelligible world. Together, the difficulties and the blindnesses, even as they distance the world and let it exist in its inherent mystery, function in an agreeable modern way to impede habituation and make our lives visible with a new immediacy.

Readers of Dickinson's poems find themselves in a realm of language density and resistant reality as they undertake the demanding task of bringing individual poems as far along as possible to a satisfactorily complex reading performance. It is a much different activity from that required by Dickinson's contemporaries. The *Springfield Daily Republican*, which Dickinson read faithfully, presented its readers with verse—sober, mellifluous, predictable—of this sort, by Adelaide Anne Proctor:

> Before I trust my Fate to thee,
>   Or place my hand in thine,
> Before I let thy Future give
>   Color and form to mine,
> Before I peril all for thee, question
>   Thy soul to-night for me.

Rufus Griswold's *The Female Poets of America* (1849) provides an abundance of the innocuous, undemanding verse of Dickinson's day. Here are lines from a poem by Sara Clarke called "The Last Gift":

> I leave thee, love: in vain hast thou
>   The God of life implored:
> My clinging soul is torn from thine,
>   My faithful, my adored!
> My last gift – I have on it breathed
>   In blessing and in prayer;
> So lay it close, close to thy heart,
>   This little lock of hair!

Dickinson's quick alien poems with their aggressive language present a radically different reading experience.

One of our aims as serious readers of Dickinson is a strict regard for the evasion of meaning. We know also that faults of banality and facile diction appear in the midst of impressive power. A reader will not praise all elements of a poem equally because of admiration for what it seems to accomplish in some parts. Other principles also seem advisable in undertaking the serious reading of Dickinson. The first is the principle of simplicity. Whatever reconstructed sentence must be made by the reader to restore Dickinson's ellipsis, that source sentence is most useful when it involves the fewest changes from the form the poet gives. The same principle ought to be invoked in the matter of meaning and coherence. What minimum of consistency, we should ask ourselves, will accommodate the elements that are important to her in a specific poem? The *tone* especially, which is so important to this deeply ironic poet, must be confirmed elsewhere in the poem. Otherwise, the ardent reader drifts in a sea of subjective possibilities and interpretive banality.

Our difficulties exist on both planes of composition, that of lexical selection, where semantic meaning and reference are established or withheld, and that of combination, where syntactical structure promotes clarity or complicates it. Dickinson's meanings are placed or withheld elsewhere as well, and we should keep the principal loci in mind: her first lines, her stanza transitions, the tone, her swerves and extinguishings, her resolutions (which are not necessarily the same as endings) or her refusal to resolve.

Disintegration of meaning comes about because Dickinson acts with arbitrary freedom and sometimes opposing impulses on these two planes of linguistic composition. She *expands* mental distance by stretching out figural connections and using highly abstract, holophrastic words on the semantic plane. At the same time, she *con-*

tracts structure on the combinational plane by syntactic ellipsis within the syllabic limitations of her hymnal form. These two pressures result in the loss of the intelligible and familiar, producing eclipses of understanding.

Readers must therefore undertake two basic activities, one with regard to the structure of her sentences and the other the motion of her figurative imagination. We must, first, construct a "normal" sentence from the cramped and inverted syntax and then, without substituting this sentence for her lines, hold it aside to see how she has contorted expected word order; second, retrace the long metaphoric path from pictorial display back to concept, in effect to summon referents she has omitted.

Restoring syntax proceeds best if we know her habit, albeit with many exceptions, of composing in two-line units. A single example will suffice to show how syntactic order can be reestablished alongside the poet's ambiguous placements.

> I knew that I had gained
> And yet I knew not how
> By Diminution it was not
> But discipline unto
>
> A Rigor unrelieved
> Except by the Content
> Another bear it's Duplicate
> In other Continent.   (P-1022)

It is a poem of bonding across the gulf of death, a topic frequently addressed by Dickinson and her contemporaries. In other hands it was the most hackneyed of subjects, but in Dickinson's closely pressed language it reacquires the force of emotional need across the barrier of mystery. Unless we establish the syntactic close at the end of line two we slide over this poem, tolerate the ambiguous phrases, and come away with an indefinite sense of weighty words in a vague conjunction: gain, diminution, discipline, and content. If there is a pattern, it is obligated in some way to the two negatives and the connectives of logic: yet, but, except. In fifty-two syllable slots there are strong words of broad meaning, connectives of definite relationship and logic, and negatives of absolute insistence.

The first two lines make a sentence of which we are largely confident because we know her habit of composing in double lines. (More will be said of this later.) The supposition helps us see the syntax:

> I knew that I had gained
> and yet I knew not how.
>
> By diminution (loss) this gain was not obtained
> but by discipline of
>
> a rigor relieved
> only by the contentment (consoling knowledge)
>
> that another (the lost person) practices a
>   similar rigor and discipline
> in the other world.

The meaning is recovered in the underlying utterance and it is, alas, banal. What Dickinson's cloistered syntax, ambiguous structure, and grave word choice accomplish is to make out of the bathos an authentic matter for emotional investment and, above this, a rendering anew of the ignorance of existence, its termination, and what remains behind in consciousness.

The second activity a reader must undertake is to retrace the metaphorical leaps, the fractional metonymic inferences, the privacies. Sometimes it is accomplished through the variant words or phrases she entered on her worksheets and even on fair copies. In the short poem just quoted, we must discover that "content," as signified, is not purport, but the emotional state, that is, "contentment." Further yet, a reader intent on opening the concealed intention here will know from other poems that the "other Continent," a sign of her typology, is the world of the dead. What we know after this interpretive labor is that there is a strong personal investment in the language of even this commonplace sentiment. Out of the contorted expression comes our sense of emotional immediacy and, most important of all, of a *consciousness coming to terms with final deprivations.*

Language as persistently mannered and difficult as this is surely not a deferential language. Rather it holds apart, resisting in every way a prosaic meshing with perceived reality. It is language conscious of its own artificiality, self-involved with its troubled construction and private lexicon, its metonymic riddles, its eclipses of meaning, and its downright difficulty. It is not a language of confirmation where syntax serves by its inherent reasonableness to recognize pattern and consequence in the world. The lines "Here once the embattled farmers stood / And fired the shot heard round the world," both simple and grandly idealistic (and deeply consistent with Emerson's mind), are language that gives unquestioned assent to the world. Dickinson's language is stubbornly itself and not a clear mirror of mimesis for the world she inhabited. Dissenting, disjunctive, it is language, one begins to sense, covering hysteria. With its outlandish character, cramped syntax, semantic grandiosities, and lexical violations, it is a language ready to collapse into chaos. Trembling with nervousness and need, it performs manically on the brink of the final modernity, silence.

In this extremity of language making, Dickinson ignored the familiar connectives, the necessary qualifications and abundance of context we need for communication, leaving only the *nodes* of her concern. She came early in her writing to compose, to think, and finally to see in these linkless terms. Hers is a voice without slack, proseless. It is the kind of spareness Pound sought in poetry, but it is beyond the compaction Pound could reasonably attain. There are, to prove the rule, some rare narratives in Dickinson. Poem 1061 is one of them, and it begins with this uncharacteristic leisure: "Three weeks passed since I had seen Her." Eight syllables, but so prolix that most of the words seem now to us, as readers of the inside, wasted.

Here is one of those poems as tight as a mathematical equation. It begins in ignorance but builds briskly, with thirty-nine words, an extravagant figural display with a simple conceptual drama of the severest economy:

> An ignorance a Sunset
> Confer upon the Eye –
> Of Territory – Color –
> Circumference – Decay –
>
> It's Amber Revelation
> Exhilirate – Debase –
> Omnipotence' inspection
> Of Our inferior face –
>
> And when the solemn features
> Confirm – in Victory –
> We start – as if detected
> In Immortality –   (P-552)

The Puzzling Idiom

Such linguistic depletion forces sensation. Once we have recovered the lexical resonance she left out of her poems, we possess the hovering meaning she intended. We can play the full syntactic rhythm off against the minimal syntax she provided. The unheard syntax then, like Keats's unheard music, forms the aura of each of these difficult poems. The phenomenon of given and concealed expression, of radically denied expression played off against our normal competence in the language, sets up a fully resonant psycholexicological field of considerable vitality around the two or three dozen words we call poems. Another way of saying this is that her flawed language sometimes captures, as no amount of clear syntax and definitely referential metaphor can, the unyielding world and the anxious consciousness that stands before it.

4   How Dickinson Wrote

Dickinson's habits of composition, to the extent we can recover them, lead us toward the origins of the language problems. "The Dickinson practice cannot be systematized; there is not enough *there*," R. P. Blackmur wrote in 1956.[1] He was not entirely accurate, but the impediments are formidable, both in the nature of the work as a whole and in the state of the manuscripts.

With Dickinson's poetry we are dealing with an outlandish body of texts. Though she was demonstrably capable in her letters of extended and coherent writing, her poems are at the extremity of fragmented discourse. A reader proceeding through several poems at a single sitting experiences the sense of perpetual erasure of impressions, a surprising collection of new starts. There is a constant displacement of perception, the one just made displaced by the next one and both by a third one. To compound this restless setting-aside and substitution, each brief poem holds the same weight of significance. The eight-line poem on the snake displays an investment of wit and language about equal to the poem on the collapse of a person's emotional life or, for that matter, the collapse of God's world. The body of poems, in short, refuses to organize a reader's experience of it.

Manuscripts of nearly all the 1775 poems and fragments survive, two thirds of them as fair copies made by the poet and gathered into the curious packets she made in the flourishing period from 1858, when she was going on twenty-eight, to 1865 and then sporadically in 1866, 1871, and 1872. The largest number of poem manuscripts exists in single holographs, whether as fair copies with the worksheets destroyed or, as is true of the later poems, as single drafts. Because so few worksheets survive, Dickinson's method of composition, her creative ways, have been obscure. There is also the problem of knowing when Dickinson considered a poem finished. Some of the bound packet poems in fair copies seem to be merely notations. In the packets too there are several four-line pieces of slight intent which, by the evidence, Dickinson considered complete. For these reasons, seeing Dickinson's composition process is a difficult matter, but it is essential to our understanding of her mental patterns.

The printing of her poems has served to conceal the original state of her verses and thus the state of mind they mirror. In orderly print, the published texts imply qualities we associate with more conventional poets, including those of the highest rank: conscious selection and revision, development, coherence of viewpoint, a defined body of completed work. In fact, the vagaries of construction are concealed behind the straight printer's type. The poems as readers know them make a far different impression from the original Dickinson texts, which we recall she never published herself.[2] What we read in Thomas Johnson's carefully edited pages are reconstituted products, like photgraphs reproduced in a book. They are not the original thing, for they have been ordered, aligned, edited, choices made, translated into type with margins and an artful visual impact. The prior fact is, however, that besides the fair copies there are scraps, particularly for the late poems, which range in quality from trivial to piercing. Lines come attached with straight pins, on scraps of brown paper sometimes so tiny they float in the palm of the hand, others on the backs of school programs or margins of merchants' bills, one poem written in the space around a postage stamp with paper arms glued on, another on a strip of paper ¾ of an inch wide and 21 inches long, an 1876 poem in pencil on an invitation to a candy pull sent to her twenty-six years earlier, another on the back of a lemon-colored cooking-chocolate wrapper. They are exhilarating to read, being, one feels, nearest the moment when the words gripped their own poetic potency. This immediacy and incompleteness we must interpret as well as we can if we are to understand what Dickinson did when she wrote poems, what they enabled her to see, what the words promoted on their own behalf, and what in the end were the capacities for experience.

The evidence shows that Emily Dickinson worked hard at certain poems even as at certain of her letters. She ably revised, after a period of perhaps six years between 1865 and 1871, to reach the bold, abrupt language that begins poem 1177 with the deft stroke of metaphorical description of which she was a master: "A prompt – executive Bird is the Jay." The original lines were "A bold, inspiriting Bird / Is the Jay." To get the one-syllable word that satisfied her in poem 1420, she listed no fewer than fourteen words for "quick" in the line "Before the Quick of Day": ripe, peal, drum, drums, bells, bomb, burst, flags, step, tick, shouts, pink, red, blade. She wanted *all* of that impact of color, sound and physical sensation of daybreak folded into a single-syllable position. In poem 533 she worked with enormous ambition, again concealed behind the printed text, to get the special lurching flight of butterflies. The effort, as always, had more concern than just butterflies, for Dickinson was once again working out an allegory of human salvation, smooth soaring into ecstasy. The layered complications of this manuscript bear silent witness to the intensive work. But there is difficulty in understanding all of her laborts, for sometimes the effort seems unjustified, as in the second stanza of poem 1211, a slight piece on a sparrow taking flight.

Her filing system, though not systematic, was remarkable for feats of retrieval. She worked at poem 1181 in 1862, went back to it around 1868, and once again in 1871. Poem 130, in a packet of around 1859, she went back to twenty-four years later to make a copy evidently to enclose in a letter. She kept her sheets and scraps in some order or other so that she could find a stanza for a letter years later, but she did not keep a notebook. She was a compulsive writer but without a conscious objective that a notebook or versebook would have indicated. It is hard to know what is implied here, but it has something to do with the lack of an advancing, coherent, and complicated intention.

Part of her compulsion, to which I will return, is the bravado of her grand subjects. "All but Death, can be Adjusted," she begins poem 749, and then in the seven lines that follow, a total of thirty-two words, takes up and disposes of Death, Dynasties, Systems, Citadels, Wastes of Lives, and the idea of Change! She never lacked conceptual reach, though her poems barely had room in which to get the great abstractions written down.

One final fact whose significance is crucial to our fresh sighting of Emily Dickinson has already been remarked: her art in its range and technique never altered over three decades of writing. This absence of growth is the more remarkable because she wrote with impressive intensity to the end of her life, to the point where, in her sick bed, in the dark, she laboriously made words on scraps of paper.

Three basic givens operate most decisively at the heart of her composing. Before getting to them, let me first note some of her lesser compositional habits. She seems not, the evidence shows, to have written prose versions of the poems first, as so many of her contemporaries did, although certain fragments, notably PF-75 about how the seconds fly to catch the centuries, might have been jottings intended to be put later into meters. Some poems seem to have gone down whole in one gesture, such as "Tell all the Truth but tell it slant." This poem exists in a pencil holograph on a torn rectangle of paper 5 inches by 4, filling out the sheet as if it had been entirely in mind before the poet set it down. Dickinson clearly felt a strong need for segmental form even while her own script looped unevenly across inelegant scraps of paper. On a piece of wrapping paper 9½ by 2½ inches she penciled the single quatrain that contains a riveting aesthetic: "sheen must have a Disk / To be a sun." Although the common meter quatrain of alternating eight and six syllables is the containing form almost everywhere in Dickinson's verse, and in cases where punctuation is lacking can be assumed to close her syntax units, there are enough instances of carryover and syncopation across stanza breaks to make a reader cautious about reading as if syntax always concludes at stanza end. This is a good example of the syntactic ambiguity created by the lack of punctuation and the syntactic grouping implied by semantic necessity, on the one hand, and stanza containment on the other.

> The Spirit is the Conscious Ear.
> We actually Hear
> When We inspect – that's audible –
> That is admitted – Here –
>
> For other Services – as Sound –
> There hangs a smaller Ear
> Outside the Castle – that Contain –
> The other – only – Hear –   (P-733)

Dickinson's second stanzas, it should be noted as well, often serve as echoes of her stronger first stanzas, providing a pale remake of the two habitually aggressive opening lines of the first stanza either in image, metaphor elaboration, or extension of a particular sound. Poem 927 is an example of this typical structure of repetition with alteration. What will interest us in a central way later on is how we are led by these second quatrains to recognize the style calling attention to itself by the replay. In the pervasiveness of this stylistic doubling, alteration, and elaboration, we see how often and obstinately the subjects in her poems turn immediately into *matters of style*.

Parallel syntactic constructions also operate regularly to hold the poems together. It was an early compositional habit, is sometimes carelessly used, but provides the structure for more poems than we have recognized. Readers aware of the syntactic problems learn to look for these parallel structures as an aid to meaning and progression in poems lacking punctuation and clear syntax.

Alliteration is important in Dickinson's verse, particularly in essential phrases and in the most novel selection violations. For example, in poem 364 these phrases bond by alliteration: "Litanies of Lead," "Some Crucifixal Clef," "Some Key of Calvary." Variants demonstrate how important sound was to Dickinson. Combined with metrical requirements, sound sometimes determined diction to the exclusion of sense, as in the suggested variants for the phrase "your summons" (P-1325). She listed for alternatives "summits," "subjects," "substance." Though she meant them in some loose way as synonyms, for a reader they present the familiar problem of obscurity caused by her lack of interest in exact lexical equivalents.

The most revealing example of how firmly alliteration, along with syllable count, holds in the typical Dickinson process of composition emerges from a comparison of the several versions of the second stanza of "Safe in their Alabaster Chambers." Whereas images of cosmic expanse and the strangeness of the images themselves alter and the perspective shifts from outside the tomb to inside, the demands in Dickinson's ear of alliteration and meter hold absolutely. The strength of these formal constraints on Dickinson's capacity for expression and thus for perception will be brought home to us more forcefully as I turn now to her more significant compositional habits.

Paired Lines

The most basic of all Dickinson's units of construction is the two-line sentence, discernible when we look into the makeup of almost every poem. Two-liners are the way she makes her meanings; they order the poem's function as a linguistic event. Her poems begin with two-liners and two-liners are at the poem's center. The visual emblems of this conceptual frame are the scraps and fragments. Small rectangles of paper contain two lines only. In a few instances two such scraps are joined by a straight pin to form a quatrain. In poem 1309 two uneven scraps of unlike paper, each approximately 1 by 4½ inches and bearing two lines, are pinned together in homely conjunction. She rarely tried her hand at couplets. They are best worked out in poem 968, in eight-syllable lines, and this unsual text is an uncommon experiment on Dickinson's part.

Exceptions confirm the two-line habit. Poem 175 consists of a long sentence of twenty lines, and it serves by its rarity to prove the pervasiveness of the basic two-line unit elsewhere. We recognize the usual Dickinson economy in the momentary flash of this sunset piece, not written slapdash but clearly formed and with two variants on a small torn-off rectangle of paper.

> Soft as the massacre of Suns
> By Evening's Sabres slain   (P-1127)

Because the two-line frames are omnipresent, readers instinctively begin to parse syntax, movement, and meaning by this arrangement. Thus when Dickinson creates enjambment or other stanza bridges that break the two-line structures, she is very effective. But her skill with the quick frame is one of her great achievements as an artist. No one surpasses her in this. Her two-line dramas hold the cosmos: "Worlds scoop their Arcs – / And Firmaments – row"; "Creation seemed a mighty Crack – / To make me visible." The two-line glance, like TV, inevitably solicits contraries, ironies, epigrams. As Samuel Johnson remarked on the characteristic grasp of couplets that inhibit sequential accumulation, the attention that cannot be detained by suspense is excited by diversity. As Dickinson recognized, "Going is a Drama / Staying cannot confer."

Quantitative Words

Words of an absolute nature, often polysyllabic, customarily carry crucial weight for Dickinson. They form a system of focal terms in her poems with the primacy of a given as important as the two-line unit. "Thank you for remembering me," she wrote to her Norcross cousins (L-785), "Remembrance – mighty word. 'Thou gavest it to me from the foundation of the world.' " Despite her occasional protestation, as in poem 420, that intuition and not the mentalized language of consciousness is the only way of knowing, mightiest things asserted themselves for her in linguistic terms. Polysyllabic words themselves triggered poems that trailed after them in varying degrees of coherence. On the back of the chocolate wrapper, for example, the shaky penciled markings begin with two words she found wonderfully weighty to the senses: "necessitates celerity." On that 21 inch strip of paper, the poem she hastily put down begins with two of the polysyllables whose weight she adored: "The Lassitudes of Contemplation."

Examples of her use of these generating nodes occur in most poems. Poem 1295 in its twelve lines contains a veritable chart, in short words and long, of life's "absolute extent": hope, horror, eternity, velocity or pause, fundamental signals, fundamental laws, doom's consummate chart. Noon, evening, and morning were absolute terms for the crucial passages of life and afterlife. When she wrote "Our lives are Swiss," she meant to draw on the whole cultural typology of that single term. Could mortal lip, she wrote elsewhere, divine the undeveloped freight of a delivered syllable, it would crumble with the weight (P-1409). Trivial terms are crowded out by the absolutes. Her uninflected verbs are of a piece with her manipulation of first ideas. When she dropped the inflections of number and tense she pared the verbs to their nucleus, and that was the mighty core she meant to convey. She would have liked, as she wrote to Mrs. Holland in 1884, to deal as the Bible did with "the Centre."

Her composition was geared to a pattern of absolute terms and impressive polysyllables. She left three- and four-syllable openings in her lines for the big words that carried authority and sonority. An example is "A little Madness in the Spring," where the slot in the line "This whole Experiment of Green" remains open on the worksheet for the multiple-syllable words: apocalypse, experience, astonishment, periphery. Even though the viewpoint and values shift with the various words, the syllabic weight she wanted and the authoritative effect do not. Polysyllables seem to have supplied linguistic assurance when philosophical assurance was lacking.

Big words are one of the locking elements of her compositional strategy. She revised toward them because they concentrated and they made absolute. The second stanza in poem 1355 is distilled in such a manner, with no loss of syllabic count, from twenty words to fourteen, which include "emaciate," "aliment," and "absolute." Dickinson would in certain instances rather have a grand polysyllabic word than clarity. She intended in the closing line of poem 929, as her variant suggests, to make the six-syllable position say "Forbid that any know," but she wrote instead only two words, one of them vague but ostentatious.

> How far is it to Hell?
> As far as Death this way –
> How far left hand the Sepulchre
> Defies Topography.

In the dispersed syntax of poem 651, we see that she was rhyming not so much by sound as quantitatively by polysyllabic count. To chime with the single-word line "Illegitimate" she has written the line "Too exorbitant" and then suggested to herself in variants "Too extravagant" and "Too importunate." On a worksheet of the poem beginning "Two Butterflies went out at Noon," which Dickinson unraveled and reworked perhaps as long as sixteen years after she first began it, the scattered last lines of an effort that already included "firmament," "circumference," "peninsula," and "gravitation" are these:

> To all surviving Butterflies
> Be this Fatuity
> > Biography –
> Example – and monition
> To entomology –

Dickinson's emphatic attention to "the Astounding subjects," as she calls them in letter 568, are numerous enough so that we know one of her persisting compulsions was to concentrate gravitational centers of linguistic power, to get absolute states of existence into absolute linguistic terms. She wrote to her sister-in-law (L-913), speaking of the "ripple" and the "Silver genealogy" of Sue's own words, "Amalgams are abundant, but the lone student of the Mines adores Alloyless things." She tried to combine alloyless purity and power in those authoritative words that spread impressively across several syllables. It came as much from her regard for the authority of words sounding in the ear as from their meaning. Even when her meanings slip and become irresolute, the syllabic weight holds firm. Of distillation, she said in a prose fragment, "one note from one bird is better than a million words. A scabbard needs but one sword."

Her holophrastic tendency has extremely important significance as we attempt to see Dickinson's originality and her role as a modern precursor. Because words were to her heavy bodies, objects of nature, to use Hopkins' terms, they succeeded by their weight in taking the place of reality for her. Coleridge grasped this act of substitution when he said a focal word acquired a feeling of reality — it heats and burns, makes itself to be felt. Now Dickinson's absolutes as gross entities that leave out particulars exist only in language and with no reference but to *other words*. The great polysyllabics were for her palpable and contained whole constructs of meaning. She liked the sound, the complexity, and the grandeur, but by this overpowering authority, her words replaced the world, reifying conjecture and in the end, with the world blocked out, constituted a self-referring system.

First Lines

A third basic given in Dickinson's composing process is her memorable first line. Because the worksheets show that the first lines are more often than not unrevised (when other parts of the poem have been), the conclusion must be that she had these in mind prior to writing, that they had formed themselves and were waiting for a poem to which they would be the head. Their special character is familiar to Dickinson readers who know the pleasure of simply reading through the index of first lines. Her instinctive skill at opening poems is the more apparent in comparison with her opening lines of subsequent stanzas within poems. Comparison highlights the careful, surprise-seeking focus as well as the limited character of those remarkable beginnings.

The exceptional revisions show her compacting first lines, but they are rare in the worksheets. She revised poem 1433, where the lines were not settled but skillfully sharpened by the poet. Another opening-line revision occurs in poem 1626. Dickinson began "Pompless no Life can pass away," but she subsequently returned to her regular alternating meter and to draw her made-up word "pompless" into the foreground by giving it alliterative emphasis. The line became the one that is now well-known: "No Life can pompless pass away," with the tripled sound giving wry support to the irony of the statement itself. It is a typical Dickinson arrangement where the authority of meter is firm, the language play immediate.

The importance to Dickinson of first lines illustrates her priorities. She pointed her strategies of linguistic challenge at the entrance to the poem, even if the shape of the full poem suffered. In poem 927 we encounter a first line constructed of sixfold assonance, firm cadence, and sufficient suspense to engage the reader unerringly. The meaning, however, is problematic.

> Absent Place – an April Day –
> Daffodils a-blow
> Homesick curiosity
> To the Souls that snow –
>
> Drift may block within it
> Deeper than without –
> Daffodil delight but
> Him it duplicate –

The disconcerting intrigue of an absent place on an appealing April day with daffodils in bloom is tacitly reinforced by the allegory of the cruelly incongruous snowstorm when the flowers are out. The poem altogether has the habitual marks of Dickinson's technique: transposed syntax, a pronoun without a referent, an illogical personification in "Homesick curiosity," and the weight of meaning on the closing polysyllabic "duplicate." My point is that while the poem as a whole is disarranged and unclear, the opening is undistorted and an effective lead-in. Once we sort out the syntax, we see the earnest figuring of a familiar Dickinson subject. Snow (confusingly misplaced subject) in April leads to reminiscence about the dead. Drifts pile within that empty place in the heart deeper than any snow without; daffodils make no difference, for they delight only the one whose happiness they duplicate as in a mirror. The actual poem never forms a coherent gesture, even though it has the fine material of the incongruity of April snowfall and daffodils to trope the wastes of the interior life. Its moment of coherence unfolds only in those first skillful lines.

A list of Dickinson's most assertively engaging first lines would be lengthy. These that follow indicate the linguistic snare she created time after time with assurance. They range across the entire canon, early to late. Some have become indelible parts of the American literary consciousness.

> A chilly peace infests the grass
> A narrow fellow in the grass
> A route of evanescence
> A wife at daybreak I shall be
> A wounded deer leaps highest
> After great pain a formal feeling comes
> All but death can be adjusted
> As the starved maelstrom laps the navies
> Because I could not stop for death
> Behind me dips eternity
> Blazing in gold and quenching in purple
> Candor, my tepid friend
> Come slowly, Eden
> Crumbling is not an instant's act
> Dare you see a soul at the white heat
> Death is a dialogue between
> Death is the supple suitor
> Dust is the only secret
> "Faith" is a fine invention
> Further in summer than the birds
> For this accepted breath
> Forever is composed of nows
> God is a distant, stately lover
> Hope is a subtle glutton
> How soft this prison is
> How the old mountains drip with sunset
> I am afraid to own a body
> I cannot live with you
> I died for beauty, but was scarce
> I dwell in possibility
> I felt a funeral in my brain
> I like a look of agony
> I never lost as much but twice

The insistent onset of her language in each poem calls attention to itself in several ways. This self-conscious idiom takes immediate possession of reality, overpowering it, altering it, distancing it. In this disparity is created the reader's critical alertness. By ways we recognize vaguely as modern, the lines hit directly, sometimes with colloquial diction, demanding attention. They mislead, overstate, shock with apparent candor. They estrange familiar conventions and expectations and demand a critical response. What, these attention-demanding first lines pose, is to follow?

These dominating lines assault with tones of authority, confidence, a linguistic takeover. Like strong music compositions, they break the silence, interrupting the white page with an absolutely sure, apparently purposeful, force. This consistent ability of Dickinson's to begin is apparent in the earliest extant poems: "There is another sky," "Frequently the woods are pink," "There is a word / Which bears a sword," "My wheel is in the dark." She strove for surprise, for disconcertion, and for suspense that irresistibly possesses the reader's attention.

> The Snow that never drifts –
> The transient, fragrant snow
> That comes a single time a Year
> Is softly driving now –   (P-1133)

Surprise in the beginning lines sometimes forces awkward inversions of syntax: "To interrupt His Yellow Plan / The Sun does not allow / Caprices of the atmosphere" (P-591). Her lines turn on paradox to make bald statements that wrench familiar belief. Dickinson elided syntax to mislead the reader, crowding ambiguous constructs into the first line. "The Stimulus, beyond the Grave" does not mean the mystical banality it implies, but rather "The stimulus (of the thought that I will see his countenance) beyond the grave" supports the bereaved like brandy. Disconcertion is manufactured in "Promise This – When You be Dying," with its astonishing lack of logic. But as her punctuation is ambiguous with the dash, the adverbial phrase serves the illogical verb in the first line only momentarily before its proper verb "summon" appears in the second line:

> Promise This – When You be Dying –
> Some shall summon Me –   (P-648)

These ambiguities anticipate more recent verse, which similarly makes a game out of syntactical overlap, thus manipulating response,

getting more meanings out of a line than seem possible. It is a doubling of the effect of the language, and Emily Dickinson played this
language game with consummate skill. Her wit, tinged with the irony
that linguistic play commands as it takes possession of attention, is
evident anywhere one pauses in the piecemeal mosaic of the canon.

The manipulation of the line and its ambiguous carryover to second lines—exploiting the linear necessities of the language as it proceeds through time—allows Dickinson to compound meaning and
implication, offering one meaning so as to take it away in the next
line. Here is a less scrupulous example.

> To make One's Toilette - after Death
> Has made the Toilette cool
> Of only Taste we cared to please
> Is difficult, and still -
>
> That's easier - than Braid the Hair -
> And make the Bodice gay -
> When eyes that fondled it are wrenched
> By Decalogues - away -   (P-485)

The deception in the first line is plain enough. But, after the design of
that opening, the poem lapses into redundancy, as if she lost any
sense of wholeness once the gesture had begun. The stanzas are identical in statement, playbacks without effective purpose.

In a single prose fragment, Dickinson acknowledged in the technique of an unidentified woman poet, perhaps Elizabeth Barrett
Browning, this power of the precipitous start to unsettle the mind.
"Did you ever read one of her poems backward," she asks, "because
the plunge from the front overturned you? I sometimes have - A
something overtakes the Mind" (PF-30). This is significant because it
is a rare statement about form and procedure, and isolates a structure
Dickinson used to advantage. The power of words in certain orders of
encounter, she knew acutely, was like gunshot, physically incapaci-
tating.

But there is added significance to these forceful openings. As the
lines tease, imply, astonish, and withhold full sense, they necessarily
demand resolutions. They inaugurate a state of perplexity requiring
clarification. When this clarification is not delivered, we have a language experience without a completed conceptual experience. Dickinson's concentration on first lines thus indicates more concern with

beginnings than with resolutions and reflects her limited conception of a poem's wholeness. It suggests a willfulness in the face of perplexity that stops short of resolute power and control through the poem to its conclusion: a knowing how to start but without a goal in view. Suspense is created for its own sake, a virtuoso language to break the silence and disconcert, as if that were enough. In view of her attention to beginnings, we must see eventually how often she possessed a commensurate wholeness of intention to sustain this power, resolve the opening suspense, and to treat in an adequately complex way the estranged world she projected in first lines.

This is the place, finally, to observe that because her first lines carry such dramatic impact, setting up difficult needs for the poems to fulfill, her final lines acquire significant primacy as well. At the moment we raise the question of the wholeness of her poetic conception, we should look to see whether her last lines are not sometimes tacked on, disjunct from the rest of the poem. What indeed are the consequences to meaning when these openings and closings usurp to themselves the power and location of meaning in a poem? To some extent the result is fitful and thus a distraction from the complexity that a reasonable care for experience requires.

The Poet Writing and Revising

Dickinson's primary elements of composition are visible in worksheet traces. Poem 1660, extant only in a transcript made by Sue, is clearly an unfinished work, even in the loose way we use that term with Emily Dickinson. Its meter, syllabic count, and rhyme scheme, all of which are fairly unvarying requirements in Dickinson, are unsettled. What we see are the organizing elements of Dickinson's composing process: the strong opening and the regular two-line unit here concealed by redundancy and an unnaturally loose syllabic count. The possible syllable and line break between "Means" and "Dominion" highlights the two parallel predicate phrases—one beginning with "Means," the other "Warms"—which are probably variants because they are redundant in sense. The focal places are those in which sit the workhorse polysyllabic words "Dominion" and "oblivion." Through this thrice-removed text of Sue's transcript, we see the basic structuring of the poem:

Glory is that bright tragic thing
That for an instant
Means Dominion
Warms some poor name
That never felt the Sun
Gently replacing
In oblivion –   (P-1660)

We are sufficiently familiar with Dickinson's elisions to know that an
object pronoun, masculine or feminine, is needed to follow the verb
"replacing" and to refer back to "some poor name," itself a metonymic trace of what is momentarily glorified.

Of the few heavily worked sheets Dickinson left, none is more
jumbled than poem 1386, which begins with typical colloquial directness "Summer – we all have seen." The reader may want to consult
the variorum here to follow the discussion. Two pages are pinned together, the top sheet placed so that it substitutes for all of the second
stanza except its first line. We find the elements we have come to expect: syllable count and meter are steady, sound patterns take form in
the casually constructed rhymes, and the authoritative closing lines
belie the general vagueness in the body of the poem.

The three basic constituents stand out prominently in the worksheet. The first line and indeed the first stanza are complete and
unrevised. The stanza is made up of two-line units and thereafter the
two-line segments proceed, dividing fairly regularly by, first, parallel
predicates ("But Summer does not care – / She takes her gracious
way," lines 5–6), a two-line simile that swerves off to compare the
mystery of the moon's remoteness ("As eligible as the moon / To our
Temerity," lines 7–8), a modified subject phrase over two lines
("Deputed [for us] to adore – / The affluence evolved," lines 9–10),
and the final locking two lines ("Unknown as to an Ecstasy / The
Embryo endowed," lines 11–12) which, because they too are unrevised, seem, despite the inversion, to have been ready-made to cap the
work.

The polysyllables are here in profusion and fall in closing spots
with a resounding authority: "Unquestionably," "unperverted"
(with its variant polysyllables—"undiverted," "eligible," "unavail-
ing"), "Temerity" (with its own train of variant polysyllables—
"Divinity," "extremity," "adversity," "obliquity"). Now this stream

of variants for the polysyllables, besides showing us once again the connections they had for Dickinson, shows how variant they are in meaning as well. These shifts are crucial to the sense of the poem and the attitude it takes finally toward summer's beauty, which is compared to the withheld knowledge of the distant moon.

A paraphrase of the entire poem is something like this: summer does not acknowledge our regard because, like the moon, it is a closed, remote mystery; our adoration of it is as unknown to it as ecstacy is to an embryo. In this context of meaning, which is complex in its undeveloped implications, line 8 is crucial, for it locates the poet's sense of the human condition in this affair of unrequited attention. Yet the meaning slips seriously out of focus as variants pile up. If the word for the human attitude is to be temerity, that is one thing: it is our pride that demands recognition and returned love. But if the condition is "our extremity" or "our adversity," then the relationship is a cruel tragedy of undeserved exclusion. If it is "our obliquity," we are back to being guilty again. Finally, if it is the moon's (and summer's) divinity that causes our exclusion, then there is a vaguely desperate commentary on divinely sanctioned exclusion from recognition.

A similarly fugitive meaning is indicated by the adjectives proposed for the way summer proceeds on her way: spacious, subtle, simple, mighty, gallant, sylvan, ample, perfect. Although not contradictory terms in any instance, they differ profoundly in signifying the relationship, from homely and appealing to remote and inhumanly perfect.

The problem of gliding sense while the syllabic slots remain constant—that is, her need for word weight and magnitude is foremost—is epitomized by the single term "Affluence." Dickinson set this pitomized by the single term "Affluence." Dickinson set this firmly, not to be revised. But that crucial locus of meaning has to do with what it is that the creator or the observer (whoever evolves, confers, bestows, involves) has invested in the summer that he or we cannot understand. In other words, "Affluence" stands for the beauty the maker has conferred or love the observer has bestowed. The point is that this prime term is indefinite, involved as it is with a vision of the creator's intention, and leaves the reader curiously unenlightened as to the poem's stance.

What we can make of these worksheet indications of Dickinson's processes of creation is highly significant in at least two respects.

First, she revised in confined locations, seemingly without a conception of the shape of the whole poem except for the statement of love in the unrevised first lines and the condition of knowledge denied in the final lines, also unrevised. This localized revision, which has to do with the demands of a line or a single slot in a line rather than with the shape of the poem, creates obscurity that we are familiar with in Dickinson. When she revises word by word, lines begin to pull their own meanings disjunct from a larger context. It is a case of the autonomy of detail, local sounds and syllable counts without regard for the progress of the piece.

Obscurity and the problems of flow for the reader, we see, are linked to this significant phenomenon: the concern within individual lines for language, its musical and rhythmic being, prior to meaning; that is, a concentration on line-limited precincts of sound and space at the expense of the larger coherence. "Summer – we all have seen" is troubled by knowledge that never gets to its surface. It is troubled by inarticulate possibility that creates commotion, not language of adequate denotation or form of adequate complexity or magnitude to handle the weight of the mystery posited. Dickinson's formulaic composition and microrevision resulted in texts that threaten to disintegrate under intensive reading.

Dominating simultaneously the linguistic strategies and conceptual inadequacy is the formal brevity. Dickinson developed the possibilities of severe compression even as it forced the strange syntax that confuses her readers. The crowded composition is especially appropriate to urgent, spoken expression, and this she exploited with great skill. To the extent her single- and double-line units have plots, they are made of quick turns and sharp paradoxes, centering on word play: "Mid-night – Good Night! I hear them call." The compacted language by its persistent intermittence courted and caught movement, alteration, glimpses, surprise, disappearance. It is incapable of systematic coverage, but it equipped her eye for special gestures. It is an instrument of intimate speech, quick glance, quick wisdom, with profound implications for the reading of this extraordinary poet. A reader must not overlook the significance of her compartmented attention or the other difficulties I have noted, for they lead to a revealing characterization of her larger discourse—the poem as a whole, the clusters of like poems, the body of poetry itself. To seek only the meaning of the words she wrote is to miss the significance of what she did not write, the equally important meaning of what is absent.

In the amplifying order of compositional units—sign, sentence, text, corpus—where linguists stop at the sentence and critics at the single-poem text, we must be able, if we are to identify this poet who changed American poetry, to move between these levels toward intention. We shall need a grammar of her canon, which will comprise a grammar of her composition process, a grammar of her presences, and a grammar of her absences. Neglecting specific circumstances outside the poem, neglecting narrative or other spacious forms, she concentrated with an exclusiveness, a "rapt attention" that is unique. The excruciating force of language, she wrote to J. K. Chickering in 1883, was actual: "I had hoped to see you, but have no grace to talk, and my own Words so chill and burn me, that the temperature of other Minds is too new an Awe."

With utmost compaction, distorted and defective as the poems sometimes are, she made her infinite wagers on the all-or-nothing experiences the poems allegorize. Her goals—the absolute subjects she presumed to possess with her words—were as large and risky as her poems were small and unstable. The force of those quick sallies after cosmic things remains with us and ensures her place as one of the language makers. To gather her full identity and her role as an inventor of language in America, we must measure the expense in more spacious composition and capacity of experience that this small focus and extreme concentration exacted.

The Hymn

The hymnal form, to say this directly now, was the main cause of Dickinson's obscurity. The pressure she put on the limits of that formal husk resulted in the strange ways of her poems, the pent-up nature of their feeling, and the hyperbolic oddity of her voice. Line by line, the hymn constrained her syntax so severely that ellipsis became a habitual, unexamined strategy. So circumscribed was this form, and so limited its textural space, that her lexical meanings often lack reinforcing definition from an adequately detailed context.

Hymnology flourished in America between 1830 and 1880.

Americans sang hymns at home and in church, and serious theologians ranked the importance of hymns with that of sermons.[3] Dickinson adopted this ready-to-hand verse form in the same way she took the subjects of popular poetry—nature's divine plan, dying, immortality. There are few instances of experimentation with meter outside the syllabic systems of the hymn. Poem 622, for example, begins with her intention to compose iambic pentameter, but the lines waver and return to the habitual four and three stresses. A casualness of conversation bordering on free verse is discernible in poems 390 and 690, but these seem to be worksheet notations rather than conscious efforts at free verse.

Dickinson required a shape and a rhythm to hold her words and, along with literary Protestantism, the nineteenth century handed it to her. Ultimately she seems never to have seriously considered or missed a more expansive form, with all the possibilities such forms would present. In the beginning, her taking up the hymn perhaps was not at all conscious but came from familiarity since childhood. The hymn was for her the way words grouped themselves, established their bonds, and took their cadence in her mind.

Emerson understood this as a natural selection. In the late essay "Poetry and Imagination," drawing on an 1854 entry in his journal, he gave the accepted view of the physiology of versification: "Metre begins with pulse-beat, and the length of lines in songs and poems is determined by the inhalation and exhalation of the lungs. If you hum or whistle the rhythm of the common English metres—of the decasyllabic quatrain or the octosyllabic with alternate sexisyllabic or other rhythms—you can easily believe these metres to be organic, derived from the human pulse, and to be therefore not proper to one nation, but to mankind."[4]

References to hymns in Dickinson's letters and poems suggest that she knew what she was doing with the form. One mention indicates that she knew she used it ironically at times. In an 1852 letter to Sue, at a time when Dickinson was becoming conscious of her gift, she described how she put the choral form to her private use. She had gone to meeting, she wrote, and when the "worthy pastor" had "said 'Our Heavenly Father,' I said 'Oh Darling Sue'; when he read the 100th Psalm, I kept saying your precious letter all over to myself, and Susie, when they sang – it would have made you laugh to hear one little voice, piping to the departed. I made up words and kept singing how I loved you, and you had gone, while all the rest of the choir were singing Hallelujahs" (L-88). She mentions hymns in other letters, and in poem 616 she wrote of the supportive "Thews of Hymn / And Sinew from within" and how "I sang firm – even – Chants." Once in the late years Dickinson agreed to write three hymns for a local charity, feeling, she told Higginson, she "could write them quite plainly" (L-674). We can appreciate that she recognized the necessity, at least for a public occasion, to write plainly.

Her taking of this simple form also freed her for her own special aptitudes: the violations of word-selection norms which give her tropes the force of novelty, her crosscutting of one lexicon against another, her intense figural concentration by which meaning gathers in a few nodes, her plain wisdom. The hymn was simple, in several ways adaptable, and by choosing it instead of the burdens of exploratory forms, she allowed what interested her more: stylistic surprise, language upstaging reality. In visual art of the late twentieth century a comparable enterprise is that of Jasper Johns who, by choosing for his subjects the most familiar of symbols (circular targets, the American flag), frees himself entirely for style. He so alters the familiar response to these visual clichés that we can see with extraordinary clarity how his paint possesses the facts and turns them into something strange. The world's ordinary things become then not matters of reality to be mirrored, but matters of style.

Sheen must have a disk. The uncomplicated syllabic and rhyme systems of the hymn, together with its convention of projecting divine landscapes in extremely small scope, was suitable for Dickinson. The hymn that came to her from Isaac Watts had no resemblance whatever to dramatic monologue because of its short line and avoidance of personality. But its origins came to life again in Dickinson. Hymns developed appropriately enough as *apostrophes* from classical sources specifically addressed to the dead. In Dickinson's hands they began to foreshadow the dramatic monologue after Tennyson and Browning. Her spoken hymn, in short, is the precursor of the mind's monologue in its modern fragmentary form.

Rhyming was not Dickinson's forte, and the hymn never taxed that faculty. There is some evidence, as in poem 473, of Dickinson's inability to sustain a rather intricate rhyme scheme (a a b c c b). Under her pen it unraveled, came apart in the last stanza; then she copied the lines in that state to bind into one of her packets. She was content to rhyme "spurn" with "born" in poem 285, adding an exact rhyme "scorn" as an afterthought in a variant. She made this communal form, instead, intimate by direct address and immediate by tone of voice. With strategies of the vernacular, of wit and pretended confession and other stylistic determiners of tone, including punctuation, she created a voice that seemed to have immediate proximity with the mind. This voice in simple meter seemed to be closer to mental experience than writing by itself could manage.

She made a form that ordinarily celebrates immutability incorporate motion and alteration, feel intensity itself in the bald modern way without a philosophical frame. "Wonderful Rotation!" as she says in one poem. Not unlike Pound's imagism, it is freed of judgment. And, like Hopkins, she animated regular forms with a mimetic syncopation. A line in poem 653, comparable to a line in "The Windhover," likens a bird to a piece of down on the breeze, "In easy – even – dazzling pace." She used this form to trace psychological currents and descend to psychological depths. Just how much intensity is generated in her words is apparent as soon as one of her poems is *sung* as a hymn or as a folk tune. What is so intense in a written text, as in poem 502 beginning with evident desperation "At least – to pray – is left – is left," is suddenly drained of personal anguish and becomes conventional religious sentiment. The special intensity of Dickinson's poems is her own investment; it is not inherent in the form itself.

She used in the hymn form, that is, an oblique language vision that produces periodic estrangements and accelerates language's withdrawal from rationality and clarification, from its mirroring function. But though this form constrained her expression to the point of contorting syntax and forcing single words to carry impossibly complex significance, the form by the same constraint foregrounded her short, assertive lines. In her hands, the hymn became *aggressive*. Even as it denied her room to open out syntax, it heightened intensity and wit and focal gravity.

Of the four basic metrical systems in English—syllabic, accentual, accentual-syllabic, and quantitative—Dickinson worked in the oldest, most rudimentary of the forms, the one closest to the origins of patterned expression. She preserved that deep, primitive cadence and invested it with a striking new power of intimacy. With this as the template of her expression, her thoughts seemed to conform to its possibilities, falling into its shape and arranging themselves within it. The hymn's strict syllabic system and simple rhyme pattern simultaneously determined and distorted her language.

When the form required severe ellipsis, it could cost the sense. The closing lines of poem 383 are so disarranged to fit the syllabic necessities that a reader is hard put to find a meaning. The constitutive elements are familiar: the first-line impact, the violation that produces the novelty of "Outer Wine," a second stanza that recapitulates the first, a further recapitulation in the final stanza. But the closing lines drift into the baffling space-forced defects of syntax. Dickinson's strengths as well as her defects are all here in these twelve lines. One supposes, but without assurance, that the last lines are to be understood to say "the best stimulant you can offer a man is to exhale from your interior (spiritual) wine closet." The problem of meaning is created by a syntax pinched by syllabic requirement.

> Exhilaration – is within –
> There can no Outer Wine
> So royally intoxicate
> As that diviner Brand
>
> The Soul achieves – Herself –
> To drink – or set away
> For Visitor – Or Sacrament –
> 'Tis not of Holiday
>
> To stimulate a Man
> Who hath the Ample Rhine
> Within his Closet – Best you can
> Exhale in offering.   (P-383)

Poem 286 bears a similar defect of syntax caused by the hymn-line requirement. The contraction in the first line is a conventional way out of difficulty, but in line 5 the elimination of the subject and the connective, "A second more, [and we] had dropped too deep," creates serious confusion.

> That after Horror – that 'twas *us* –
> That passed the mouldering Pier –
> Just as the Granite Crumb let go –
> Our Savior, by a Hair –

A second more, had dropped too deep
For Fisherman to plumb –
The very profile of the Thought
Puts Recollection numb –

Syntax is garbled because of syllabic count in poem 450 as well. The poem is a Dickinson allegory of passage into immortality. Her term "Solid Dawn" presents a typical problem of semantics. She wanted it to mean what she said it meant: sufficient dawn, total dawn, permanent dawn. Other defects are caused by the syllabic count: it forces the misleading parallel placement of "better," one as a line stop, the other enjambed. The use of "well" as an adjective and "sweeter" where an adverb is called for is gratuitous. The final stanza must be completely rearranged to make an understandable syntactic chain: The surmising robins would never gladden a tree more sweetly than if they were confronting (singing in) a perpetual dawn leading to no day. Here is what she wrote:

Dreams – are well – but Waking's better,
If One wake at Morn –
If One wake at Midnight – better –
Dreaming – of the Dawn –

Sweeter – the Surmising Robins –
Never gladdened Tree –
Than a Solid Dawn – confronting –
Leading to no Day –   (P-450)

A last egregious case shows how much pressure the hymn mold put on Dickinson's syntax. Poem 651 displays an unusually complicated atomization. I believe Dickinson composed it initially by two sorts of rhyme—one auditory and the other by quantity of polysyllables within the 8–5 count. Least of all, evidently, was the need for straightforward meaning. The poem is nothing so much as a cubist dispersal of natural arrangement to conform to an arbitrary form. Dickinson bound it into one of her packets, satisfied with it.

3   5
So much Summer

2   1
Me for showing

4
Illigitimate –

6   7
Would a Smile's minute bestowing

9
Too exorbitant

10
To the Lady

With the Guinea

8   11
Look – if She should know

Crumb of Mine

13
A Robin's Larder

12
Would suffice to stow –

The Lady with the Guinea means a rich lady, the phrase plumped out to make the second half of an eight-syllable line. The poem is an allegory of the luxury of frugalest charity. We proceed, as we should with Dickinson, on the principle of the conservation of material—she wasted almost nothing, the rich lady here notwithstanding—to reconstruct the poem's sentence. This cubist exercise produces the order 3-5-2-1-4-6-7-9-10-8-11-13-12. It looks like the firing sequence of a weird thirteen-cylinder internal combustion engine. The poem's question is this: For showing me so much summer (illegitimate because a substitute), would a smile's minute (tiny) bestowing look too exorbitant even to a wealthy lady if she knew that just a crumb of mine would fill a robin's larder? No other poem of Dickinson's shows quite so clearly what the hymn form did to her syntax.

With all its constraints and narrow vision, Dickinson never abandoned the hymn. In it she suffered her severest limitations, made do with her worst defects of grammar and syntax—and yet on balance made this small fragmenting form shape a power in certain ways unexcelled by any other poet in the language.

5   Disabling Freedom

Dickinson's strict reliance on the hymn form reveals with new clarity the severe limits of her compositional craft. Millicent Bingham's observation in the introduction to *Bolts of Melody* in 1945—that some poems trail off into a vague limbo—is an inkling of the handicap readers sense even when it can not be defined. If we track down the significance of this confined indefiniteness, we can address the most vexing technical mysteries in her verse: its lack of outside reference, its refusal to tell a story, its piece-by-piece arrangement; indeed, why she wrote voluminously, but did not speak.

Although there are many instances of larger structures in her work, the norm is small segments rather than carefully organized contexts of magnitude. The body of 1775 poems is the exhibit of this fragmentation, defying most avenues of critical approach. It seems an extraordinary privation, this absence of any sustained, architecturally intricate, carefully unfolding poem. But in truth the lack of a poetic design is implicit in cryptic pronouncements, such as the one she made to Higginson, that "My Business is Circumference": it reflects need without a definable goal. The fact is that she had no large structure for her poetic energies and had difficulty with the construction of a whole poem.

The characteristics of her work have suggested this essential unfinishedness, but we have all been too pleasurably distracted by the local brilliancies of her work to remark the larger significance. The manuscript scraps, the tendency to revise in small discrete parts of individual poems without attention to broader rhythms, her practice of sewing unfinished poems into her packets: this points to a poet without an urgent sense of structural wholeness. She seems to have been a thinker without final thoughts, to take a phrase from Wallace Stevens. Lacking finality, her works remain a calculus measuring motion and variation, but without bringing one vector of attention to meet another.

Nor did she ever classify her interests. They crowd in together and, like a drawer full of photographs taken over the years, make an unorganized collection. Photography, in fact, whose development in the 1840s and 50s was contemporary with Dickinson's coming of age, is a striking analogy to her own appropriation of reality by pieces, without a grand design. Her taste for individual excitements as against overall design, evident in her mid-twenties as she chased her enthusiasms and talent, is indicated in a letter to Austin concerning some poems he had sent her by the Scottish poet Alexander Smith. After remarking that the poems "are not very coherent," she then praised them because they had a "good deal of exquisite frensy, and some wonderful figures, as ever I met in my life" (L-128). It was a prescient description of her own poetry, constricted in form, flawed and disjointed, but evincing what one must call brilliant impurity. These textual, technical, and attitudinal elements, then, are evidence of the central truth of her artistic endeavors: strenuous linguistic wit without even latently an informing design.

No poet can compose the whole of his poetry himself, R. P. Blackmur said of Hardy's limitations, arguing that Hardy relied for authority of idea and language less than he should have on the great poetic tradition and too much on his own philosophical and narrative penchants. But, except for Watts's hymns, this is the rash autonomy Dickinson exercised. Her reliance on the hymn form relieved her of the obligations of a more demanding and contingent craft. It avoided the harsher responsibility that Frost said must follow feeling or the "inner mood" that first carries a poet part way into his poem. Dickinson had freed herself of almost every exterior discipline except the one she needed most—a line and stanza form that did not require an intricate program or an architectural procedure.

In addition to the cumulative significance of the fragmentation of the work as a whole, specific poems illustrate the absence of a controlling design. Poem 501 is representative. It proceeds almost entirely in the familiar two-line steps, and instead of developing the initial thought, the succeeding lines repeat in new terms the basic idea of an invisible but beckoning second life. To be sure, it is a tight expression with no digressions. With the word "Faith" at the opening of what would normally be the fourth quatrain, however, this intensity is suddenly released, diverted here into the coy personification that is so frequent a part of Dickinson's work.

> This World is not Conclusion.
> A Species stands beyond –
> Invisible, as Music –
> But positive, as Sound –
> It beckons, and it baffles –
> Philosophy – don't know –
> And through a Riddle, at the last –
> Sagacity, must go –
> To guess it, puzzles scholars –
> To gain it, Men have borne
> Contempt of Generations
> And Crucifixion, shown –
> Faith slips – and laughs, and rallies –
> Blushes, if any see –
> Plucks at a twig of Evidence –
> And asks a Vane, the way –
> Much Gesture, from the Pulpit –
> Strong Hallelujahs roll –
> Narcotics cannot still the Tooth
> That nibbles at the soul –   (P-501)

The variants include one for the next-to-last line that deflates what in the original version is a spare, experience-wise metaphor. Dickinson thought to change "Tooth" to "Mouse," letting the poem trail off into that playfulness that sometimes defeats her effects. The poem weakens as it goes into the final two stanzas, slackens its own tension, gets painfully wordy even in so small a compass ("Faith slips – and laughs, rallies – Blushes"), and ends where it began, the sequel to life having beckoned, baffling and riddling, and still at the end nibbling. With four variants appended, and in this repetitive and loosening tone, the poem went as it was into one of the packets.

Similarly, for all its concentrated sensation of autumnal strangeness, "Further in Summer than the Birds" depends on nodal phrases in each of its four stanzas which actually are repetitions of the single theme of haunting change: "unobtrusive Mass," "pensive Custom," "spectral Canticle," and "Druidic Difference." The second and fourth stanzas indeed, as do the first and third, mirror one another as paraphrases with no increment of meaning. Indefiniteness in Dickinson also results from the sharp swerves in poems that signal their lack of organization. In this poem from the middle years the syntactic mystery that opens between stanzas following the word "Countenance" (is it verb or noun?) obscures and deranges that space. Punctuation necessary to an understanding of what constitutes the closing statement is missing.

> So the Eyes accost – and sunder –
> In an Audience –
> Stamped – occasionally – forever –
> So may Countenance
>
> Entertain – without addressing
> Countenance of One
> In a Neighboring Horizon –
> Gone – as soon as known –   (P-752)

"Entertain" in the company of "accost," "sunder," and "Stamped" is only the most pointed of the disorganizing detours. This shift together with the abstractness of unidentified Eyes, Audience, Countenance, and One makes the poem seem targetless, sounds without definite purpose, speech divorced from design. Entered in such a state of gravityless suspension without a center, without the lines connected, we are unable to complete the sense.

When this tendency of stanzas to float free of a precise overarching purpose or intent combines with rococo playfulness, we have egregious efforts of a sort that no amount of revision can set right.

> The Bird did prance – the Bee did play –
> The Sun ran miles away
> So blind with joy he could not choose
> Between his Holiday
>
> The morn was up – the meadows out
> The Fences all but ran,
> Republic of Delight, I thought
> Where each is Citizen –

From Heavy laden Lands to thee
Were seas to cross to come
A Caspian were crowded –
Too near thou art for Fame –   (P-1107)

The last stanza again creates the problem because it takes a turn rather than completing what has gone before. When we anticipate closure we get a veering into indefiniteness. Her ending in this semifinal draft is never brought under the control of a design that reaches back to the first line. A paraphrase: from careworn circumstances ("Heavy laden Lands"), if there were oceans to cross, people would crowd the seas to reach the land of Delight. Yet the final line doesn't summarize but baffles the more. She intends to say that this outdoor republic of delight is so close at hand and familiar that it goes unnoticed. The worksheet version is little help because there too the intention is in doubt. It seems that Dickinson brought the poem to a close without the mold of a clear idea of what the poem was to say in its totality. It ends short of completion, the result of writing cut loose from discipline and the challenge and check of a design.

One of the major poems I discussed earlier seems to have come to closure almost by chance. The variant versions of "Safe in their Alabaster Chambers" occupied Dickinson and her sister-in-law, certainly her most valued reader through the crucial middle years, in 1859 and again in 1861. The variants show the indefiniteness of the poet's purpose as she attended to her worksheet versions in response to Sue's carefully tactful criticism. "I am not suited dear Emily with the second verse," Sue wrote. "It is remarkable as the chain lightening that blinds us hot nights in the Southern sky but it does not go with the ghostly shimmer of the first verse as well as the other one." She referred to the closing stanza beginning "Grand go the Years" which Dickinson had substituted for the original closing that, in the 1859 version, began "Light laughs the breeze / In her Castle above them." Dickinson then made at least two other attempts to complete this poem, one of the endings starting out "Springs – shake the sills" and emphasizing the cold finality of the life inside the tomb: "Hoar – is the window / And numb the door"; "Staples – of Ages – have buckled – there." The other ending swept out inexplicably to distant places: "Frosts unhook – in the Northern Zones – / Icicles – crawl from the Polar Caverns." This is impressive imagery of finality, impotence, absolute loss, and the end of hope, but it is a world away from the tenor of the original version with its pleasurable imagery ("Light laughs the breeze / In her castle above them") and the only sign of hopelessness in the single reference to "a stolid ear" of the dead. In considering a second stanza to balance what had obviously been a satisfactory first stanza, Dickinson shifted from the state inside the tomb to both close- and wide-angle visions of what went on outside, and there, in turn, from Bees to Doges to icicles. The tone shifts correspondingly, contrasting enough to make questionable any idea of a fixed purpose on the poet's part.

Poems clearly incomplete, not matured in either the fullness of their expression or their intent, even so are put into the packets. This poem is bound into packet 91.

> Each Scar I'll keep for Him
> Instead I'll say of Gem
> In His long Absence worn
> A Costlier one
>
> But every Tear I bore
> Were He to count them o'er
> His own would fall so more
> I'll mis sum them.   (P-877)

With its syntax inversions and ellipsis, the syllable count is the only fulfilled element in this contorted poem. The rest is jerky in movement and in the second stanza unnecessarily nervous with shifts back and forth between the unidentified participants: I bear, he counts, his tears fall, I mis sum. A paraphrase shows the difficulty of flow in the poem's single sentence: I will keep each scar for Him, I'll say, instead of a costlier Gem worn in his long absence, but if he were to count every tear I bore his own would fall so much more that I could not count them. Except for the simple strength of the first line the poem is undistinguished.

Like impressionist music, Dickinson's poems search for a resolving chord, but the poet seems not to have undertaken the complicated work of achieving it. Dickinson's letters, more and more, took on the same disjointed aphoristic qualities. (One to Mrs. Holland in January 1871 is an instance.) The poetry is a discontinuous body of work, which in turn presented a discontinuous world lacking a dominant resolve. The whole is made up of particles, impressions, attitudes of more or less equal weight that were never arranged by the poet so that an attitude might take form toward the world. Dickinson could have written, that is to say, with only time itself to stop her, an infinite number of verses. Without, to use a term of Pound's, a major form for all of her poems or an appreciable part of them or even individual poems, there was no natural positioning of her poems, no inhering emphasis. Samuel Johnson thought Pope's line on wit— "What oft was thought, but ne'er so well expressed"—reduced the meaning of that useful term "from strength of thought to happiness of language." Matthew Arnold believed that some of Keats's poems "seem to exist merely for the sake of single lines and passages; not for the sake of producing any total impression." Something of the same is true in the case of Emily Dickinson.

Unity is not, despite their compactness, a quality of Dickinson's poems. The truth is that they disperse rather than hold. This is the effect of their activity. As readers we sense that her poems are roiled by a knowledge for which there is no adequately complex structure or sufficient magnitude to grasp. "I hardly know what I have said," she wrote to Joseph Sweetser, a relative of her neighbor, in 1858. "My words put all their feathers on – and fluttered here and there" (L-190). Inevitably, this unorganized activity that takes place in so compact a space—troubled, instinctive, unformed knowledge—disturbs any possible balance between reality and the imagination. We confront a poetry of great strength and no direction, the loaded gun without a target. The absence of a grand design and the resulting absence of architecture in the individual poems was a grave but characteristically unelaborated vexation for the poet herself. She touched on it in one of those enormously telling disclosures so brief that it has gone unremarked. She gave Higginson an impulsive account of her aesthetic dilemma: "I had no Monarch in my life and cannot rule myself, and when I try to organize – my little Force explodes – and leaves me bare and charred" (L-271).

Though up to now it may seem that Dickinson's motive in writing to Higginson was her desire to get her poems published, she was in fact pleading for his help to find control, to find some indwelling design by which her poetry might cohere. It is a penetrating announcement half concealed, perhaps only partly conscious, by Dickinson. It is as close as she ever got to defining her own central poetic identity for herself. It was, as well, the minutest glimpse of a lawless poetics that was to characterize some of the literature in the age that succeeded hers.

In Dickinson's poems, rhetoric leaves off its mimetic function to make what Harold Bloom has usefully called in another context the dance of tropes. Altogether uniquely, her rhetoric persistently makes that quick passage into the excitement of language without the authority of structural craft. It is a style, to borrow Samuel Johnson's judgment of Milton's style, which T. S. Eliot happily repeated, that is not modified by its subject. In place of structural and ideational finality, instead of an arduous engagement with facts, with, that is, prose, we have in Dickinson language pyrotechnics. Her atomized components necessarily court intense states of emotion. Besides movement and novelty, they solicit contraries, ironies, and inevitably epigrams and abstractions. It is a poetry of brilliantly concentrated firepower but no movement forward, no design beyond the moment's display.

> My Soul – accused me – And I quailed –
> As Tongues of Diamond had reviled
> All else accused me – and I smiled –
> My Soul – that Morning – was My Friend –
>
> Her favor – is the best Disdain
> Toward Artifice of Time – or Men –
> But Her Disdain – 'twere lighter bear
> A finger of Enamelled Fire –   (P-753)

Overnourished language, this is hyperbole that threatens to erupt in hysteria, or at least has a knowledge of hysteria. It makes single probes without the obligation of extended analysis. The fact that mattered was the poem. At its extreme, this supercharged language turns sententious, as here in poem 779. Its terms are nothing less than the unalloyed absolute Hopelessness against the equally abstract opposites of Gain and Goal. Even the unlikely word "tenderest" is an absolute in this poem made up of insupportable weights.

> The Service without Hope –
> Is tenderest, I think –
> Because 'tis unsustained
> By stint – Rewarded Work –

Has impetus of Gain –
And impetus of Goal –
There is no Diligence like that
That knows not an Until –

The astonishment in poem 769 at life's and death's totality seems adolescent because of the overblown language on overblown subjects, without qualification, without coming to terms with complexity. What she presents is not life and death and the everlasting, but the absolute words. The first line is gimmicky:

One and One – are One –
Two – be finished using –
Well enough for Schools –
But for Minor Choosing –

Life – just – Or Death
Or the Everlasting –
More – would be too vast
For the Soul's Comprising –

One intention of modernist poets is to retard the process by which language effaces itself in meaning. The poet avoids denotation in order to keep language itself centered, performing in the foreground. No other modern precursor so instinctively yet so intensively concentrated on the words to the exclusion of other matters of form and subject. The Dickinson idiom, to use one of her own phrases, was "Accomplished in Surprise" (P-1371). Her linguistic flair transformed everything at the center of her delight. She took words in preference to reality.

Surprise is like a thrilling – pungent –
Upon a tasteless meat
Alone – too acrid – but combined
An edible Delight.   (P-1306)

In her sick bed, the end of life near, in addition to some poems on death and the seasons, she wrote in tortuously formed letters on the inside of a slit-open envelope a poem about a drunk. But it is really a poem about how her *words* transform the ditch where the drunk lies, taking it up into language until its reality disappears. The absolutes are all here:

> The Ditch is dear to the Drunken man
> For is it not his Bed –
> His Advocate – his Edifice –
> How safe his fallen Head
> In her disheveled Sanctity –
> Above him is the sky –
> Oblivion bending over him
> And Honor leagues away   (P-1645)

Sue's obituary for Dickinson caught this extraordinary impatience of hers to name. "Quick as the electric spark in her intuitions and analyses," Sue wrote, "she seized the kernel instantly, almost impatient of the fewest words." The poet's language pleased itself in the way mathematics does, without much concern for the other, prosaic, self-consuming function of mimesis.

In the end then, instead of proceeding by the reasonableness of syntax or the obligations of representation, her poems dart and posture. There is a wholly linguistic excitement removed from experience. We see it epitomized in the poem that follows. The motion outward extends to eternity, the compaction to thirty-nine words. The subject is another word, eternity. The single phrase "Periods of Seas" shows us how this hermetic language can force a surreal vision with no referent in reality.

> As if the Sea should part
> And show a further Sea –
> And that – a further – and the Three
> But a presumption be
>
> Of Periods of Seas –
> Unvisited of Shores –
> Themselves the Verge of Seas to be –
> Eternity – is Those –   (P-695)

Withdrawal

The autogenerative concentration on language both reflects and was caused by Emily Dickinson's withdrawal from the world. She withdrew in all the physical ways with which we are familiar, and we must at long last consider what the effect was on her poems. Most crucially, her language became idiosyncratic, disengaged from outside authority, and thus in its own way inimitably disordered. The lack of architecture is a consequence of the linguistic reflexiveness, and both are part of the harsh artistic freedom that opens up when reality and language undergo a separation.

Dickinson's poems have remarkably few references to a social reality, to particular events, to politics, to real people in a verifiable way. There is, astonishingly, no Civil War in the flood of poems from the war years. Instead, a considerable part of the language is inwardly parabolic in the way we have noticed, having detached itself from the authority of experience and become, in its cramped form and selectional daring, self-regarding and hyperbolic. It has freed itself from the familiar function of representation at the cost of its own sporadic contortions and fragmentation. In those accumulating idiosyncrasies, Dickinson's true artistic character was composed, and they exist, when we comprehend the signs, as our chief way of identifying her as a poet. When she disengaged her idiom from the complicated texture of social existence, she made it self-conscious, private, and momentary in its grasp.

Unfastened thus from contingent exterior reality, the language frequently slips easily enough into the autogenous code, as I pointed out earlier, of "Dots on a Disc of Snow" or of suddenly surreal combinations of the sort depicting the song of the wounded bird that closes poem 514: "the Music crashed – / Like Beads – among the Bog." It was a language sometimes formed of complacent abstractions into a kind of pseudo-representation, as here:

> Myself – was beggared . . .
>
> I clutched at sounds –
> I groped at shapes –
> I touched the tops of Films –   (P-430)

For the hymn form to confine her language so decisively, there could have been no countering and affective pressure on that form from outside the poems. But there is as well a disregard for commonplace reason which involved, in turn, an escape from the constraining patterns of syntax. In this extravagant freedom Dickinson could collapse transitive and intransitive verbs into a confusing intermediate state and as willingly leave out a crucial subject noun even while retaining its adjective, winding up with disjoined words in a kind of closet language:

> The Flesh – Surrendered – Cancelled –
> The Bodiless – begun –   (P-524)

Similarly, her language generates stanzas like the second one of poem
1291 which suddenly goes opaque and requires intense study and the
insertion of punctuation to get to the rudimentary syntax and the fit
with what has gone before.

> Until the Desert knows
> That Water grows
> His Sands suffice
> But let him once suspect
> That Caspian Fact
> Sahara dies
>
> Utmost is relative –
> Have not or Have
> Adjacent sums
> Enough – the first Abode
> On the familiar Road
> Galloped in Dreams –

Dickinson's withdrawal of language was perfectly, even predictably, consistent with her life. When she went into reclusion in her father's house in Amherst, she took her language with her. That is why
words like "circumference" or "wife" have no ties to reality. They
are language talking to itself, not negotiating with the outside world.
In this separated state, Dickinson's idiom existed not as representation, but rather in its exclusive state only as literature.

This is why much of the world in Dickinson's verse is impalpable,
why there are so few poems about what it is to maneuver in a world
of people and events, even what it is exactly to knead dough, put your
hands in soil, smell flowers, walk in grass, feel water on your hand.
"Almost all these poems are strangely impersonal," Higginson wrote
in *The Christian Union* in 1890, the year Dickinson was first published, "but here and there we have a glimpse of experiences too intense to be more plainly intimate." Mabel Todd, the earliest editor,
defined that difficult privateness in a preface to *Poems: Second Series*
in 1891: "In Emily Dickinson's exacting hands, the especial, intrinsic
fitness of a particular order of words might not be sacrificed to anything virtually extrinsic; and her verses all show a strange cadence of
inner rhythmical music." Samuel G. Ward, a writer for the *Dial* and

Dickinson's near-contemporary, writing to Higginson shortly after the first edition of *Poems,* linked her self-enclosed language to its Puritan origins in one deft sketch. "She is the quintessence of that element we all have who are of the Puritan descent *pur sang.* We came to this country to think our own thoughts with nobody to hinder. Ascetics of course and this our Thebaid. We conversed with our own souls till we lost the art of communicating with other people."[1]

Almost everything in her poems is allegorized, removed from sensation into words of a privately encoded intent. "The Soul selects its own Society," that famous poem with its deeply ambiguous perspective, heads a crucial cluster of some twenty poems about withdrawal. It is time we attended to their implications for the quality of her autogenetic art. The sum of this unusually numerous group of linked poems on separation and self-enclosure is in two lines from poem 753, where her speaker says of her Soul, "Her favor – is the best Disdain / Toward Artifice of Time – or Men." Closing the valves of her attention was an obsessive state, and her language came back and back again to give it a name.

> The Soul's Superior instants
> Occur to Her – alone –
> When friend – and Earth's occasion –
> Have infinite withdrawn –   (P-306)

>   subject
> To Autocratic Air –   (P-306)

> There can no Outer Wine
> So royally intoxicate
> As that diviner Brand

> The Soul achieves – Herself –   (P-383)

> Itself – it's Sovreign – of itself   (P-683)

"Deprived of other Banquet, / I entertained Myself," she says in P-773, and that business of sustaining herself with words instead of experience is the source both of our pleasures and our problems with Dickinson. It is also what freed her to hammer up a language whose peculiar processes now seem consonant with our own postmodernist literary expectations.

Disabling Freedom

For Dickinson, the soul's strict economy was superior to fate. It was a loneliness that is richer than any numeral can measure. Obsessive, valued, courted surely, deliberately chosen perhaps, this state of sovereign oneness separate from a demanding reality is a central fact of Dickinson's life, and we should now see that the sovereignty of the language it produced is crucial to the character of her poetry.

The resultant qualities of a language taken into reclusion have effects on us as readers that we have come to recognize as modern in the general sense. The language is difficult, uncommon, even roughened and impeding, and with the marks of being strenuously formed. It is, in fact, a language strenuously foregrounded, anything but automatic. Further, the effect of these qualities is sporadic blindnesses in the language where illumination, the coupling of words and the world, gives way to withdrawal and opacity. With this clouding come also modern feelings of doubt and mystery, impressions of the unspeakable depths of our ignorance about the unspoken world. The familiar then becomes strange. When forms become difficult, our perception seems lengthened because attention is prolonged. In this pleasurable defamiliarization, we also feel turbulence and intensity out of sight, unexpressed. In these ways Dickinson's poems, with their hyperbolic language, haphazard ambushes, and sudden darkenings, agitate without ever quite bringing issues to clear articulation. There seems to be a troubled, unclear knowledge all the more powerful because of its agitation in so confined a space. While they do not characteristically achieve clarity or magnitude or experiential complication, the poems suggest the chaos out of sight with which they are not equipped to contend. In this agitated language, we receive what the best poetry gives us: we recover in its silences the sensation of life itself. Some experience that was automatic, habitually perceived, we now see against her language in its utter novelty, and we feel the novelty of our situation. Such fresh, disturbing perception is one of the great achievements of art and Dickinson, when she took her language into the house with her, opened up this perception again. "Art is a House that tries to be Haunted," she declared to Higginson, and by her odd unfastening of words and word order from the complications and rigidities that experience puts upon our language, she was able to accomplish this ghostly effect. The warping of language into private expression, words breeding their own phrases, "Reorganizes Estimate," as she wrote in poem 906, and we "mostly – see not / What We saw before."

When Dickinson took the language inside with her, she evaded the obligations to experience and to common perception that a public language must ordinarily meet. It is not enough to say, as Adrienne Rich does, that Dickinson "chose her seclusion, knowing she was exceptional and knowing what she needed." Nor is it convincing to say as well that "given her vocation, she was neither eccentric nor quaint; she was determined to survive, to use her powers, to practice necessary economics."[2] The language distortions, the exclusive use of the hymn form, and, most of all, the dissociation of words from things were not separate, chosen modes of art but the stylistic consequences of her seclusion. The seclusion chose the art rather than the artist the seclusion.

The breach that opened in Dickinson's work between language and reality has haunted American poetry ever since. It might be said that she created the problem of the separation of imagination and reality that by Wallace Stevens' time had become the critical dilemma. He labored incessantly to portray it, so much so that he began his Harvard lecture "Three Academic Pieces" in 1947 with an insistence that reads like an ultimatum:

> The accuracy of accurate letters is an accuracy with respect to the structure of reality.
>
> Thus, if we desire to formulate an accurate theory of poetry, we find it necessary to examine the structure of reality, because reality is the central reference for poetry.

But the breach was too wide for Stevens, and thus his poetry holds little of the common workaday public world. Stevens was writing his own *ars poetica*. His reality was of his own making, the reflection of his art, and, like Dickinson's poetry, was oblivious to a social morality or politics or life with its hair down.

Autonomous Discourse

The gap that opened up when Dickinson took her language into seclusion is manifested everywhere in her work. The poetry does not regard the actual world so much as words that stand for that world.

Similitude no longer being the dominant form of knowledge in the poems, they become nonrepresentational and allegorical. Verbal presence involves the concomitant loss of objects and events. This dissociation from outer reality accounts for the indefiniteness of her subjects.

It is not, I said earlier, a language of assent. All the elements of dissociation are linked to the problematics of her technique and language: the way she disturbed grammatical regularity by extreme ellipsis, lost referents, and uninflected verbs required by the constraints of the hymn form; the violations of lexical selection which made chains of meaning confused and circuitous; the figures that opened long metonymic distance from any possible origins in experience. Because the poetry is thus distanced, it refuses again and again to make a clear statement. "This is my letter to the World / That never wrote to Me," Dickinson began poem 441. Her famous declaration, universally interpreted as her proud expectation of a public place later among her "Sweet-countrymen," is more centrally a declaration of this exclusive inwardness I am tracing.

In its exclusion of interest in circumstantial reality, Dickinson's writing was defensive, technically disturbed, closed off. Self-absorbed, her poems, innocently enough at first, exacerbated the psychological and aesthetic problem of the relationship of the complicated sensate world not only to her own markings on scraps of paper but to writing as an art. Withdrawal into words creates the sort of surreal word-world that is figured in the fourth stanza of "I felt a Funeral, in my Brain." The steady assurance of the poem and its extended figure of psychic death compensate even for Dickinson's characteristic repetition and the anticlimactic final stanza. But it is in the fourth stanza and the line that leads into it where we watch the language in the act of displacing reality.

> Space – began to toll,
>
>> As all the Heavens were a Bell,
>> And Being, but an Ear,
>> And I, and Silence, some strange Race
>> Wrecked, solitary, here –   (P-280)

This is pure deixis, a reality that can be projected only in the world of language.

In fact, it is useful to say that at moments in most of Dickinson's poems *language is speaking itself.* In these cases, Dickinson's speech is the performance of language and not representation of the world. The stanza from "I felt a Funeral, in my Brain" can stand as an example of this. It is hermetic language and the poems themselves become hermetic enclosures. The evidence of that hermeticism rises now to our attention: texts as traces of nonspecifiable states, referents that are indeterminate, poems about death and the afterness of immortality which are states that can exist only in language, definition poems that are actually poems about language itself. These are exemplary instances of the major crossing from outside to inside, from world to language, from mimesis to performance. Dickinson's penchant for words as heavy objects is apparent in her skillful use of those polysyllabic abstractions that carry so much weight of indefiniteness in her poems. The unique hermetic quality of the language—narcissistic and autosuggestive—calls attention to itself in the many poems where the tone and meaning are made by languages confronting each other, evaluating each other. Dickinson puts the lexicon of commerce up against the lexicon of religion, or a formal group of Latinate words up against the Anglo-Saxon, each cluster commenting on the other.

When language breeds, removed from exterior referents, it becomes almost pure locution, and meaning cannot be established. Poems then open onto a space that is their own, entities that stand against nature, and their internal network gives rise to whatever meaning they have. Take, for example, Dickinson's invention of "a dotted Dot" in poem 617. No seamstress could envision what has existence only in Dickinson's words. The poem's speaker is describing the sort of sewing she can do when her sight, which has "got crooked," is repaired. The words carry by their own momentum into language that is air-tight.

> I'll do seams - A Queen's endeavor
> Would not blush to own -
>
> Hems - too fine for Lady's tracing
> To the sightless Knot -
> Tucks - of dainty interspersion -
> Like a dotted Dot -

These words are coupling by their chemical affinities with no restraint from things. The phrase "Periods of Seas," in the poem defining eternity, I have already noted as an example of how the pressure of language forces a crossing into anomalous metaphors. Other examples occur in the coupled brilliance of two figures of pure locution in poem 1431: "electric gale" and the impossibly bald assertion, "The body is a soul." Language here is audaciously accelerated to the point of non-reference that impresses powerfully even as it defies understanding. It is language in seclusion obeying its own affinities unrestrained by a regard for facts. We note once again how language of power is managed with a remarkable vagueness of palpability or specific visuality. A late draft, it is a pure Dickinson exercise in the discourse of language itself. The single particular, the feather, is metonymic and thus deprived of specificity. What is left is a remarkable extravagance of language.

> With Pinions of Disdain
> The soul can farther fly
> Than any feather specified
> in Ornithology –
> It wafts this sordid Flesh –
> Beyond it's dull – control
> And during it's electric gale –
> The body is a soul –

In her nonsophisticated way, she risked as much as Hart Crane and with a similarly mixed success. The phrase "paragraphs of Wind" is a telling instance. For her it was a figure of the remembrance of fear, and yet the reader's mind cannot visualize it. It is, again, sheer locution, language orbiting away from reality, speaking itself. The stanza's most noticeable quality as it opens the poem is its impalpability:

> We like a Hairbreadth 'scape
> It tingles in the Mind
> Far after Act or Accident
> Like paragraphs of Wind   (P-1175)

So natural in Dickinson's work is this pressure of language to displace reality that in certain poems we can watch the common language of representation yield before our eyes to an interplay of tropes. That is, we can see language passing momentarily from its instrumental connection with the world to its self-enclosure removed from experience. One of poetry's main techniques of affective expression is to call attention to its corporeality as an artful medium. In Dickinson's work, this release from its purely observational role seems to have been forced to its extreme by her physical withdrawal from the referential world. It is a sample of what pure language might be, language writing itself, making only what language can make, that is, a reality that is undetectable by other means. It unfolds in Dickinson's poem beginning "Best Things dwell out of Sight," which proceeds from characteristic, fairly identifiable figures and abstractions at the beginning—"The Pearl," "the Just" (meaning the blessed dead), "Our Thought," the cherished things that are invisible—to the mid-poem anomaly "The Capsule of the Wind" and ends in the closet figure "Germ's Germ" where Dickinson let her language make something never observed. Here are words moving from partial reference into a purer realm by the end where they speak themselves:

> Best Things dwell out of Sight
> The Pearl – the Just – Our Thought.
>
> Most shun the Public Air
> Legitimate, and Rare –
>
> The Capsule of the Wind
> The Capsule of the Mind
>
> Exhibit here, as doth the Burr –
> Germ's Germ be where?   (P-998)

The poem demonstrates Dickinson's language moving into the realm of referentless, quasi-mathematical expression. Meaning, if such a word is even applicable here, of "The Capsule of the Wind" and "Germ's Germ" lies almost completely within the enclosure of language. It is the sort of virtual meaninglessness, in fact, that language only as object instead of instrument is capable of, most especially when that language is taken into seclusion.

Linguistic analysis is beginning to demonstrate some of the syntactic marks of Dickinson's withdrawal. Of the thirteen poems beginning with the construction "There is a . . . ," it has been deduced that "the existential sentence and its accompanying verbs in the generic present tense construct a context of intense feeling from which a

participating lyric actor and specific poetic occasion are conspicuously missing."[3] It is a linguistic case where reductive verbal arrangement takes the place of life's accidental occurrences.

Dickinson's language in such cases foreshadows poetry as closed
discourse. She is the first American to manifest in rudimentary form
what was to become a widening breach between words and things,
words and experience, as language was amplified at the expense of
representation of a commonly experienced world. The effect is a tendency toward logocentrism in which language is not a transparency
of reality but word domination, an extravagant performance of naming. Word-centeredness, displayed in sporadic bursts such as we see
in the Dickinson idiom, seems bound to proceed to still further separation. Language thus affirms its own existence, and that concentration is its content. Roland Barthes has written of modern poetry that
it "destroys the functional nature of language . . . Grammar is bereft
of its purpose, it becomes prosody and is no longer anything but an
inflexion which lasts only to present the word." That radical strain of
modern poetry as nondiscourse is a self-advertising refusal to mean.

As Dickinson begins "Because I could not stop for Death," the
domineering selectional stroke "stop" so calls attention to itself that it
usurps the reality that might otherwise be represented in the poem.
This is self-regarding language that is the beginning of negative discourse. It occurs as well in Dickinson's day-glo words that coat reality with extravagant color and so cost the reality itself. In the hummingbird poem, the bird has disappeared without a trace into the
virtuoso performance of "A Resonance of Emerald," "A Rush of
Cochineal."

Words were more important to her than social experiences, epi-
phanies without association. "They come a single time," she wrote,

> Like signal esoteric sips
> Of sacramental wine . . . (P-1452)

I have already noted the way the sunset disappears into the few
words she jotted down: "the massacre of Suns / By Evening's Sabres
slain." And so we are not surprised, in this context of the movement
in her poetry of language towards self-absorption and autonomy, that
poetry to her was the most palpable of mediums, more so than reality
itself. It was not its transparency that struck her, but rather its physical force. It froze her, maimed her. She told Higginson, we recall,

how she knew what poetry was: "it makes my whole body so cold no fire ever can warm me . . . I feel physically as if the top of my head were taken off. These are the only way I know it."

Her poems establish their linguistic dominance immediately by those assaulting first lines. This sheer power makes us reconsider with care the use of her autotropic language as biographical fact. Most of the texts that are invariably read as biographical revelation—religious anguish, psychic distress of the person Emily Dickinson—are patently language performances, patently literary texts. John Cody, in his otherwise provocative study of Dickinson, misses this basic caveat, that life described is, at the least, life altered. Language is the center of her poems and that is why subject and circumstance are not only absent from the attention of the poems but unnecessary to them. And that is why there is so little narrative about the outside world and experience in it. The regard for the world that is common for people who live in it is, for this poet, displaced by an eccentric, surprise-filled, sometimes contorted word system that takes the place of that world.

Biographical inquiry based on the poems, therefore, is an unsubstantial business. But, as Dickinson criticism amply demonstrates, it is irresistible. The most persistent fallacy is the sexual one. Dickinson's ambiguity, indefiniteness, and lack of reference create mystery that invites, indeed traps, readers into sexual speculation of a predictable and even self-revelatory kind. Beyond this pitfall, however, are more profound reasons for being wary of biographical bridge-making in Dickinson's case. As I have suggested, the severely inward poems could not regard the complicated world in a faithfully detailed way. Why then, we must ask, should we think the poetry is any more faithful in mirroring her life? The root of the fallacy is the seemingly ineradicable belief still fostered in literary study that most poetry is essentially an expression of the poet's emotions.

Dickinson's frequent use of the first-person voice, while obviously making resistance to biographical interpretation most difficult of all, will lead us to essential observations of some of the radicals of language. We must recognize that the I-speaker locution entails semantic and syntactic consequences that have more to do with the structure of language and reader response than the poet's intention. The "I" imitates an authentic memoir, so that a reader postulates an actual "narrator," taking what is written as fact not needing to be verified, indeed incapable of verification. The I-speaker seems free to say whatever she wants, and we as readers accept linguistic and perceptual idiosyncrasies because they seem to be the speaker's personal voice and vision. It is flow of consciousness, manufactured, modern.

Instinctively, Dickinson distinguished the autonomous nature of language in her poetry. She stated it with absolute clarity in an early letter to Higginson, no doubt in reply to his own questions about her life: "When I state myself, as the Representative of the Verse," she wrote, "it does not mean – me – but a supposed person" (L-268). It is time we believed this statement without suggesting that she was deliberately hiding herself from her readers. I believe it, as I do other statements of hers we shall come to. It is accurate because the language has determined that it be so. "The exemplary or model 'I' in autobiography," one theorist has written, "*ipso facto* belongs to writing: it is an explicit 'dummy' ego by which the autobiographer is kept aware of or acknowledges the discrepancy between his 'life' and life."[4]

Dickinson was aware, it seems clear, that the first-person pronoun necessarily becomes in writing—as opposed to speaking—something other than a strictly self-referring sign, in fact, a *de facto* third-person pronoun. She recognized, as indeed we must, the inevitable impersonating effect of discourse. Life *is* revised by the simple act of writing, and certainly by the use in that writing of the first-person pronoun. Necessarily constructed and selective because it is a determining structural element of the medium, the "I" is in fact a third person, as Dickinson said. Anne Sexton phrased the truth of this "supposed person" for herself: "I've heard psychiatrists say: 'See, you've forgiven your father. There it is in your poem.' But I haven't forgiven my father. I just wrote that I did."[5]

With some of the radicals of language in sight, we see that, as tempting as the biographical interpretations are, Dickinson's poetry is not and cannot be confessional in a strict or even usefully approximate sense. Aside from the problems caused by the absence of a reliable chronology of composition for Dickinson's work, there is this nature of the medium itself. The discrepancy between the life and the words inheres in writing itself. Richard Ohmann reminds us that writing has neither the illocutionary intention nor the effect of speech. Poems exist independent of the immediate motive that a spoken sentence possesses by its nature. Writing releases language from its communicative function, allowing other functions of language to be presented in their pure, that is, authentic, form.

There are more reasons yet to resist the hazardous leap to biographical interpretations of Dickinson's poems, especially those that, employing the first-person voice, seem most autobiographical of all. Her poems are *pretended speech acts* and as such deceptively induce some of what speech does: a circumstantial context for the speaker, a set of events. This inducement to the reader to provide the contexts (say, for "I cannot live with You") is particularly strong for all the reasons I have put forward. There is another, perhaps strongest of all: the Dickinson canon has no fewer than seventeen hundred instances of her use of "I." And yet we cannot ask a Dickinson poem if its speaker really has these feelings because the poems are only mimetic of a confession and not a confession itself. A real speaker we can interrogate directly, but we cannot ask this of a novel or a poem.

Literature changes everything into literariness. Life is revised by writing. Thus faced with the autonomy of language as I have tried to define it, in Dickinson's case—perhaps the most intransigent case in our literature because of all its linguistic marks of personal confession—psychobiography is not only manufactured and impressionistic, it is beside the point. It is like trying to find the apples in a Cezanne still life: they have no existence but in the paint.

Language-centeredness is a Dickinson phenomenon, finally, that will enable us to understand one of the aspects of her work that has always evaded attention. The poems equalize every subject. Poems nominally about love and death and immortality have an equal emphasis with poems on snakes and bluejays and butterflies. The leveling occurs because it is the language and not the content or representation that is central to the art.

Hers is the purest kind of proficiency in language, if not in formal structures. The gift can be located even more precisely than this. It operates on the axis of lexical selection where her violation of commonness disturbs the words we speak. Of all her brilliant gestures—from metaphorical aptness to expressive concentration, candor, and wit—this is her basic skill, the root of art she touched with instinctive sureness. Death is the demonstration subject, although one might point as well to sunsets, birds, storms, light, seasons, or doubt. In her seemingly inexhaustible ability to put words in the place of death we find the heart of the reason we can go back and back to Dickinson and read her with surprise. The language performs, the subject stays the same. A list, not complete by any means and not even including her striking figure of death as a country squire, gives us the feeling of being overwhelmed by selectional ingenuity. Here, then, over the years, in metaphor, adjective, and verb, again and again, is Dickinson's death:

Death, but our rapt attention   (P-7)

soldered mouth
awful rivet
hasps of steel
listless hair
adamantine fingers   (187)

the postponeless Creature   (390)

The Mold-Life   (392)

Mortality's old custom –
Just locking up – to Die   (479)

As far from pity, as complaint   (496)

Death's etherial scorn   (521)

To put this World down, like a bundle   (527)

a truth of Blood
the livid Surprise   (531)

          the little Tint
That never had a Name   (559)

Art of Snow
Trick of Lily
Crystal angle   (649)

a famous sleep
an independent one   (654)

Silver Reticence
Solid Calm   (778)

out of story
that strange Fame

That lonesome Glory
no omen here – but Awe   (1370)

this Alabaster Zest
the Delights of Dust
recusance august   (1384)

Bisecting Messenger   (1411)

Death – so – the Hyphen of the Sea   (1454)

On that specific Pillow   (1533)

The soul her "Not at Home"
Inscribes upon the flesh –   (1691)

Paid all that life had earned
In one consummate bill   (1724)

A linguistic tide such as this, with the ability to create anew constantly, calls attention to itself and does not disappear in the representation of death. It is the words that remain and not the idea of death. A whole linguistic environment envelops us and costs us a view of reality itself. But that ingenuity, however narrowly exercised, is what engages us. Furthermore, this fresher language atomizes the language that we use, shows us its possibilities, and in its usurpation of experience gives back to experience its mystery. No mean accomplishment! She destroys habitual encounters, and for this we cherish her.

Dickinson lived in the primacy of the written word not just as any poet must center his world in words but in the extreme state created when she took the words inside to live with her, away from reality, and made them perform in her deliberate handwriting on odd shapes of paper. There she was able to concentrate on the signs themselves and practiced her pure art of lexical surprise. To Yvor Winters' charge that her poems of life after death are fraudulent, the necessary answer is that *anything* can trigger and exist in language, most potently so when language dissociates itself from things, from experience, and from its functional role to represent either of them. Her language progressively became the silent subject of her medium, and in that enclosed activity almost any freedom was possible. The lack of a reality principle is what Winters failed to recognize in her work. Dickinson had no subject, least of all reality. She had instead a magnificent, limited instrument without a target, without an end other than itself.

What is the consequence of this inwardness of discourse that reduces representation to a problematic? The answer is in one of the truths of Dickinson's artistic consciousness as it takes its form in her poems and that must surely emerge to us now: a ferocious need to live fully but apart from experience in the world, joined fortuitously (but not inexplicably) with the acutest sort of linguistic imagination in which to live that separated life.

Reality Disappearing into Language

Things existed for Dickinson because they could become the words of a poem. Like her life and the selective traffic she maintained with the world through her letters, her poems were a way of refusing experience by limiting her subjects to what her language could dominate. What remained invisible or was necessarily rejected was action or story that proceeded over time. The poems, because their two-line units needed movement and surprise and the hymn frame required abstract hopes to make up in breadth what the form lacked in size, addressed only what was visible to them according to their capacities. Rejected was any cumulative action involving subtlety, such as a character portrayal, anything of philosophical intricacy, anything of a large coherence, anything that needed time for its identification. If Yeats, when he looked out, saw only symbols, Dickinson saw only allegories of denial and, to anticipate my discussion, incomprehension. Her devouring linguistic imagination converted everything to allegory. Nothing, one might say, in the outside world had an existence independent of her words. A sunset was always the enactment of soft massacres. Spring, vivid as it might be, was always resurrection.

In this word tyranny we see the beginning of a process by which reality disappears into language. Words for Dickinson had an absolute privilege. The ultimate linguistic implosion exemplified for her by the word *death* she once described with characteristic extravagance: "I hesitate which word to take, as I can take but few and each must be the chiefest, but recall that Earth's most graphic transaction is placed within a syllable, nay, even a gaze" (L-873). That usurpation by words or by gaze exacted a price she knew with profound accuracy.

> Perception of an object costs
> Precise the Object's loss –
> Perception is itself a Gain
> Replying to it's Price –
> The Object Absolute – is nought –
> Perception sets it fair
> And then upbraids a Perfectness
> That situates so far –   (P-1071)

Like photographs of exotic places, or even of our own place, the poems make us feel the world is more available than it really is. They have converted experience into a souvenir of words and refused the rest of the reality. Because her poems, even so compressed and exclusionary as they are, appropriate the thing or feeling they name, taking power over reality by their aggressive language, they feel like knowledge to us. It is one of the curious qualities of her poems that they pretend an authoritative relationship to the actual world even though they flee from that world.

One of the consequences of this disappearance of reality into language is a large number of poems that are unabashed word displays. Like some of Marianne Moore's, these poems are occasion for a polysyllabic avalanche. In Dickinson's bobolink poem, the bird becomes a matter of hyperbolic style.

> Of impudent Habiliment
> Attired to defy,
> Impertinence subordinate
> At times to Majesty.
>
> Of Sentiments seditious
> Amenable to Law –
> As Heresies of Transport
> Or Puck's Apostacy.   (P-1279)

I have called certain of her poems occasions of pure style. A four-line poem on the sea which she placed in a packet, evidently satisfied it was finished, provides the barest minimum of visual effect and gives instead a sort of conceptual seascape. It is the idea of the sea and not the sea itself. She had little or no firsthand experience of the sea, so not surprisingly it is almost absent from the words. The poem is sheer style, without observation, composed of metaphor, an abstract image or two (silver, ropes), an oxymoronic twist, and a bit of irony. The poem is all style except for "effacing," with its presumption of a specific action.

> An Everywhere of Silver
> With Ropes of Sand
> To keep it from effacing
> The Track called Land.　　(P-884)

Most of her poems are mixtures of meaning and mode, with the style more insistent than the meaning. Dickinson's style is part meaning but in larger part the dance of tropes where otherwise purposeful rhetoric passes into verbal display without association. Such poems have places of meaning in them and places of style (defect being an element of her style, as we have seen), and the two do not intersect at many points. In poem 881, for instance, the meaning is strung on simple threads: I have only Thee, but you are gone; tell me if you would seek me the way I am seeking you, and I will then follow your voice to find you. This somewhat mawkish meaning rests in four phrases:

> I've none to tell me to but Thee
> Thy sweet Face has spilled beyond my boundary . . .
> If things were opposite would'st Thou seek so? . . .
> Just say, that I may pursue the answer unto the lips, so overtaking Thee . . .

All else is word play, including instances of defect, but mainly in the metaphors: thy sweet Face has spilled, Me and Me, some unanswering Shore, the lips it eddied through. Here is the poem altogether, with its places of meaning (solid line) and its many more places of style (broken line) marked.

> I've none to tell me to but Thee
> So when Thou failest, nobody.
> It was a little tie –
> It just held Two nor those it held
> Since Somewhere thy sweet Face has spilled
> Beyond my Boundary –

If things were <u>opposite</u> – and <u>Me</u>
And <u>Me</u> it were – that ebbed from Thee
On some <u>unanswering Shore</u> –
Would'st Thou seek so – just say
That I the Answer may pursue
Unto the lips <u>it eddied through</u> –
So – <u>overtaking Thee</u> –

Poems have a permanence that creatures do not. Certain creatures—the snake, the hummingbird, the cat—exist most memorably
in Dickinson's poems, as birds do in Audubon's paintings or in the
heightened representation of color photographs. But Dickinson's
mode is more selective even than photographs and her words are capable of greater focusing of effect. She was fully conscious of this
quality of her word dominance, for when Higginson asked for her
photograph, she wrote back with characteristic ellipsis to say: "I noticed the Quick wore off those things, in a few days, and [I, by not
sending you a photo] forestall the dishonor" (L-268). She gave him
instead a description that no visage could possess, let alone a photograph. The metaphors are brilliantly mixed and jostle for attention.
"Could you believe me – without? I had no portrait, now, but am
small, like the Wren, and my Hair is bold, like the Chestnut
Bur – and my eyes, like the Sherry in the Glass, that the Guest
leaves – Would this do just as well?" She thus disappeared into her
own words.

By replacing reality this way with words, she could retreat from its
complications and invent her own. Enormous realms were displaced
by the scraps of paper with a few penciled words on them in her irregular hand. Note these seven: "Worlds scoop their Arcs – / And
Firmaments – row." Like hymns they take the place of impossible referents, becoming the signs of the absent—the Dead, God, Immortality.

This hunger of the word makes Dickinson's poetic speech, at its
strongest, full of dread, withdrawn from the world and overnourished in its autogamous state. It is a discourse that persuades us,
like zero at the bone, even though the reality remains dim if not impossible. Her devouring language grips and startles, not because it
represents a world but because the words have a closed, invulnerable
authority.

Disabling Freedom

Dickinson's style broke off from social experience and entered into a lonely sovereignty. Its brilliance is not to be gainsaid. The concentration, intensity, animation, and voice with which she imbued the hymn form is a triumphant achievement of imagination and primitivist daring. She accomplished it in part, as we have seen, by the striking first lines, by the lexical and figural shocks that her selectional boldness produced, and by an extraordinary adeptness charged by wit in her use of polysyllables. In the latter, where she employed a fine rhythmic art, she showed impressively the inhering authority of language. More broadly than this, her genius shows in her linguistic control—however clipped and compartmentalized by her twenty-eight-syllable quatrains—over the emotionally disabling responses to death, despair, and ecstasy. It shows in her psychological accuracy. Behind the penetration of her figural sense and her unsurpassed faculty for concentration, behind all the stylistic quirks, lay a simple, hard wisdom of human existence and the swings of consciousness.

The significant difficulties we have seen up to now are linked to her freedom: primarily the lack of architectural response to outer reality, the absence of a large technical design, and instead the whipsaw effect of abstract metaphors within the severe limitations of the hymn constraint. She made no interpretive pact with her readers, gave them no plan of the whole. Capable of shocks and surprises, her characteristic poem is repetitious, lacking in development, sometimes petering out in the closing stanzas, often incapable of endings, and riddled with the obscurities of private reference, syntactic ellipsis, and grammatical distortion. The peculiar withdrawal of her idiom is reflected as well in her compositional habits. Dickinson seized her intentions with two-line assaults and by her localized revision, heightening individual parts at the expense of cohesion and intricacy.

The obscurities in her poems are linked to specific problems we have seen: syntax distorted to fit the syllabic and stanza restrictions of the hymn form; uninflected verb stems that blur both tense and number and cast a gnostic aura over the phrases; lost referents that result in ambiguity if not obscurity; metaphors and parables that are transfigured so far from their origins that they have displaced their intentions. All of these difficulties are then made more problematic by the willful peculiarity of Dickinson's punctuation. Sentences are left scattered in a do-it-yourself kit, with no assembly plans.

The idiosyncrasies produce a fundamental unfinishedness. This is most noticeable in cases when she placed her compositions, transcribed, in the packets bound with thread. The unfinishedness of her language projected accordingly into the narrow field of experience that was available to her. Because her art lacked a large or complicated organizing capacity, it was peculiarly without mature expectations or a worldly vision. The same is generally true of her letters. They fragment experience, sometimes mystify it, parade their mannerisms. In letter 264 to the Norcross cousins, Dickinson lurches from fright ("I am still hopeless and scared") to humor ("the rooms were marble, even to the flies") all in an instant, until the whimsical turns and jumps bewilder and entertain equally, jolt and engage.

The not seeing in a great many of her poems, due to their disorderly spontaneity, her lack of an overall compositional intention and, generally, the distortions forced upon her by her procrustean form, made her writing a revolutionary moment in American literature. Her language, in the gravityless condition of her impulsive freedom, began the profound and consequential turning of language from its representational function to its self-regarding and willful condition as literature, separate from experience and of an autogenous energy that worked deliberately to create its own corporeality.

What remains constant and awesome in this inordinate freedom of language secluded from the world is significant: it is the intense, restless consciousness aware of its presence in the world, determined to speak that presence in heightened language. At the center it is hypersensitivity coupled with linguistic art of accelerated force. Neither the Dickinson consciousness nor the wit diminished. Thomas Johnson said with understandable conviction that "the wellsprings of her creativeness dried up after 1865," but it is not so.[6] All her life what was important to her was not the representation, the content, but the *telling.* Toward the end of her life, sometime between 1879 and 1882 when she was approaching or in her fifties and ill, perhaps confined to bed, she sent a characteristically pert, characteristically conglomerate poem to her nephew Ned, then an undergraduate at Amherst College. It bears presentation here in full because even so late it is a catalogue of her own subjects, parabolic to be sure, jumbled together, stemming from the source among all others she never turned her back on.

The Bible is an antique Volume –
Written by faded Men
At the suggestion of Holy Spectres –
Subjects – Bethlehem –
Eden – the ancient Homestead –
Satan – the Brigadier –
Judas – the Great Defaulter –
David – the Troubadour –
Sin – a distinguished Precipice
Others must resist –
Boys that "believe" are very lonesome –
Other Boys are "lost" –
Had but the Tale a warbling Teller –
All the Boys would come –
Orpheus' Sermon captivated –
It did not condemn –   (P-1545)

Even this late she had not forgotten that she had been a "lost one" at Mount Holyoke Female Seminary thirty-five years earlier. The choice she made then is still the choice in the poem, that is, the preference for what gives pleasure instead of what instructs, for the self instead of reality, for what would captivate but not condemn. Her search for the word for that artistic captivation reveals to us now how primary the telling was to her. Unfinished as her thinking was and lacking as the poetry was in compositional wholeness, still the vitality of the telling remained her central concern.

The unmanageable consciousness and heightened need for language are reflected all through the canon by her shadowy, unidentifiable speaker. She employed voice after voice, from bee to boy to Queen and God. But no matter what the shift in voice or the lack of a steady identity of speaker in Dickinson's work, she emphasized to the end the vitality of the telling. Her speakers do not have names or places or bodies or biographies. Those absences are an unmistakable corollary of a poetry that is lacking in formal craft but is spontaneous in gesture and language-centered.

When she went back, perhaps in 1882, to rework the poem before sending it to Ned, she wrote down thirteen alternatives to describe the ideal teller of the tale. While referential intelligibility was almost never a serious concern of hers, as we have seen in the poems, the vitality, intimacy, and arresting power of the speaker were. What was important was not so much the material or its orderliness, but the intensity of engagement. "Had but the Tale a warbling Teller" she had sent to Ned, but only after she had found the other names too for that heightened language she excelled in: thrilling, typic, hearty, bonnie, breathless, spacious, tropic, ardent, friendly, magic, pungent, winning, mellow.

Some Technical Mysteries Solved

Seeing the profound consequences of a thoroughgoing freedom helps us now to solve some of the persistent Dickinson mysteries. Tracing back to find Dickinson's poetic identity has been necessary to take us this far. We have had to pierce each barrier that has concealed her: her silence about her life and her reclusion, the myths surrounding her that took the place of the missing facts, the orderly print of the poems whose publication she could never bring herself to authorize and which now recast her disorderly creative ways, through that print to reach the fair copies and then the worksheets, back to the immediacy of the scraps with the penciled words on them. It is a journey from the myth to the dance of language itself and from the surface of the art to the reality concealed behind it. When we confront the actual character of her composition and the ways the hymn form and the allegorical abstraction distorted her syntax and obscured her referents, we come upon the phenomenon most basic of all in her technique: the absence of connective webbing in her work.

What we recognize is a language as well as a life withdrawn from contingent experience. The idiom of this reclusion is private and without adherence to the authority of either the actual world or literary tradition but eccentric in a fierce freedom. With this recognition that emerges from the larger semiotic context, we see we are dealing with the nature of a new experience of language and things.

The reading has taken us from words, images, phrases, and sentences, where most literary criticism is situated, to the level of the texts themselves and to the canon these texts constitute. At this encompassing level a significant context, presently unfamiliar to criticism, is apparent. Here we see the peculiar grammar of absence and the way her poetic identity begins to take form in a network of avoidances. Many of the technical mysteries in Dickinson's writing both signify and are accounted for by the seclusion of her art. She made a poetic language unaccountable to the outside world, with limited bearing on actual experience in that world, and thus without sufficient architectural design to create a technical wholeness fully responsive to such a provisional world. Out of this knowledge come our clearer perceptions of the mysteries, and then our comprehension.

1. *Dickinson's poems have extraordinarily little specific outside reference.* With one or two exceptions, there are no identifiable individuals referred to, no lovers, no actual circumstances behind the pain and desolation. There is no causation signified directly by her poems. This mysterious remoteness, what Higginson called the poems' strange impersonality, which has troubled readers for so long and induced so much speculation and void-filling fantasies, occurs because the language requires no proximate reality. Unconcerned with the full texture of existence and its own representational function, the language becomes private, self-observing, and momentary. Outside impingements have fallen away, especially those that require a language of magnitude, coherence, sustained attention, complexity, and the capability of accumulation. This closure explains why her poems have no dates, why no dates were necessary, and why it never occurred to Dickinson that the dating of her poems, what we miss so crucially as readers, was necessary. She could not have thought of herself as a personage, a figure in history, for she threw most of her worksheets away. Subjects and circumstances were unnecessary except as triggers for the language to speak itself. There is simply no dialogue with her time. Instead, in this reclusive language, there is indefiniteness, the unique Dickinson allegories without experience.

2. *The poems are rarely narrative.* Dickinson's compact quatrains undertake no ordinary observation of experience—physical, social, descriptive—that requires extended and qualified language and structure. This absence of close social or perceptual texture is a direct corollary of the hymn form that restrains her vision and her possibilities simultaneously, while it accommodates most easily her allegories of hazy reference. An extended engagement with unfolding human existence would have demanded a story-telling form with a narrative worldliness, but this circumstance she repudiated in her life and left unexplored in her art. Given her means, she focused on a limited set of aims.

3. *The poems have no magnitude.* There are few long poems in the Dickinson canon. Rather, there are scraps waiting for occasions to

speak. This habitual piecemeal quality is reflected in her sometimes casual regard for her art, in her habit of taking poems already written and inserting them, sometimes only parts, in letters with the most tenuous relationship to an event alluded to in the correspondence. Discontinuous in their combined effect, the poems are for us, as they were for her, momentary means of perception. Magnitude depends on deliberately deployed structure, and it was her lack of architectural interest that made her incapable of—even uninterested in—an art that composed a large reality. It was as if plans were too taxing, as if long poems had an indecent ambitiousness and vanity about them. "Spasmodic" was Higginson's word for her lack of continuity. His letters kept asking if she had a plan in mind. What had she read, he asked. How many poems had she written? What was her life like? He sought in vain the coherence we seek and the lack of which we now recognize as the mark of the withdrawal of her art from experience. Incoherence is thus the primary fact of her poetic identity. The lack of long poems is in this new light the very essence of her identity. It is also the inseparable adjunct to her lack of structural sense.

4. *There is no cumulative wholeness in the body of writing.* "Everything," as Elizabeth Bishop wrote in "Over 2000 Illustrations," is "only connected by 'and' and 'and.' " Perhaps no other quality has so vexed critics into seeking the figure of coherence in Dickinson. The work simply has no self-defining character, no fate of its own. It is a brick-by-brick procedure that produces no building, only a quantity of bricks. Even the bound packets have no discernible plan and thus no magnitude in the sense we mean by the term. Dickinson's language, a forceful but focusless instrument, had no reason for a sustained regard of anything. Rather, for Dickinson, the motive of her poetic speech did not lie outside of language but is to be discovered within the language itself.

5. *The poems make no natural ranking.* Each poem has an equal claim on our attention as readers. The experience of reading Dickinson in large batches emphatically bears out this curiosity. The brief, nonreferring poems, coming one after the other (she is represented by dozens of poems in anthologies where other poets have a few sustained poems), produce a perpetual erasure of impressions as we read her. I have assigned Dickinson reading to students for a full semester and have seen the distraction come in the third week. Her poems equalize all the subjects. The ones on love, death, snakes, and immor-

tality engage in the same way as those on bluejays, pain, desperate separations, trains, doubt, the seasons, and June bugs. They occupy the same level of attention, seek the same space in the reader's mind. The special experience of reading Dickinson is that there is an unprecedented lack of leading, of organizing, of general direction. It is like driving in a shopping-plaza parking lot. This lack of self-selected emphasis, attention or intensity, is the evidence, once we can comprehend it at the level of texts, that it is the language and not the subject that is crucial in this body of brief poems. There is no preferred perspective on experience, no bias with which to enter the world or make its data visible, no dogmas to be argued. Rather, the poems have equal value because each is a pretended speech act, the content but the excuse for speaking. In a condition of reclusion, the making of toast and tea is as important to the maker as the running of a railroad. Deciding to write a letter has the same importance for the recluse as deciding whether to commit the troops to battle or hold them in reserve. In reclusion, the claims are all the same.

6. *Dickinson, unlike every other major American poet, wrote no ars poetica.* The letters provide no more than the slightest commentary on the poetic art. It is an unusual absence, one would suppose, in this poet who wrote to the end. There are scattered bits as I have pointed out elsewhere, but essentially there is a startling absence of self-consciousness as an artist, of self-positioning, and of space making that major poets undertake. We must conclude that the lack of a body of discourse on her art is another reflection of the mind of a poet who took her art into the house with her, did well what she could do within severely drawn boundaries, and was not forced by the contingencies of experience to develop an architectural sophistication, let alone a grand design for her writing. There are poems on fame, to be sure, but Dickinson seems to have exchanged the possibility of a public name for her freedom from the authority of literary tradition. Far from being a master craftsman in revolt against tradition, she was utterly free in a radical privatism. Her fame rests on the skill with which she made a reclusive language, within the severe confines of a simple art form, shock with seemingly inexhaustible brilliance. In the end hers was a poetry and an idiom of partial ripeness. The evidence lies in each of the absenses I have outlined.

7. *The deepest technical mystery is that Dickinson wrote.* Why she

wrote is the most difficult of all the questions. Why did so much of her existence and all of her artistic expression take the form of written words? Why was hers a textual art? The answer is that she could not have spoken these poems or anything like them. Speech is phenomenal, an activity in the world, inherently contingent on the world and in active intercourse with it. "All men say what to me," she once said. Writing, hermetic by its nature, allowed her to be still, to offer others from the start the last word. Writing freed her language from its communicative function and allowed some of its other possibilities—surprise, ellipsis, privateness, obscurity, risks, its visual features—to be enacted. It possessed both malleability and stability (control, that is) that the impermanence of speech did not. If she could not speak to strangers, she could at least write. And so writing had absolute privilege for Dickinson, above speech, above a social life, above the Boston ladies' conversation club to which Higginson once invited her. Not in speech but only in writing could the Dickinson words wield power. And they went down on scraps of paper, in pencil, crammed in margins, scribbled along strips.

What should be clear to us now is that the only expression where all the idiosyncrasies could be accommodated, given her withdrawal from the world, was writing. Texts necessarily are removed from reference, while speech cannot be. Dickinson's knowledge of this difference was instinctive. "A letter always feels to me like immortality," she wrote to Higginson in 1869, "because it is the mind alone without corporeal friend. Indebted in our talk to attitude and accent, there seems a spectral power in thought that walks alone" (L-330).

Dickinson couldn't have got away in conversation saying what she wrote so cryptically in her poems and letters. Pure writing, her poems could not have been in any other form—not speech, certainly not painting, which requires wholeness; perhaps only music or mathematics—because she had no context, no narrative, no circumstance. Germ's germ be where? Indeed, there is no record of Dickinson reciting her verses, even for her family. On the other hand, there is the deliberate physical exertion of making fair copies and binding all those packets. Quintessentially, hers was a textual art, and in the nature of those texts—scraps, untitled, unfinished—we can read the significance of her poetic identity.

Removed from the world, writing furiously with a language she had removed from its representational and responsive function in a contingent world, Dickinson did not know what she had wrought. And so she paused on April 15, 1862, at the age of thirty-one, in the tidal stage of her writing career, and wrote to Higginson to ask: "Are you too deeply occupied to say if my Verse is alive? The Mind is so near itself – it cannot see, distinctly – and I have none to ask."

6   *A Finless Mind*

Her letters to Higginson after that first one, nearly always with poems enclosed, seek from him a definition—"nomination" she called it in 1870—that will bestow on Dickinson an identity within her disorderliness. In the light of their barely masked pathos, we can see clearly for the first time, with all thoughts of departed lovers aside, the searing need in those letters for identity.

"While my thought is undressed," she wrote to Higginson ten days after the first letter, "I can make the distinction, but when I put them in the Gown – they look alike and numb." Near the end of the letter she wrote the genuinely plaintive phrases that plead for identification: "I would like to learn – Could you tell me how to grow . . . I could not weigh myself – Myself" (L-261).

The real intent of those early letters, never self-pitying, created a stark existential drama. Everything was at stake for the poet without a project or a path. "You think me 'uncontrolled' – " she said to Higginson. "If I might bring you what I do . . . and ask you if I told it clear – 'twould be control, to me" (L-265). That was in June. In July, with only partial concealment, she showed Higginson the extent of the need. "Will you tell me my fault, frankly as to yourself, for I had rather wince, than die. Men do not call the surgeon, to commend – the Bone, but to set it, Sir, and fracture within, is more critical" (L-268). By August of that first year's searching correspondence, the exaggerated figurative diction protecting her ego but with more revealing openings now, Dickinson is still painfully serious. She enclosed two more poems. "Are these more orderly? I thank you for the Truth – . I had no Monarch in my life, and cannot rule myself, and when I try to organize – my little Force explodes – and leaves me bare and charred – . I think you called me 'Wayward.' Will you help me improve?" And then the plea again: "You say I confess the little mistake, and omit the large – Because I can see Orthography – but the Ignorance out of sight – is my Preceptor's charge" (L-271).

Eight years later, after Higginson's visit to Amherst, she made a rough draft of a letter which, the lack of evidence indicates, she did not actually send. (She had expected him the day before he actually arrived. I find it moving to imagine her state of mind through that day she waited and he didn't come—and then again on the next.) Perhaps in that conversation, but probably in a subsequent letter, while certainly encouraging her, he had echoed what she had been declaring all along. She wrote in her draft response: "You speak of 'tameless tastes' – A Beggar came last week – I gave him Food and Fire and as he went, 'Where do you go,' 'In all the directions' – That was what you meant" (L-353). Higginson's role for her was the person with the sustenance, and she was the wandering beggar at the door, still after all those years going in all the directions.

In November 1871, almost a decade after she initiated the correspondence with the question that still arrests us—"Are you too deeply occupied to say if my Verse is alive?"—Dickinson closed her letter to Higginson simply, "Would you but guide" (L-368). By 1873, not long before her father's death, which was to be followed by her mother's paralysis in 1875, and when the intensity of her appeal to Higginson had gone slack with the years, she wrote two single-sentence notes to him. The first may have enclosed three poems; the second perhaps was posted when there was no reply. Dutiful, it seems, in language, yet piercing still because of the deep permanent need of her life, the first note said, "Could you teach me now?" and the second, "Will you instruct me then no more?" (L-396).

The technical and canonical disorderliness that prompted such insistent pleas to Higginson for definition inevitably urges upon us the question as to what deeper circumstance, linked to her withdrawal from the discipline of experience, lay at the origin of her artistic dilemma. I propose that the lack of architecture in individual poems, itself the result of the lack of an encompassing poetic design, comes from the absence of an abiding, life-centering angle of vision in the poet's mind.

A more comprehensive portrait is required to bring into view the nature of the Dickinson matrix. Our question of her starting point, the original creative movement at the center of her poetic consciousness, may very well turn out, as with the body of poems, to be a question of what is absent from that generating center.

The evidence, when we look from a fresh viewpoint, is unexpectedly abundant and begins with what I now believe to be one of Dickinson's crucial outsetting-bard compositions, a text in the tradition of which "Lycidas" and "Out of the Cradle Endlessly Rocking" are notable examples. It is a letter written in 1856, when she was in her twenty-fifth year, to her distant cousin John Graves who, a year younger than Emily, had graduated from Amherst College in 1855. He was an honor student at the college, had delivered the philosophical oration at commencement time, an address entitled "Philological Philosophy," and then moved to New Hampshire to become principal of Orford Academy. Graves had recently become engaged to be married, but the letter is more concerned with eternal matter. Much is displayed although the letter, while earnest, is typically oblique and partly concealing.

It stands out from the hundreds of letters that sustain troubled or bereaved relatives and friends, that console, pontificate, or simply gossip, because it sets a scene with herself as principal actor and defines clearly the issues that engage her. Most interesting to us in our inquiry, it gives glimpses through her skepticism of traces of hysteria and anxiety. Generally, as we know, her letters are remarkably free of explicit reference to her art, yet despite its veils and evasions, letter 184 to John Graves rivets our attention with its brave purpose.

At the beginning it establishes with two artful strokes, one boldly explicit and the other disarmingly self-deprecating—she and some hens sit together—her utter independence.

> It is Sunday – now – John – and all have gone to church – the wagons have done passing, and I have come out in the new grass to listen to the anthems.
>
> Three or four Hens have followed me, and we sit side by side – and while they crow and whisper, I'll tell you what I see today, and what I would that you saw –

In this independent, if not mildly rebellious state, and weighted with some nineteenth-century existentialist melancholy ("We, too, are flying – fading, John – and the song 'here lies,' soon upon the lips that love us now – will have hummed and ended"), Emily Dickinson is announcing her new maturity, her obligatory Christian concern, and her *vocation:* "To live, and die, and mount again in triumphant body, and *next* time, try the upper air – is no schoolboy's theme!" Her sense of forcing with rude fingers the laurels before they are ripe in the mellowing year is hardly Miltonic, but it is here all the same, in April, slantwise, in a fetching country lass, in a seemingly unrehearsed way. It is neither strained nor Bloomian to think that Prufrock, decadent by his time, his trousers rolled, has a forebear here in Dickinson's offhand self-portrait: "will you trust me – as I live, here's a *bumblebee* – not such as *summer* brings – John – earnest, manly bees, but a kind of a Cockney, dressed in jaunty clothes."

Dickinson conceives here both her role as a presumptuous poet and the primary nodes of her interest. Simply but earnestly, the letter constructs the field of Dickinson's consciousness and thus of her texts—the observing person, the mutable world, the now somber, now ecstatic word. We can see in retrospect a determining field of reference that endured and outside of which a Dickinson poem could hardly be conceived. Emily in this field, upon the April grass, is a primary vortex of the most ponderous elements: *faith* in the form of the anthems heard on the spring air; the *life principle* in nature reborn; *death* in the things that faded or crumbled in the vacant nests, in the wings turning to dust; and *promise* in the blue sky fairer than Italy's. They are all here, with nostalgia, humor, and a lively visualizing power, but most of all with a primitivist simplicity, the need to be intense, and the naiveté to be profound.

Our attention turns to what is *not* included in the Dickinson field of reference, here by the homestead where she sits on an April Sunday. There is, remarkably, no social role for herself, although there is one for Graves: "I am glad you have a school to teach ... and shall feel – I know, delight and pride, always, when you succeed." There is no social realm at all for her outside the hens and birds and insects. There is no politics, indeed no history. The past is already crumbled, faded, flown "far from us," perhaps to heaven! Her letter has focused on *saying*, on performing, on self-dramatization—"I'll tell you what I see today"—and the deliberate choice of reference makes it almost a parable of her basic elements: life, death, faith, nature, and memory. So near to banality are these primary materials and the medley of conventions she employed that the reader turns back to this voice that somehow keeps the melange from dissolving into stock graveyard vapidities.

The solitary figure, giving the world names as if for the first time: that is quintessentially the American voice. She is the betrayed innocent, the keeper of both the dream and the loss of it. She is the dying maiden in the promised land but also, amid wings of dust, the dying maiden in the wasteland. She is the sayer of lost dreams in the place of death. Above all, the Dickinson voice is unconsciously and without sophistication doing what ambitious poets have done before—attempting to make a place for herself in the company of poets. "Remember, early friend," she says to Graves with studied melancholy, "and drop a tear, if a *troubadour* . . . may chance to sing."

The scenario serves in varying detail for a great many Dickinson poems. The elements of it should be kept in mind: the part saucy, part dejected voice, the conventional topics that are shared with the most trite writing of her time, the sense of deprivation, but also, however disguised or unconsciously put forward, the independence and sense of purpose and need. Conspicuously absent is the experiential density of a life lived fully in the world.

Over all is the faint smell of anguish, a latter-day Gethsemane of one. She was to find a host of expressions for that interior wilderness more than barely visible in the Graves letter when she was twenty-five. "Gethsemane," she wrote in a poem five or six years later, "Is but a Province – in the Being's Centre . . . newer – nearer Crucifixion" (P-553). The setting in the letter, where contradictory feelings flow, half transport and half trouble, is itself a bucolic Gethsemane with its focal consciousness the intersecting point of all these currents. It is a setting too of afterward, the happiness of youth, as she notified Graves here and her brother Austin repeatedly, the closeness and the love consigned already to an ideal past now lost.

But there is a deeper sign in this Gethsemane set forth so disarmingly in the Graves letter. Deeper than vocation, than lost youth and Aprils gone, is the ignorance at the center where the resistance of conviction should be forming. That same condition is disguised, winsomely, in a letter to Mrs. J. G. Holland, three months before the Graves letter, in which she describes the family's change of household: " 'Moved' . . . It is a kind of *gone-to-Kansas* feeling." Dickinson described her reaction to her mother's disabling illness that descended almost as soon as the family had settled in the newly

purchased homestead on Main Street in November or December
1855. "Mother has been an invalid since we came *home*," she told
Mrs. Holland, and then she commented on this profound change
from behind her child-person mask (continual childhood was one of
the roles open to women in the nineteenth century): "I don't know
what her sickness is, for I am but a simple child, and frightened at
myself. I often wish I was a grass, or a toddling daisy, whom all these
problems of the dust might not terrify." In the letter to Graves there
are the traces of a deeply insecure existence. What is left out of the
letter, once again typically in this identity of absence, is a fixed position, a secure way of seeing, a sustaining conception of a relationship
between the profundities she took up: faith in the form of the anthems, death in the crumbling wall and dried-up insect wings, and
life as the cockney bee. There is no resolution, system of belief, even
tentative on her part, to hold these contraries. There is, in short, the
lack of a center. The promise of life is everywhere denied by the evidence of death. It remains a persistent contradiction for which she
had no reconciling idea as a securing pin. To say she had no philosophy is accurate but unfair in its presumption for this country-bred
and domestic young woman. The fact of the matter as it comes
through the philosophical vacancies in the letters, through her theat-
rical poses, and in offhand remarks, is that the contradiction between
the biblical promise and the evidence around her left Dickinson per-
manently at the mercy of its disjunction. That absolute division
without reconciliation is barely concealed in the carefully casual but
skeptical central line in the Graves letter: "It is a jolly thought to
think that we can be Eternal – when air and earth are *full* of lives that
are gone – and done . . . a conceited thing indeed, this promised Resurrection!" Dickinson placed her text in April, in the time-honored
season of contradictions, of renewal and remembrance, as did poets
from Chaucer to Eliot and after. Her April took the place of faith and
made bearable for the moment the deepest contradictions. There was
no philosophical center to hold her steady amid the problems of the
dust, but there was April, and most of all a past April when youthful
friendship overrode all the lurking disparities. Wallace Stevens came
later to that same situation of the consoling poet putting April against
death and words against ignorance which Dickinson created in her
unschooled way in her own "Sunday Morning" letter. Stevens' lines
are apt:

There is not any haunt of prophecy,
Nor any old chimera of the grave . . .
            . . . that has endured
As April's green endures.

Death was in the world when Dickinson came to consciousness
and she seems never to have got beyond her astonishment. There is a
curious American quality to this surprise, especially in its pastless-
ness and personally borne anguish over the whole human condition
and the problems of the dust. What is most American, perhaps, is a
mentality in which the Fall of Man is encountered each occasion as if
for the first time. Foreshadowing the modern with this combination
of doubt and astonishment, Dickinson, like other American poets,
was nothing less than astounded by the sentence of Eden.

With anguished concentration in the last decade of her life, she
confirmed in a prose fragment what emerged only faintly in the letter
to Graves, before that in the letter to Mrs. Holland, and elsewhere in
all the Gethsemane and Microchristus situations. Death and ignorance faced each other in the voided center of her consciousness. The
fragment is her bleakest statement of the aftermath where the victim
of the ultimate alteration is still exclaiming. The idea is the motor of
her art. Free of mystifying allegory, it is a rare statement because of
its high philosophical self-consciousness.

Death being the first form of Life which we have had the power
to Contemplate, our entrance here being an Exclusion from
comprehension, it is amazing that the fascination of our predicament does not entice us more. With such sentences as these
directly over our Heads we are as exempt from Exultation as the
Stones –   (PF-70)

Exclusion from comprehension: this is the stark vacancy at the center. The disabling, decohering ignorance streams through her entire
canon and forms time after time the significance of her allegories. The
primal consequence of such ignorance is that it gave her no place to
stand in addressing the experiences of the world. The impotence of
ignorance, the utter lack of an organizing vision, left the outer world a
swarm of events and a jumble of sensations without an ordering perspective. Nature thus was indeed a haunted house. Here in one of
those allegories of the central absence is the indecisiveness of ignorance:

"Nature" is what we see –
The Hill – the Afternoon –
Squirrel – Eclipse – the Bumble bee –
Nay – Nature is Heaven –
Nature is what we hear –
The Bobolink – the Sea –
Thunder – the Cricket –
Nay – Nature is Harmony –
Nature is what we know –
Yet have no art to say –
So impotent Our Wisdom is
To her Simplicity   (P-668)

In late 1883, the death of her beloved nephew Gilbert bared the old ignorance again. Dickinson, as deathbed convention dictated, described the last moments of the boy. But she ended with bewilderment.

"Open the Door, open the Door, they are waiting for me," was Gilbert's sweet command in delirium. *Who* were waiting for him, all we possess we would give to know – Anguish at last opened it, and he ran to the little Grave at his Grandparents' feet – All this and more, though *is* there more? More than Love and Death? Then tell me its name!   (L-873)

At the age of fifty-three, three years before her own death, the exclusion from comprehension troubled her still. No system, however latent, philosophical or aesthetic, had ever established itself. She echoed here what had dogged her from the early years. If we go back to a letter she wrote her Uncle Joel Norcross soon after she turned nineteen, we see that curious sense of her own separation from events and her lack of control over them, even of the rocks she has thrown: "Harm is one of those things that I always mean to keep clear of – but somehow my intentions and me dont chime as they ought – and people will get hit with stones that I throw at my neighbor's dogs – they insist upon blaming *me* instead of the *stones*" (L-29). She insisted on this peculiar disjunction for the rest of a long paragraph, playfully coming back again to the separation of herself from her actions and from the world of consequences: "if I stab you while sleeping the dagger's to blame – it's no business of mine – you have no more right to accuse me of injuring you than anything else I can think of." Then the ignorance, the void at the center, comes into view as the obsessive absence: "it's so trying to be read out of the wrong book when the right one is out of sight."

The worst experiences of incomprehension were the moments of stone when, without a sustaining bias from the beginning and having filled the void with no convention of faith or even resolute cynicism, she was as exempt from exultation as the dead. More sterile even than the snowman moments Stevens enacts, hers was a bald view in its pure state in which the real stops the heart instantaneously. There are signs everywhere of her condition. Without a principle of organization, she felt every current of emotion across this void of understanding. "I cannot tell how Eternity seems," she wrote to the Norcross cousins in November 1882. "It sweeps around me like a sea." With that lifelong indecision that made her impotent to face the contingency of the world and live in it, helpless therefore to make a program of her poems, she yet forced words into the face of her doubt. Reality became her *words*—because she had a certain extraordinary control over them—yet they had withdrawn from the exterior world where individuals confront life and death, love and faith. It was one way of existentialist survival, but it seems to have been renewed each moment with the same intensity. "The Mind is so near itself," she had written in her first letter to Higginson, "it cannot see, distinctly – and I have none to ask." That remark, we see now, was a stunning perception.

With its ambitious declaration of the setting-out poet making even more prominent the pathos of her deeper circumstance, the Graves letter is a window onto the void at the center of her consciousness. Several other pieces that reflect this state of absence at the origin of her disorderliness become visible now, and more will present themselves as the consequences of this word-intense consciousness. The letters to Higginson, in this new light, are to be understood as the sincerest sort, a genuine cry for an identity she could not discover for herself. The world was displaced by words of her superb selection, but the poems formed no meaning. There was intensity but no light, sensation but no idea. The void startles us, for we have assumed in our interpretive eagerness, with our formalist assumption of inevitable coherence in any poet's makeup (it is the fundamental assumption of the formalist approach), that Emily Dickinson too might be seen to have a way of looking at the world. Not so. We like to think of poets standing in a place where attitudes intersect to make an integrated self, but the Dickinson center is a void, with no genetic connection even to forestall, as Santayana said of Pound, utter miscellaneousness.

The Absent Center

Emily Dickinson is the only major American poet without a project. That vacancy at the heart of her consciousness provided a tragic freedom that constitutes her identity. It is the circumstance in which she was free to enact that peculiar human attitude that makes her unique in our literature.

Willy-nilly, that decentered and passive stance constituted a perception of the world that was inevitably chaotic. One of the manifestations of that disorderly perception is the idea of compensation familiar to her readers and mistakenly seen as an Emersonian equation. "Success is counted sweetest / By those who ne'er succeed": there, readers say, is her inescapable Emersonianism. But Emerson meant always in his compensating formulas to illustrate a metamorphosis from fact into truth, from the present circumstance into the ideal essence of it. To Dickinson the give and take is quite otherwise, never resolved. Every rapture is stolen simultaneously by the Death and Ignorance of which she writes in prose fragment 70. What is given, as Georges Poulet remarked with penetrating insight, is in the same moment taken away. Every emotion is two-edged and thus every triumph is qualified, every ecstasy comes at a full price. " 'We conquered, but Bozzaris fell.' That sentence always chokes me," she wrote to Louise Norcross in 1871, referring to Fitz-Greene Halleck's poem on the hero of the Greek war of independence. It is Dickinson's primary perception, this constant displacement, because there was no immovable place on which she had come to stand. The vision is part of a basic moral confusion that is the inevitable sign of being excluded from comprehension. While Emerson's poet could turn the world to glass, as he wrote with a Romantic superficiality in the essay "The Poet," employing the higher imagination to convert the material world into its Platonic idea, for Dickinson—grievously, painfully—life is interlocked and utterly dependent, but not understood. "Mysterious human heart," she intoned in another fragment, "whose one mistake in Eden has cost it all its Calm to come" (PF-39). Because she reenacted in her poetic self the trials of humankind, making them personal encounters in her poetry, this last fragment is also one more concentrated description of the ceaselessly disquieting denial of comprehension.

A poet without a project, I have called her. She had no subject because she had no scheme, philosophical or poetical. Thus she had no way to address the world and no entry to experience. This startling disability has always lain embedded but unnoticed in her much-quoted definition of poetry to Higginson in 1876: "Nature is a Haunted House – but Art – a House that tries to be haunted" (L-459a). Read alongside the Graves letter and the other fragmentary distillations of her predicament, the quality of hauntedness meant the pervasive mystery that existed for her in her exclusion from a clarifying faith or an order of perception. If her cryptic remark is a poetry program, an abbreviated *ars poetica*, it is testimony simultaneously of a basic incomprehension; as for the part about art trying to be a haunted house, the statement is of a vagueness and indecisiveness that parallels what we have seen so far: poems that lack an architectural craft commensurate to the world outside the closeted consciousness. Dickinson's declaration to Higginson in the end is a poetics that unconsciously reveals an unprecedented withdrawal of poetry from reality. The world, haunted and unintelligible, is to be pantomimed by words that themselves have been taken into the house and into the fierce but autogenerative mind of this withdrawn poet who married herself.

Very late in her life, still amazed at all that eluded her, she sent the Norcross cousins another telling concentration of the disability she had turned into an antiphilosophy of ignorance, exclusion, and alienation: "I believe we shall in some manner be cherished by our Maker – that the One who gave us this remarkable earth has the power still farther to surprise that which He has caused. Beyond that all is silence" (L-785). She reached in an intuitive way in a poem of her thirties a conception of the final consequence of this denial on a person's ensuing perception of the world. It is a poem so bleak in its acquiescence to fated ignorance that wisdom itself seems irrelevant. Characteristically, the poem has a confusing ellipsis in the third line where crowding of the octosyllabic frame required deletion of the verb itself. We can read the line's sense this way: "Whose Will [became] a numb significance." The poem's experience of ignorance is so deep that it conjectures on the uselessness of knowing what it is that removed heaven and the loved one. It is a poem of the paralyzed will, the extreme of the haunted-house poetics.

> Denial – is the only fact
> Perceived by the Denied –
> Whose Will – a numb significance –
> The Day the Heaven died –
>
> And all the Earth strove common round –
> Without Delight, or Beam –
> What Comfort was it Wisdom – was –
> The spoiler of Our Home?   (P-965)

Art as a haunted house, then, in the light of what we know to be the absence at the center of the Dickinson consciousness, is in fact art without a subject.

Was there no structure at all by which Dickinson grasped some portion of the world to take into the house with her? Of course there is: it is a principle of conservation that is pathetic in the weakness of its holding power and self-limiting in its ability to perceive an abundant and social world. Not surprisingly, it is part of the Sunday school teaching of her time on which she depended so often for departure points in her poems. Again, the essential statement is in a prose fragment. Memory, simply enough, is the nucleus of the rudimentary concept. She wrote in the fragment: "Were Departure Separation, there would be neither Nature nor Art, for there would be no World" (PF-52). It is an existence where the past is present and the world exists in the mind, in remembrance. Memory and Art preserve all that Death takes away. This afterlife is clearly a further meaning she attached to "haunted." Memories of the dead keep the dead present in a sentimental, dutiful way. The fragment says, then, the same thing as the haunted-house poetics. What Dickinson naively willed into being was a continuous universe through the medium of an unceasing consciousness. Memory holds the world together, preventing what is lost from disappearing. This is a simple substitute for a philosophy or a poetics, but it served Dickinson. Although exclusion from comprehension disabled her in many respects, this elementary faith in the memory's stewardship of continuity, of *holding the world from dissolving utterly,* while astonishing to us in its pathos and far from a strong ordering principle, is the enabling fiction of her poetry.

But even memory cut, in Dickinson fashion, both ways, took away as it preserved, pained even as it consoled. That is, even this semblance of an angle of vision, of a binding and perceiving power, was subject to the ceaseless disorder that constantly kept displacing one emotion with its opposite. "Memory," she wrote to Mrs. Holland in 1882, "is a strange Bell – Jubilee, and Knell."

Dickinson's poetic consciousness came to its strange maturity in the mid-nineteenth century at the point of a sharp swerve in the capacity and matter of American poetry. The age when fundamental questions human and divine could be linked by the tradition of a simple protestant belief was in sight of its end. Dickinson came of age at the point, as Allen Tate cogently argued a long time ago, where the shared confidence of a privileged perception was breaking up. And so, like some of her contemporaries, Dickinson found herself without the support of a comfortable, unexamined Christian design. Fundamentally, it was the loss of outside authority, and for Dickinson this loss of an ordering power was particularly vivid and personally disabling. Her predicament was the experience for a naked and candid biography that combined personal and historical revelation.

Uncertainty was a fact not only of her life. What operated of the authority of Christian faith for many served mainly to remind them that death was a constant companion, life was precarious, and the need for some measure of composure in the face of this demanded what one historian of death in America, Lewis O. Saum, has called the psychology of bereavement. Dickinson's supreme need, always part of her figure of the bisected hearse that separated the living from the dead, was to bisect certainty from uncertainty. In this we know she was never successful. Samuel Bowles didn't help dispel the confusion when he called the Dickinson family's attention all the way from Paris, where he was visiting in 1862, to the hypocrisy of Amherst's Sunday rituals. "Yesterday," he announced, "while all Amherst was praying, and scarifying the body and torturing the soul into affected humility all Paris was in a frolic. Half the town went out to see the races."[1] The contradictions were part of the disintegration underway in the culture, and Dickinson, despite her physical withdrawal from its society, was a child of that confusion. No doubt, the natives of the rain are rainy men, as Stevens said, and Dickinson raised the experience of philosophical drift and disappearing authority ("I had no Monarch in my life"), the skepticism and the in-comprehension, to a private, high, excruciating pitch.

Some evidence of her felt loss appears in poems that project an ideal state where uncertainty and change—all the things she named with such elan—had ceased. It was a lost, ideal state in poem 646 from her middle, most active period of writing. There she created a time when there is

> No numb alarm – lest Difference come –
> No Goblin – on the Bloom –
> No start in Apprehension's Ear,
> No Bankruptcy – no Doom –
>
> But Certainties of Sun –
> Midsummer – in the Mind –
> A steadfast South – upon the Soul –
> Her Polar time – behind –
>
> The Vision – pondered long –
> So plausible becomes
> That I esteem the fiction – real –
> The Real – fictitious seems –   (P-646)

When she was twenty-three, she wrote to Austin at Harvard: "I wish we were children now. I wish we were *always* children, how to grow up I don't know" (L-115). The plaint still reaches us with the force of pathos, for we know that her inability to reach the firm ground where an ordering perspective could accommodate a worldly social experi-ence was a lifelong failure, and the one need Higginson might help her fulfill. In that inability which limited her poetic breadth even while intensifying her poetic force, she reflected the larger culture she had turned her back on. But by raising that loss of comprehension and that disappearance of a central project to a personal Calvary, in the shrillest words she could command, she found herself most truly strange.

"How Conscious Consciousness – could grow"

The syndrome of the lost center was especially marked in Dickinson because the lack of a structure of belief was emphasized by such in-tense consciousness. She seems to have been affected in an uncommon way by her feeling of the fearful privilege to be alive. Denied the reassuring structure of a systematic belief and therefore of a mode of dwelling in the world, she was herself the best example of what she called "Costumeless Consciousness." It was her term for God or Fate, for whatever "schedule" operated out of sight. She was all the Fate she knew, and thus the capacity of consciousness amazed her. Pain revealed that capacity, expanding time so that she could assert with evident authority, "Ages coil within / The minute Circumference / Of a single Brain" (P-967).

"What was it that Proust sought so frenetically?" Walter Benjamin asked in an essay on Proust's "unconstruable synthesis" of personality and art. "What was at the bottom of these infinite efforts?" [2] We ask the same with regard to Emily Dickinson. Yet we will certainly discover that it does not resemble what Benjamin called in Proust a "paralyzing, explosive will to happiness." We find, no matter with what ingenuity we look, no solar system into whose gravitational field all her experiences were attracted.

What one senses instead of a conceptual center in Dickinson is the phenomenon of pure activity. There seems to be a concentrated field not of pooled belief but of ferocious needs and a tireless imagination. It was this uncentered swirl evidently that Higginson reacted to when he made the most revealing of all the remarks on Dickinson the person. The comment of this experienced and social man after meeting her stops us in our tracks with its implication: "I never was with any one who drained my nerve power so much. Without touching her, she drew from me. I am glad not to live near her" (L-342b). Later in his preface to the 1890 edition of the poems, he defined in his own way that combination in the poetry of power and incoherence: "the main quality of these poems is that of extraordinary grasp and insight, uttered with an uneven vigor sometimes exasperating, seemingly wayward, but really unsought and inevitable." She had said the same, as we know, in those remarks in her first letter to him: "the Mind is so near itself – it cannot see, distinctly."

Dickinson associated the state of heightened consciousness, predictably and by Christian sanction, with death, when all the veils are to fall. She posed the question on the capacity of the grasp of consciousness in a poem that originates in the tired convention of the deathbed watch and the signs of grace. She starts out in the most predictable way, except for the typical snag of a paradox in the first line:

> To know just how He suffered – would be dear –
> To know if any Human eyes were near
> To whom He could entrust His wavering gaze –
> Until it settled broad – on Paradise –

The observer then touches the rift of knowledge where Dickinson herself was caught: "Was Dying as He thought – or different." But Dickinson inserted her freedom into the convention as, toward the end in the way we recognize, she made a moment of word sophistication. The words, unobtrusively, measure out to its boundary the question of the capacity of consciousness:

> Was He afraid – or tranquil
> Might He know
> How Conscious Consciousness – could grow –   (P-622)

It was a frenetic consciousness that forced the single most noticeable characteristic of her poems: their displacement, the perpetual erasure of impressions, and the constant going on to new ones. In a way, activity was her project, words of power and surprise but loosed from any gravity field in which they could, like magnetic roses in steel dust as another poet was to put it, cluster to create the patterns of their deeper cohering signification. The radical modernity of this phenomenon of freely forming and freely striking power will occupy us in a later chapter. The activity issues from the irrepressible will to speak, to make the words in which one can exist. In Dickinson's case it was her main mode of existence. All those words were the record of her existence, the terrible privilege, as I said earlier, of being alive.

The mode of her existence clarifies now as a marvel of force and of power to destroy. Her world is one of deprivation and denial and, as in the letter to Graves, she is alone in it, the intersection of its strongest blows, both ecstatic and destructive, because she is excruciatingly conscious. If we consider this situation with its closed-in forces, we understand better the dimensions of the metaphorical quip that Dickinson married herself. That irreverent figure begins to indicate the concentration of power coming in on itself in a way we can hardly conceive. Hyperconsciousness against ignorance: she, not another, not Emerson, not even Elizabeth Barrett Browning, was her own Flaubert!

George Eliot died on December 26, 1880; in noting her reaction to the news Dickinson chose the single observation that applied as well to her own centerless condition. "Now, *my* George Eliot. The gift of belief which her greatness denied her, I trust she receives in the childhood of the kingdom of heaven" (L-710). It seems to be as close as she ever got to a prayer for the resolution of her own need. Lacking the gift of a centered self, her poems one by one spell out the intensest kind of consciousness of existential being. What is it to be alive? What is it to love and then to lose what one loves? What is it to die? Each elemental question she confronted with unabashed plainness. But they linked one to the other by the overriding question: What is it to conjecture and not to know? This is where Dickinson is a world away from Emerson's confident Platonism. For she sought not examples of his reassuring metamorphosis of fact into Truth but rather the design of experience itself of which she was ignorant.

Her words inevitably sought discrepant experience, the space between supposition and reality, between the second-hand beliefs of a received faith and the strange life lived apart from the world. The primary rift, as she said with crushing finality in that scrap of prose (PF-70), is death and the exclusion from comprehension. Like probing a sore tooth, she sent her sharp, steely words into this rift between the parables and fact, the disjunctions of labels from the fearful life within.

Poetry, as I have said in an earlier essay, is what Dickinson did to her doubt and incomprehension. The absence of a center is what her poetry centered on, sometimes coyly, as if it could not be faced.

> Trust in the Unexpected –
> By this – was William Kidd
> Persuaded of the Buried Gold –
> As One had testified –
>
> Through this – the old Philosopher –
> His Talismanic Stone
> Discerned – still with[h]olden
> To effort undivine –
>
> 'Twas this – allured Columbus –
> When Genoa – withdrew

> Before an Apparition
> Baptized America –
>
> The Same – afflicted Thomas –
> When Deity assured
> 'Twas better – the perceiving not –
> Provided it believed –   (P-555)

She lived under the shadow of the end with no secure place to stand. With this knowledge we see the primary condition of her art. The absence was the sacred poverty out of which her verbal imagination leaped. The poverty made the poetry possible, even justified it. For she heaped words in the void as her kind of consolation. What power was left to her lay in her restless art, and it possessed a wildness she sought Higginson's help to put under control. "Cherish Power," she wrote to Sue in 1878. "Remember that stands in the Bible between the Kingdom and the Glory, because it is wilder than either of them." To Higginson she had written so many years earlier, "You think me 'uncontrolled' – I have no Tribunal."

Ignorance at the center of power: that is the Dickinson syndrome of hyperconsciousness without system or order. That hyperconsciousness had its life in those risky acts of linguistic violation by which she seized words that surprise and then joined them in willful combination. Otherwise the phenomenal activity within would have had no medium, and for us no being. With the most colossal irony, the hymn was the site of that activity, the place where language turned away from the harmonies of belief and the symmetries of conceptual order. She had no steady faith and yet she wrote in the forms of faith. Her impatient, strenuous, rough-edged language turned in the smooth, old hymnal socket of easy faith. Her defective, programless language, striking out with no belief to guide it to a target, to give it the gravity of an identity, was seated with fierce unconscious symbolism in the hymn – that last vestige of the greatest program of all.

Stone Moments

One of her spears of doubt closes a letter of late 1882 to Mrs. Holland: "Is God Love's Adversary?" (L-792). Epitomized in that concentrated question, but mostly out of sight in the consolatory letters, was the massive iceberg of doubt. The extreme moments of her ferocious needs that lacked a strategy were inevitably her snowman times, stone moments when "all the Earth," as she wrote in poem 965, "strove common round – / Without Delight, or Beam." In an earlier letter to Mrs. Holland, to whom for reasons not clear to me she was occasionally willing to raise the optimistic veil, she wrote this trenchant supposition: "we cannot believe for each other. I suppose there are depths in every Consciousness, from which we cannot rescue ourselves – to which none can go with us – which represent to us Mortally – the Adventure of Death" (L-555). One comes to see that Dickinson's "finless Mind" (her expression in an 1866 letter, 319) not only must inevitably have gone repeatedly to the ends of the knowable, but that her language itself began with the void. To use Maurice Blanchot's insight into how language removes man from the world's wholeness and unitary embrace, it was almost always true that plenitude and certitude for Dickinson did not speak. She starkly set out in another fragment the problem at the core: "When it becomes necessary for us to stake our all upon the belief of another in as for instance Eternity, we find it is impossible to make the transfer – Belief is unconsciously to most of us . . . an Untried Experience" (PF-53).

The exceptions to Dickinson's litany of doubt, of joy instantly counterbalanced by its price, are conspicuous because they contrast so vividly, proving the rule of the underlying desperation. "My period had come for Prayer" moves first through some condescending skepticism in which God is "this Curious Friend" the speaker searches for, then opens upon a great silent space of incomprehension. Surprisingly, then, Dickinson brings the poem into a triumphant Dantesque fusion of the self and Creation. The ending stands out as a rare moment of high Emersonian transport:

> Vast Prairies of Air
>
> Unbroken by a Settler –
> Were all that I could see –
> Infinitude – Had'st Thou no Face
> That I might look on Thee?
>
> The Silence condescended –
> Creation stopped – for Me –
> But awed beyond my errand –
> I worshipped – did not "pray" –   (P-564)

Such exceptional moments of pure exhilaration only emphasize the other, paralyzing times of snow, of absolute doubt and exclusion from understanding. She wrote this on the back of a draft note to Sue in 1884 to make the anniversary of Gilbert's death (PF-49). It chills so deeply because the language comes straight out of the void: "Tis a dangerous moment for any one when the meaning goes out of things and Life stands straight – and punctual – and yet no signal comes. Yet such moments are. If we survive them they expand us, if we do not, but that is Death, whose if is everlasting." The point of her attention, the core of her urgent language, was an absence. It was this absence that allowed her to see as much as she did. Like darkness for William Carlos Williams, a thing known has value by virtue of the dark. We remember that Dickinson wrote in the Browning poem, "The Dark felt beautiful."

Because Dickinson saw by absences, by endings, by, that is, death, she courted this condition in her poetry and letters. Her language made visible decline, doubt, the exclusion from comprehension. It sought, in short, man deposed, the gray slate of Fate in dominance when death gives "Dominion room." Her sense of the ending seems to have been brought to a heightened pitch by hyperconsciousness and absent faith. She called the overthrow of man, in a variant of uncanny power, the "denuded Pageant." It is a typically concentrated poem, thirty-five words of an utterly common lexicon that court death, catching up death in its simultaneous colossal aspect and its fastidious destruction as "The Glory of Decay." "Forget" parallels "Depose" as a verb. The poet crosses into irony with the word "Glory."

> The harm of Years is on him –
> The infamy of Time –
> Depose him like a Fashion
> And give Dominion room.
>
> Forget his Morning Forces –
> The Glory of Decay
> Is a minuter Pageant
> Than least Vitality.   (P-1280)

Her language of incomprehension not infrequently resorted to stock sentimentality by the evasion of meaning, as when she sought out the drowning of a child.

> How the Waters closed above Him
> We shall never know –

How He stretched His Anguish to us
That – is covered too –   (P-923)

For want of philosophical development that would carry her by a progression to deeper understanding rather than deeper doubt, like Keats's persistent movement toward meaning despite his inability to find a subject, she was doomed, while possessed of unmatched ability and a persistence that is almost beyond our belief, to see her exclusion from comprehension afresh each moment. Every time anew, her poems were destined not to know but to discover ignorance, enact it time after time with surprise.

In the homeliest of sites, Dickinson's language could find the great ignorance. Poem 742 has an architecture that is typically lacking in her poems, and this order leads skillfully, inexorably it seems, into the absolute ignorance of the final line. It is a language of uncharacteristic flatness, interrupted in its prosaic flatness by no pyrotechnics.

Four Trees – upon a solitary Acre –
Without Design
Or Order, or Apparent Action –
Maintain –

The Sun – upon a Morning meets them –
The Wind –
No nearer Neighbor – have they –
But God –

The Acre gives them – Place –
They – Him – Attention of Passer by –
Of Shadow, or of Squirrel, haply –
Or Boy –

What Deed is Their's unto the General Nature –
What Plan
They severally – retard – or further –
Unknown –   (P-742)

Elsewhere, her chronicles of anguish contain language of a hyperbolic weight that suggests in other ways the darkest side of her grappling with the absent center. The poem that follows is constituted exclusively of heavy elements almost entirely unqualified by a distracting adjective. It is language right at the bone, that is to say, a language of absolutes that seems to me to be the surface display of a latent hysteria caused by doubt.

> Water, is taught by thirst.
> Land – by the Oceans passed.
> Transport – by throe –
> Peace – by it's battles told –
> Love, by Memorial Mold –
> Birds, by the Snow.   (P-135)

Her language gives every indication of existing in a condition of final uncertainty. That Dickinson herself, as we have glimpsed her so far through the interstices of her language and consolatory poses, existed in a trial of doubt, even desperation, seems clear in a note she sent to Sue in 1865 on the news of the death of Sue's sister. Dickinson is relying on her knowledge of loss and her skill at living with incomprehension: "You must let me go first, Sue, because I live in the Sea always and know the Road. I would have drowned twice to save you sinking, dear" (L-306).

The darkest of her poems is of a piece with fragment 70. The repetition of the hollow pronoun "it" at the beginning leads into the terrifying view even as the language flashes. Line 10 normalized would read: "And neither opens the eyes."

> We dream – it is good we are dreaming –
> It would hurt us – were we awake –
> But since it is playing – kill us,
> And we are playing – shriek –
>
> What harm? Men die – externally –
> It is a truth – of Blood –
> But we – are dying in Drama –
> And Drama – is never dead –
>
> Cautious – We jar each other –
> And either – open the eyes –
> Lest the Phantasm – prove the Mistake –
> And the livid Surprise
>
> Cool us to Shafts of Granite –
> With just an Age – and Name –
> And perhaps a phrase in Egyptian –
> It's prudenter – to dream –   (P-531)

But what was abhorrent to one who seemed now to pride herself on her ability to endure in pure consciousness, without a raft of belief or a place to stand, was extinction. More particularly, it was the extinction of consciousness, which, as we know, she usually depicted as extending beyond death. But there were thoughts of obliteration. In the representative poem of annihilation that follows, we find the idiosyncratic ellipses, particularly in line four, where the normal phrasing "Cease to be identified" or "Cease to have an identity" is forced by the rigid limitation of the six-syllable hymn count into the phrase "Cease to identify," a distortion that is typical of Dickinson's labors inside the form. Another forced ellipsis distorts sense in line eight as well.

> This Dust, and it's Feature –
> Accredited – Today –
> Will in a second Future –
> Cease to identify –
>
> This Mind, and it's measure –
> A too minute Area
> For it's enlarged inspection's
> Comparison – appear –
>
> This World, and it's species
> A too concluded show
> For its absorbed Attention's
> Remotest scrutiny –   (P-936)

To fail of faith in immortality, on the one hand, or to be forgotten by the living on the other, seemed to her to be the two sides of the most complete misery. Ignorance, then, was linked to the possibility of extinction, and not to exist as consciousness was at the heart of her apprehension. It was the central doubt, "the Instead," as she wrote in one poem.

> the Instead – the Pinching fear
> That Something – it did do – or dare –
> Offend the Vision – and it flee –
> And They no more remember me –   (P-462)

Extinction of identity made up the artist's horror of the imagination's death. For Dickinson, withdrawn into her consciousness, alive mainly in the activity of words, that death was the ultimate of the snowman moments.

In the inert moments, fearing the extinction of the imagination, she touched in a tentative and not wholly conscious way one of the associated dilemmas of the modern poetic consciousness: How is poetry to be made out of sterile ground? How is poetry to be made by the man on the ashheap? What are poems to consist of in the absence of a building project under a way of seeing the world? The fragmentation of Dickinson's work is the visible wrestling with this problem. "For the sensitive poet, conscious of negations," Stevens wrote, "nothing is more difficult than the affirmations of nobility and yet there is nothing that he requires of himself more persistently" ("The Noble Rider and the Sound of Words").

What is it that withstood the winter within her? What faced against the haunting and incomprehension? It was the enactment in words of the life of the imagination. This was the life of the consciousness, restless, fertile, agile, able to devour the world, to take it into the language as her emblematic bee took the flower's nectar. Knowledgeable about winter, lacking a project that would allow her to confront experience let alone organize it, Dickinson did not embrace the night and dissolution, or even embrace the God of the organized Church. The sinking man does not drown so as to be with his God, Dickinson knew. The repeated rising to life and to consciousness was her vital activity. The weighing of hope against certainty, life against death, is in these homely terms.

> Drowning is not so pitiful
> As the attempt to rise.
> Three times, 'tis said, a sinking man
> Comes up to face the skies,
> And then declines forever
> To that abhorred abode,
> Where hope and he part company –
> For he is grasped of God.
> The Maker's cordial visage,
> However good to see,
> Is shunned, we must admit it,
> Like an adversity.   (P-1718)

A way of recognizing her connection to the modern dilemma of poetry on the dump is to see how much Dickinson made individual consciousness in the poems the nexus of attention, with suffering unmediated by institution or philosophy. In part it was an inherited Romantic manner: the individual inwardly attending to the private emotions, chaotic, fearful, mysterious. When Emerson celebrated the individual, he found order and harmony, a neo-Platonist inner world. But Dickinson's personae lived their most terrible moments in her poems. Her poetic language and the experience it could perceive are beyond Romanticism in the way religion in her writing was no longer a habit but each time a new, directly lived encounter.

It is this juncture where we shall see whatever signficant relationship there is between Emily Dickinson and the American Puritans with whom she is often indiscriminately merged. The link may be wholly fortuitous and untraceable, but the Puritans' ways of finding meaning for themselves, a Puritan semiology of how and where they found the significance of their lives, enable us to uncover one of Dickinson's preoccupations. The crucial term is *microchristus*. I rely here on Bercovitch's discussion of Christology.

Dickinson's emblematic term for the passion of Christ was Calvary, which she used a dozen times in poems from the early period to the latest. The person in the poems called herself "The Queen of Calvary" (P-348) and "Empress of Calvary" (P-1072). Her personalizing of Christ's passions of doubt and ecstasy, however, involved more than simply the tropes that clergymen took from the Bible and applied to their American setting. Dickinson's perceiving of experience has to do not with the tropes themselves but with the transfer of the experience of Christ and other biblical figures to one's own immediate experience. Dickinson created personae who reenacted as if for the first time and without mediation the passions and circumstances of the biblical accounts. The Puritans had transferred the Bible stories to America in a wholesale manner. They had, as Bercovitch says, "discovered America in Scripture; and had proceeded from the thing to the things signified—from Noah to Abraham to Moses to Nehemiah to 'Americanus.' Along the way, they changed the focus of traditional hermeneutics from biblical to secular history."[3] Dickinson changed the focus more, to personal history. She discovered scripture anew in her imagination, in the selves of her poetic voices. For her, the private nexus was where experience existed, where meaning, if not to be found, at least was frantically sought. All experience, and meaning if it existed, for this poet was to be found in the solitary sufferer. That extraordinary Puritan transfer of Christian parable into personal affairs had produced a private typology of affairs.

The closed-in personal nexus appears conspicuously in a Dickin-

son poem that is representative of her whole group of private enact-
ments of Christian allegory. This poem, endlessly anthologized I sus-
pect because of its verbal intimacy, the chill fear that invades it, and
not least the psychoanalytical titillation involved because of its connection to the Amherst spinster, derives directly from the parable of
the ten virgins in the Book of Matthew. There, we recall, Christ
speaks of the Second Coming and how believers must be prepared.
"Watch therefore," Christ admonishes, "for ye know not what hour
your Lord doth come." And then he continues with the parable:

> Then shall the kingdom of heaven be likened unto ten virgins,
> which took their lamps, and went forth to meet the bridegroom.
>
> The wise took oil in their vessels with their lamps but the foolish
> took no oil with them.
>
> While the bridegroom tarried, they all slumbered and slept.
>
> And at midnight there was a cry made, Behold, the bridegroom
> cometh; go ye out to meet him;
>
> . . . the bridegroom came; and they that were ready went in with
> him to the marriage: and the door was shut.
>
> Watch therefore, for ye know neither the day nor the hour
> wherein the Son of man cometh.

Here is Dickinson remaking the parable into a private experience, immediate and urgent, imagining the moment, without ritual distance
but as felt on the senses.

> A Wife – at Daybreak I shall be –
> Sunrise – Hast thou a Flag for me?
> At Midnight, I am but a Maid,
> How short it takes to make it Bride –
> Then – Midnight, I have passed from thee
> Unto the East, and Victory –
>
> Midnight – Good Night! I hear them call,
> The Angels bustle in the Hall –
> Softly my Future climbs the Stair,
> I fumble at my Childhood's prayer
> So soon to be a Child no more –
> Eternity, I'm coming – Sir,
> Savior – I've seen the face – before!   (P-461)

The penciled draft reads "Master" for "Savior." Dickinson's parable once again had within it her plea for coherence: "I had no Monarch in my life."

Christ's passion in the wilderness is the parabolic source of her version of the individual in the wilderness. The poem quoted below is more powerful for its less obvious association, linked only in the words "wilderness" and "divine." A reader does not know what the circumstances are, only the desolation. The first words, with the severe compaction of which Dickinson is capable, take the reader into desolation so deep it is varied only by further desolation. It is a remarkable emotional space to travel in sixteen words. Here, with a mirror image anticipating Prufrock, is the particular Christology of Dickinson at the midpoint of the nineteenth century when the mediations of an habitual faith had, for her it seems, broken down.

> Like Eyes that looked on Wastes –
> Incredulous of Ought
> But Blank – and steady Wilderness –
> Diversified by Night –
>
> Just Infinites of Nought –
> As far as it could see –
> So looked the face I looked upon –
> So looked itself – on Me –
>
> I offered it no Help –
> Because the Cause was Mine –
> The Misery a Compact
> As hopeless – as divine –
>
> Neither – would be absolved –
> Neither would be a Queen
> Without the Other – Therefore –
> We perish – tho' We reign –   (P-458)

My discussion of these moments of extremity leads to a crucial observation at this point: Dickinson's poems of desolation do not depend upon her loss of a lover. That supposition trivializes the life, perceiving it with a banality that misses the complex truth of the woman. Feminist interpreters, moreover, might recognize, as they have not, that it is simplistic, even sexist, stereotyping to regard these poems as the evidence of psychological throes caused by cultural oppression of women. Dickinson's desolation is a fully human one of the complexity I have been trying to make visible in her work. It is uniquely painful because it is in her case an aspect of a restless and demanding consciousness. Her desolation as an artist lies at the terrifying depth of thought where she finds Nothing at the end, where the final No is reached. In her intuitive way she gave her own definition to this absence that existed where authority should have stood and which was the origin of her *unmanageable art*. She brought the vacancy momentarily into view in that aside to Mrs. Holland we saw earlier: "There are depths in every consciousness . . . which represent to us . . . the adventure of death . . . no one can accompany us there."

Allegories of Ignorance

The Puritan idea of the plain style recurred in the vernacular directness of Dickinson's language, but her reliance on metaphor is an even more noticeable quality that she and the Puritan writers as well as American writers share. Bercovitch's definition of the Puritan plain style quoted in full in Chapter 3 is to the point on both counts. Dickinson's use of parable, practiced over the full span of her writing years, holds a prodigious irony, however, and one that is modern at its core: her parables are not of faith but of ignorance and incomprehension. She had, we know not precisely how or why, turned some absolute corner since the Puritan dispensation and faced the prospect that the moderns have faced ever since, a stark existentialist state bereft of coherence.

What was it that Dickinson saw through her instrument of a latter-day parable when she looked on existence? The letter to Graves is especially revealing. She saw death and nature's seasonal renewal of life, but in ignorance of any design that linked, as she said, what is sad and what is gay. In short, with death and beauty and ignorance her triad, she saw constantly the parable of the Fall of Man. When Dickinson looked out on the world she saw the allegorical language of denial, incomprehension, and great beauty. It was a prohibiting perception of an astonishing simplicity.

It is this simplification of existence into parables consisting of all-or-nothing terms in all-or-nothing wagers that brings readers up short. She came to the mystery of death and ignorance—that problem of the dust that, as she said, terrified her—as if no one had confronted it before. Hers was a brilliant simplification associated with a peculiar

brand of American artistic amateurism. In the pervasive Adamic tradition, Dickinson wrote as if man were a recent invention. Thus her
parables are propelled by a need that overpowers us. They embarrass
us by drawing from us with their enactment of need. That desire appears in the repeated Dickinsonian transformations from midnight to
dawn, from maid to wife. The major allegory is an endlessly generating typology for death in the face of ignorance.

Dickinson was like Hardy in her regard for simplicity. He too had
escaped early schooling in more sophisticated thought and the conventions of literary tradition and so intuitively focused on the essen-
tials of existence, the elemental rounds of birth and death, of love and
suffering, quite out from under the more artful modes of concealment. Like Blake, too, she lacked the impulse to conformity which
education confers, as Eliot reminded us. It was this provincial wisdom that enabled Blake to escape merging by endless qualifications
into the attitudes of his culture. Like both Blake and Hardy, Dickinson with her parabolic eye for the essential passions and mysteries of
life gives her poems their symbolic richness and, in turn, their indefiniteness and lack of circumstance. Because of their simple gravities,
facing on the issues of death and ignorance reduced to their main
outlines, I just called her poems all-or-nothing visions, all-or-nothing
wagers.

When Dickinson's allegories express momentary elation, employ
the language of exhilaration, they also carry with them the aura of incomprehension. To use her terms from a prose fragment referring to
the knowledge the dead kept to themselves, they are about "that great
Romance still to us foreclosed." She added: "while coveting their
wisdom we lament their silence" (PF-50). This was the ultimate ignorance, but it would have been a most commonplace concentration in
the dear, dear dead school had she not made her central contemplation the ignorance at the heart of all existence. Her poems are about
lost redemption. In short, the most important element in her poems is
the very thing that is absent. All the lines of inquiry circle about but
never converge with assurance or with any sense of a plan on the
comprehension that is absent.

This aspect of her work reveals again how different she is from
Emerson. Seeing likenesses between them is to judge on the superficial evidence of formal brevity, partial rhymes, stock ideas of compensation, and shared tropes, and to miss the deepest and contrary

realities of their dispositions toward experience and the disparity of their languages that perceived these different worlds. Those worlds are different realities separated by different languages.

The centrality of Dickinson's doubt becomes apparent in a great many poems when we are sensitive to it. In the dying-person and death poems, for example, the not knowing is the core of interest. Here it is explicitly in an early poem on the death of a woman whose assurance of immortality never registered on her face: "Had not the bliss so slow a pace / Who knows but this surrendered face / Were undefeated still? (P-58). The end of the poem comes down directly on the incomprehension to form a parable of denial.

> Oh if there may departing be
> Any forgot by Victory
> In her imperial round –
> Show them this meek appareled thing
> That could not stop to be a king –
> Doubtful if it be crowned!   (P-58)

This same ignorance is the core of the great poems too: in the marvelous poem of secular deflation, "I heard a Fly buzz – when I died"; in the baffling sterility and isolation of the blessed dead of "Safe in their Alabaster Chambers"; in the endless surmise at the close of "Because I could not stop for Death"; in the collapse of consciousness in "I felt a Funeral, in my Brain." Even "The mail from Tunis" (P-1463) is an emblem of indefinition. Can we afford to evade any longer the knowledge as readers of Dickinson that her poems are parables of incomprehension? Her figural grasp of this desperate state of absence is nothing short of brilliant where the stumbling fly stops us instantly with its emblematic concentration of restlessness and incomprehension that exist after all the conventions have done their mediating:

> I willed my Keepsakes – Signed away
> What portion of me be
> Assignable – and then it was
> There interposed a Fly –
>
> With Blue – uncertain stumbling Buzz –
> Between the light – and me –
> And then the Windows failed – and then
> I could not see to see –   (P-465)

Dickinson's odes on the intimations of immortality are consistently anti-odes on the exclusion from comprehension; they hide the dilemma of her lack of a coherent vision, a place to stand, or a project in the mind. Some are extraordinarily explicit. Lines two and three of this poem, if the ellipses were restored, would read: the first thing I could recollect was that I was bereft of I knew not what.

> A loss of something ever felt I –
> The first that I could recollect
> Bereft I was – of what I knew not
> Too young that any should suspect
>
> A Mourner walked among the children
> I notwithstanding went about
> As one bemoaning a Dominion
> Itself the only Prince cast out –
>
> Elder, Today, a session wiser
> And fainter, too, as Wiseness is –
> I find myself still softly searching
> For my Delinquent Palaces –   (P-959)

If we seek an explanation of why Dickinson resisted so firmly and to her discomfort the religious revival at Mount Holyoke Seminary when she was a student there some eighteen years earlier (this poem may be much closer in date to 1848 than we can tell from the surviving fair copy), perhaps we have part of that explanation here. Yet it is not, characteristically, an explanation at all. It is a poem about absent knowledge, an absent plan, a loss, an omission.

As explicit as the poem seems in its assertive language, there is simply no definition of the loss. What we have instead is bravery that conceals beneath its surface the turbulence and impediment, the inhibited intensity, the chaos out of sight but felt, the failure even as the emotions suggest an articulated meaning. In place of meaning, as in her life, we have commotion, intuitive knowledge mixed with ignorance. The poems are animated by the knowledge they seek but which they never manage to possess. In the place of a bias that orders experience, we have words of emotive power strung over an obscure region of confusions. With few exceptions the major poems are the parables of this anarchy.

As each poem is an allegory of exclusion, each poem works an estrangement. I called it autistic discourse earlier. In the place of comprehension, language opens the rift between figure and fact. Thus it might be said that in Dickinson's intense practice, words take the place of the sustaining order of belief that she lacked. Without the authority of an attitude, words protected her from the uninterpreted being of things. "I sing as the Boy does by the Burying Ground," she wrote to Higginson when he inquired about her motivation, "because I am afraid" (L-261).

Coincident with this generative ignorance of hers was an outrageous appetite for the sensations of language and the power with which she fed it. It was, as she wrote in a poem in a moment of high self-consciousness, "a finer famine." The entire poem shows the power and urgency of the appetite without an object. Characteristically, the poem operates by hyperbolic absolutes. Here is a maelstrom, a vulture, a tiger, and blood lust, and then the famine finest of all, craving an exotic berry and a single glance of—what? the erotic? It is a poem of craving and appetite, of instinctive need, but without understanding. The metaphors of the "Berry of Domingo" and "Torrid Eye" take the place of comprehension:

> As the Starved Maelstrom laps the Navies
> As the Vulture teased
> Forces the Broods in lonely Valleys
> As the Tiger eased
>
> By but a Crumb of Blood, fasts Scarlet
> Till he meet a Man
> Dainty adorned with Veins and Tissues
> And partakes – his Tongue
>
> Cooled by the Morsel for a moment
> Grows a fiercer thing
> Till he esteem his Dates and Cocoa
> A Nutrition mean
>
> I, of a finer Famine
> Deem my Supper dry
> For but a Berry of Domingo
> And a Torrid Eye.   (P-872)

Dickinson's poems were a continual calculus of absent knowledge. She speculated in the coyly juvenile poem about Heaven and immortality that begins "There is a June when Corn is cut." The poem measures out difference in an attempt to understand. It is a poem of unsophisticated speculation but of language precision that creates high wit. These are the second two of the four stanzas:

Two Seasons, it is said, exist –
The Summer of the Just,
And this of Our's, diversified
With Prospect, and with Frost –

May not our Second with it's First
So infinite compare
That We but recollect the one
The other to prefer?   (P-930)

Dickinson was not so completely captive of her Sunday school age as we might conclude. Wallace Stevens' "Sunday Morning," as I have suggested, is our modern gloss on many of Dickinson's poems of speculation on the absent knowledge. In that poem, for the woman who speaks, words take the place of comprehension. Her contemplation is the linguistic imagining of a possible world: "Does ripe fruit never fall? Or do the boughs / Hang always heavy in that perfect sky?"

Existential ignorance is linked inextricably with Dickinson's life-long role as a consoler. The words of consolation, if not in fact the faith itself, by sustaining others was no doubt a way of assuaging her ignorance. A single poem of pointed satire which joins scientific theory of the conservation of matter and religious belief is a marvel of compression. It is also characteristically distorted in language by the hymn's procrustean bed. The second stanza, ellipses restored and inversions rectified, would read this way: If, after death, I shall see the atoms that had departed this earth, with how much more [delight, rapture] I shall see my loved ones, their lives completed by immortality, who had departed from me in death. Here is the bridge Dickinson made from her condition in ignorance to her role of consolation.

The Chemical conviction
That Nought be lost
Enable in Disaster
My fractured Trust –

The Faces of the Atoms
If I shall see
How more the Finished Creatures
Departed me!   (P-954)

The Role of Consoler

Consolation literature was an important part of nineteenth-century
American culture. Dickinson's conscientious production of consolation quite beyond the conventions actively pursued in her time came,
it seems, directly from this abiding personal anarchy. The anarchy
and the sustaining are an extraordinary division in her even so, her
doubt making strength for others. But consolation is of a piece with
the aftermath syndrome I outlined earlier. Dickinson drafted a letter
to Otis Lord late in her life in which she joined the two elements, the
aftermath being the time when consolation is most needed. It was the
"engulfing '*Since*,'" she wrote around 1882. "Antony's remark to a
friend, 'since Cleopatra died' is said to be the saddest ever lain in
Language – That engulfing '*Since*'" (L-791). Earlier to Lord, she allowed that courage is but a dress put on for show, for she said, referring to how lost she felt after her mother's death, she was writing
"without that Dress of Spirit [which] must be worn for most" (L-
790). She paraded a conventional faith for all who needed it, for she
knew personally what anarchy could descend when a coherent faith
disappeared. She maintained faith for others, saying to the Norcross
cousins with firm finality in her role as consoler: "God made no act
without a cause" (P-1163).

She practiced a "Dover Beach" attitude as well, the replacement of
faith with earthly love, with friendship and particularly with remembrance. Emerson had set out a consolatory credo for the time:

> Try the might the Muse affords
> And the balm of thoughtful words;
> Bring music to the desolate;
> Hang roses on the stony fate.
> (Fragment, W, IX, 329)

A consolatory role for the poet extended back, of course, to antiquity.
Gorgias had said, "The inspired incantation of words can induce
pleasure and avert grief."

The connection between skepticism and consolation was a contemporary recognition. "Dover Beach" appeared in 1867. Two years earlier J. A. Symonds had candidly written in his diary the facts of the
situation: "Scepticism is my spirit. In my sorest needs I have had no
actual faith, and have said to destruction, 'Thou art my sister.' To the

skirts of human love I have clung, and I cling blindly. But all else is chaos – a mountain chasm filled with tumbling mists."[4]

Dickinson sustained "with Thews of Hymn / And Sinew from within," as she wrote in poem 616. It was also a perfectly natural role for her, in her time, as a participant in what was called Christian stewardship. She was fully conscious of this role of the artist. Quite deliberately in poem 544 she set out the simple poetics of encouragement:

> The Martyr Poets – did not tell –
> But wrought their Pang in syllable –
> That when their mortal name be numb –
> Their mortal fate – encourage Some –
> The Martyr Painters – never spoke –
> Bequeathing – rather – to their Work –
> That when their conscious fingers cease –
> Some seek in Art – the Art of Peace – (P-544)

The letter to Graves in 1854 with its garden scene had already expressed the instinctive recognition that in the face of all that departs and in the absence of a connective understanding or a place to stand within the crushing contradiction of the Christian promise of life through death, there was only love left to sustain one. And she had written to Mrs. Holland even as late as her forty-seventh year, "Had we the first intimation of the Definition of Life, the calmest of us would be Lunatics!" (L-492).

Thus some of Dickinson's energies were sublimated into channels of domestic consolation. The role was one of her great triumphs. "Let us be true to one another" is everywhere declared with great urgency and affective power. All of her poems on death are a part of this role, so that a major part of her poetry and her letters constitute a "Dover Beach" transplanted to America. Her profoundest comment on the poet's role in this regard shows her perception especially of the poet's job in creating a heaven with beauty and power—the kingdom, and the power, and the glory. In a letter to Higginson the year she died, she grasped the heart of the matter in a characteristic parable: " 'Audacity of Bliss,' said Jacob to the Angel. 'I will not let thee go except I bless thee' – Pugilist and Poet, Jacob was correct" (L-1042).

Five lines, written late and evidently sent across the yard to Sue, hold in their cryptic phrasing an essential linkage of the ignorance at

the center of her restless consciousness, the consolation role by which
it was displaced, and the simple recognition of the poet's role. Precisely here shows that cutting division between incomprehension and
sustaining art. "Nothing," I take it, is the mystery of immortality of
which there is no proof and yet its promise sustains. The poem is one
of the most curious pronouncements in our literature. Essentially
Dickinsonian, its power comes from assured words surrounding thematic mystery. The mystery has to do with what it is that would
sustain; the absence is the source of the strength.

> By homely gift and hindered Words
> The human heart is told
> Of Nothing –
> "Nothing" is the force
> That renovates the World –   (P-1563)

With such a poem, the reader comes full circle of the Dickinson phenomenon: no project but assertive strength. Camus in his youthful
writings made a similar connection between loss and loving. It was
for him the crux of the matter to know how to suffer, how to love,
and, when everything collapses, to take everything up once more.

Consolation for our ignorance in a fallen world called forth Dickinson's best efforts and her greatest candor. "No one surpassed her in
that delicate art," Richard Sewall has written with justification. It is
an art, moreover, in which she has few equals.[5] She could be cloying
as she was sometimes in her poems. She could write to Samuel
Bowles's son in 1880 on the second anniversary of his father's death
and say, "I congratulate you upon his immortality, which is a constant stimulus to my Household" (L-651). But she could also write to
her cousins on her mother's death this masterful work of self-conso-
lation in which doubt sits at the center of her strength.

Dear cousins,
    I hoped to write you before, but mother's dying almost
stunned my spirit.
    I have answered a few inquiries of love, but written little intui-
tively. She was scarcely the aunt you knew. The great mission of
pain had been ratified – cultivated to tenderness by persistent
sorrow, so that a larger mother died than had she died before.
There was no earthly parting. She slipped from our fingers like a

flake gathered by the wind, and is now part of the drift called "the infinite."

We don't know where she is, though so many tell us.

I believe we shall in some manner be cherished by our Maker – that the One who gave us this remarkable earth has the power still farther to surprise that which He has caused. Beyond that all is silence . . .

Mother was very beautiful when she had died. Seraphs are solemn artists. The illumination that comes but once paused upon her features, and it seemed like hiding a picture to lay her in the grave; but the grass that received my father will suffice his guest, the one he asked at the altar to visit him all his life.

I cannot tell how Eternity seems. It sweeps around me like a sea . . . Thank you for remembering me. Remembrance – mighty word.

"Thou gavest it to me from the foundation of the world."

Lovingly,

Emily. (L-785)

Amid the deprivations of life, she created with her language strength and ecstatic possibilities and did it with wit, courage, and a love of this world. It was a feat of sustenance in a fallen planless world. The possible world she imagined with her language shows the way she displaced an incomprehensible world with words, making a reclusive discourse of great consolatory strength. She seems to have taken upon herself in her letters and verse the keeping of the archives of all that was lost to incomprehension and death. This is why forgetfulness seemed to her so devastating an omission. "Nothing is so resonant with mystery as the friend that forgets us – the intricacy and boundlessness of her . . . so dwarfs Heaven and Hell that we think of them if at all as tepid and ignoble trifles" (PF-95 reconstructed). She summed up in poem 995 that same role she took so seriously and for which language was the only possible medium.

> Retrospection is Prospect's half,
> Sometimes, almost more.

7 The Curse of Spontaneity

Without an active prejudice, no characterization of experience is possible, let alone a planned revolution. To face Dickinson's miscellaneousness, we ourselves seek the pattern of a bias marking her intelligence, her attention, her existence. But that enabling tendency does not exist. Her mind possessed no homing instrumentation. When she wrote to Higginson in 1866 inviting him for the first time to visit her in Amherst, she located with incisive metaphoric language the truth of her condition. He had evidently asked about her interest in immortality. She replied: "You mention Immortality. That is the Flood subject." And then she made that keen self-estimate: "I was told that the Bank was the safest place for a Finless Mind." For her as an artist, the finless existence carried the affliction of spontaneity.

Without a line of vision, lacking an axis of conception, there was no Archimedean stance by which to pry the world. The world thus, as her work attests, was always a surprise. Near the end of her life, in a letter to Joseph Chickering, she still bore witness to that incessant novelty in the unbiased eye. "Life," she wrote, "never loses its startlingness, however assailed" (L-786). And so a reader becomes familiar in both her poems and prose with the diction of persistent surprise. A draft letter to Higginson following his first visit to Amherst was preoccupied with contingency. Her choice of words makes up a lexicon of tentativeness: Riddle, Surprise, Risks, enchantment, Haunted, distant, alarm, precious, harrow, possibility, interrogation, experiment, pungent, tameless. The counterbalancing vocabulary is a light ballast: stale, secure, intimate, a neighbor's cottage, obtained (L-353). The diction attests to a fundamental truth of her existence, that she had no way of addressing the world of exterior experience, let alone entering that world. The consequence for her as an artist is a fundamental aesthetic dilemma.

It was a lifelong condition contrary to what her critics assert. In early letters to Mrs. Holland, partly pose but revealing all the same, she portrayed herself as scatter-brained, talked of "getting wild" and forgetful, and in a letter of 1856 signed herself "mad." As late as 1877, she used the words by which we must characterize her intellectual stance as well as her poetic consciousness: inordinate and unruly. When she attempted in the fullness of her poetic activity a larger definition of her purpose, she left us only in mystery. I believe her word *circumference* meant to her the visible, natural periphery of all of God's realm to which the Bible's wisdom was the center. Yet at the center of her bold assertion lay only the vagueness of her self-identification. In two letters in the intensity of that summer of 1862 when she first sought from Higginson a definition of her power, she came figuratively, and of course cryptically, to that statement of purpose. "My Business is Circumference." She wrote then to the Hollands: "*My* business is to love," "*My* business is to *sing*" (L-268, 269). Amid death and ignorance, her role was indefinite in a most intense way.

The evidence shows she came short of finality in her work. There is no regular movement of the imagination toward an obsessive truth, as one traces in other poets. Higginson described the incoherence accurately in 1890 in his piece in *The Christian Union*, where he said her work was "without proper control," it made "wonderful strokes and felicities, and yet an incomplete and unsatisfactory whole." It was not that she was impatient with finality, for that in itself demands a choice and a strong bias. She suffered from a profound inability to effect finality because at her mind's center, in the parable of the Fall that she reenacted, she had been excluded from knowing. The lack of a settled mind accounts for the brevity of individual works, their conceptual fragmentation, and the variants that were never decided upon. The lack of design, of duration, then, is the manifest sign of the lack of authority with which to stand against reality if not to enter fully into it.

Her art therefore was not an instrument to perceive daily affairs, let alone society in a larger aspect or history at all. Instead it was a running chant, word making to interrupt the silence of incomprehension. A canon of odds and ends, a chatter of word play that disengages from and replaces outside reality, contradictory in attitudes, it evinces what the artist was able to create: an identifiable style and an identifiable but undefined presence, that is, a word system, word masks.

Discrete parts, impressions and attitudes, more or less of equal weight, the poems could not be arranged by her to make an address toward or a priority about the world. In theory she could have written, I repeat, an unlimited number of her poems. Only mortality could impose a limit. The significance of this is astounding: she could have written endlessly because she had no way of knowing when she was finished. There could be no *summa*. There was only this impressive linguistic power, startling, but free of the defining pressures from outside reality or from inside purpose. It was an art independent and in endless orbit. In that loose dynamic, as we shall see later in a discussion of Dickinson and contemporary women poets, lies a unique and destructive prospect for the art of any who follow her.

Solving the Conceptual Mysteries

The Dickinson affliction of inordinateness had its own interior imperative. Her intense linguistic consciousness rose from irrepressible need, but she was unable to give the poems definition, individually or as a body. Instead, these aggressive poems are hermetic speech without exterior reference; they are their own end, life is outside and the only act that matters is the poem.

We mistake Dickinson therefore when we expect her to show a rigorous coherence or systematic thought. Her true presence is to be found not in the explicit content of the discourse but in the revelations that emerge from the absences in the poetry canon itself. This, in effect, is a semiotics of the Dickinson evasions. It is more terrifying, more stunning to contemplate than any of the schemes that critics or psycho-biographers have devised. Hers was a life, a consciousness, and an art of extreme intensity but without a goal that could assuage those urgent needs. The artist's life was a noted case of modern frustrations, of the unaccommodated poet after the Fall. It was existence in a free-fall zone, without gravity, weightless.

With this knowledge we can begin to solve the most vexing conceptual enigmas that lie wrapped inside the technical mysteries that I discussed earlier. The revelation must begin with a clearer view of the absolute novelty of this woman. To that end, a basic assumption must be dismantled. "Works of literary art," Donald Davie has written, "are conditioned by economic and political forces active in the society from which those works spring and to which they are directed, forces which bear in on the solitary artist as he struggles to compose."[1] The stark exception to this conventional and therefore accurate wisdom is Emily Dickinson. In this she no doubt proves the generalization. It is a remarkable role to fill as the unique case. The consequences of her exceptional position are manifest in the avoidances that mark her poetry.

1. *There is no history in the poems.* Certainly the main omission in the poems is the Civil War. Not only is there no history in the poems, the poems have no history. Almost without exception Dickinson did not date her poems. The outside world and the war, notice of a historical sense of dates, or calendar dates for the poems themselves remained invisible to the poems or irrelevant for the reason adduced: she had no basis for entering that complicated space of social experience, of events, or of dates, but rather faced entirely inward. There was no way for these poems of pure style and screened eye to see or to take in the historical world.

2. *No social consciousness informs the poems.* Not even a handful of circumstances seems to have given rise to poems. The reason is that Dickinson had no mental path by which to order social experience. Thus the poems are divorced from society, oblivious to it in a reclusive, self-delighting way. Frost's homely wisdom in his essay "The Constant Symbol" helps us to account for the inherent, experiential ignorance of the poems. He writes about the urgencies that move poems into being and shape them. Dickinson's artistic autism is defined in the simple truth of his argument. He speaks of the "freshness of a poem" when the poet is "having a thought while the reader waits a little anxiously." This "inner mood" is the instinctive gesture with which the poem begins—it is "feeling before knowing"—and this carries a way into the poem. Then "the harsher discipline from without" begins, the pressure of reality and the authority of experience. Frost's conclusion is that "He who knows not both knows neither."[2]

3. *The poems present no identifiable speaker.* We realize that Dickinson partly defined her representational predicament when she told Higginson it was "a supposed person" in the poems. The voice

rarely has an age and often no gender; it emerges from no background and has no purpose beyond the speech of the moment that is the poem. The speaker is the language and does not exist outside of the utterances, does not exist before or after the poem itself. It is a markedly pure language voice, bereft of an identity.

4. *The poems show no ranking according to importance or other modes of self-selection.* There is no difference in weight, no self-defining priority by which one or the other poem is put forward with inherent decisiveness or specially intended significance. Dickinson's canon holds nothing like *Tintern Abbey* or *Four Quartets.* It comprises instead poems centered on language and not on events. Each manifestly the same phenomenon, together they are of equal gravity, equal in performance, indistinguishable in signifying value.

5. *There is no ars poetica.* There is almost no consciousness in the poems of the art of poetry. This absence of abstract aesthetic musing is novel in the extreme. The reason we now know is that she had no definition of art to reproduce in the poems, no large design, no abstract cognitive sense of the possible ranges of artistic construction. There is only limited consciousness of the craft of poetry and the problematics of putting up language against a powerful, complex and opposing reality. Because she was not self-conscious in the way literary critics presume, she evidently did not see her art as an accumulating, developing process. A reader finds infrequent going back, little maturing of the sort we expect. The raw materials of a synthesis, though she surely worked energetically at her compositions, did not mean enough for her to preserve. She did not keep her worksheets, destroying them we presume as soon as they were copied over. The worksheets were as dispensable as the calendar. She had sought her self-definition from Higginson and, failing to find it because it did not exist, she remained in need of a way to arrange the world. Without that essential starting point, she had no motive to date her poems, keep her worksheets, or contemplate her art. It is an eerie absence of artistic self-consciousness, and most so perhaps because of its absence in the letters. A reader going through them carefully finds no discussion, not even with Higginson, of what it is to be a poet.

6. *Although she did not stop writing, her art never changed.* Its form, its language ploys, its unarranged mosaic of glimpses did not alter, did not evolve. The body of poems, that is, has no plot. If we overlook the significance of this phenomenon, we will not recognize

the unique identity of this poet. We have needed the full textual picture with its peculiar omissions to see what her way of writing signifies. The answer to the mystery of suspended development now seems clear. Just as there were minimal bonds between the poet and the world, there was no binding of the art by a conceptual project. In this void of solipsism, there was no dependency of the art or the mind on experience. Because a fully lived concurrent experience did not impinge on the art demanding adequate mirroring forms and capabilities, no evolution of structure occurred in the poems. To take Frost's term, there was no harsher discipline from without. And so there was no maturing formal sensitivity to contingency. Without experiential density the poet and her language faced no demand that the mirroring art change to capture the harsh complexities without.

Because reality did not impinge and no conceptual center held, no structural craft beyond the most rudimentary was called for. Her poetry was produced by explosive personal needs and the fortuitous possession of a simple hymn form. This closed condition produced an extraordinarily willful primitivism in which the style swallows the reality. All reality then looks alike, has equal gravity, and in turn forces no change.

7. *Dickinson did not give titles to her poems* (except for the nineteen she named in accompanying letters and the five actually penned on individual works). She as a poet and her art in each instance were incapable of the kind of finality that calls for titles. It is that simple. Because she had no definable purpose, and was without a sense of mastery carried through to its conclusion, she was unable to recognize the definiteness involved in putting a title to a poem. With no particular subject to her parabolic sweeps, no presiding project, and no sense of form fulfilling itself, there were no titles. The absence is emblematic of the artistic career.

8. *Dickinson did not publish her poems.* We can understand now, I believe, that her approach to Higginson was not made with a view to publication, but to the prior desperate necessity of finding a definition of purpose. Without that identification of poetic stance, she had no principle of selection by which to sift through the cherry dresser filled with poems. Because she recognized no determining cause she saw no determined effect. The poetry was incapable of characterizing itself. Locally there was no architectural plan so that she could determine when a poem was finished; generally there was no project so

that she could tell when a *body* of poetry, thematically or formally, was finished. At no moment of development might she have been able to say her project was complete, its character accomplished. Instead, this fragmented writing remained irreducible, a disorderly calculus of her exclusion from comprehension, the unorganized grammar of an absence, a fall from knowledge. It is, we shall see, pure modernity, the aimless energy of mind of the modern predicament.

An audience for her poems was, even so, a matter of occasional concern to her. She wrote the lines that follow in her early thirties, in the most productive period of her poetry years. Metaphoric and indirect, they are a simple, undeveloped reflection on fame and a public. The poem's manifest need is tellingly different from that in its paradigm "Lycidas."

> The Bird must sing to earn the Crumb
> What merit have the Tune
> No Breakfast if it guaranty
>
> The Rose content may bloom
> To gain renown of Lady's Drawer
> But if the Lady come
> But once a Century, the Rose
> Superfluous become –   (P-880)

The question runs tangential to that in "Lycidas": what use is it to write poetry if there is no reward and no reader, or only an infrequent one, say once a century? Although the Dickinson syndrome of centerlessness seems to explain why she did not publish, the issue here is more excruciating. It is not merely Milton's questioning of artistic purpose in a randomly destructive world; it is the question "Who am I?" a plaintive seeking for a purpose to hold the extraordinary power and to make a target for the words. Dickinson asked all her life the question she addressed to her loyal but helpless friend Higginson, "Who am I?" No other quest could exceed the dimension of this tragedy.

From this extended discussion of Dickinson's nodes of power and voids of purpose we come to an understanding of her existence as an artist and what is meant by the curse of spontaneity. Her act of writing was as signficant as the poetry that was a product of that act. We must make this shift in perception to seek the places of meaning in the phenomenon we call Emily Dickinson. We then come to recognize her—what is signified by *Dickinson*—as the act of writing itself, but of a very special sort. It is the act of writing in which the compulsive corporeality of language is dissociated from incomprehensible experience. Understood in its full pathos, this is the modern situation of literature in pure form. It is a far harder economy, this consciousness without plan, than the artist's bravado, say, in "The Idea of Order at Key West." Compared to Dickinson's position, Stevens' is an exaggerated and now ancient-seeming optimism. To see her clearly, we must even get beyond the optimism of Frost's faith in the possibility of momentary stays against confusion. Dickinson's situation was in the heart of confusion itself. Not only did her language not order confusion, it sprang from purposelessness itself and compounded it. Unarmed by a vision, she had her existence in purposelessness and language.

If, in a Lacanian way, we go back through the Dickinson language, retracing the tropes and the crossings, we find not an original reality at the source, only a void of mystery that changes its appearance as the reader's various approaches create this or that origin. Her tropes are everything, the expressive medium and the content itself, the signifiers and the signified inseparable.

Death as a Problem of Style

Decades of exegetical criticism, my own included, have projected Dickinson as a highly conscious, technically adept, sophisticated craftsman. The reading of her poetry benefited from this supposition because the intense linguistic activity in the poems became evident. Now our insights into her inordinate writing, conceptual vacuum, and canonical anarchy make possible new approaches to clusters of her problem poems. Broader understanding comes as we see more distinctly the problematics of Dickinson's artistic coherence and the emerging dissociation of her language from experience in the outer world. The first application of this knowledge can profitably be made to the significance of her preoccupation with death.

Yvor Winters, in that notorious judgment I have referred to, concluded that all of those poems that deal with experiences in the afterlife—toward which the horses' heads were turned—are fraudulent. Yet so many of her poems address or assume that state implicitly that his characterization might extend to the largest proportion of the canon. What are we to do with the sunset poems, for example? They are not simply about sunsets, but about the promise of immortality in these vivid, emblematic endings. The vision of death or, to use her own somber metaphor, "the Drift of Eastern Gray," pervades her writing.

Dickinson's death poems in fact are more a matter of style than of idea. To put it concisely, death is the occasion for her language performance. A poem of Donald Davie's on the death of friends, including Theodore Roethke, puts the matter for me in terms very useful in a discussion of verbal art. His poem "July, 1964" begins "I smell a smell of death," and comes to this disclosure in the final stanza:

> The practise of an art
> is to convert all terms
> into the terms of art.
> By the end of the third stanza
> death is a smell no longer;
> it is a problem of style.

In the mid-nineteenth century it would have been impossible for any artist to claim death as her peculiar property. It was a cultural obsession. Dickinson was not immune to the conventions that gave expression to the preoccupation. Her death poetry is always on the verge of it, working with the stock attitudes.

Added to this pressure of convention was the inescapable fact of death in her time and place. For everyone in that age of typhoid and tuberculosis, horse accidents and unattended childbirths, it was an immediate specter. It came suddenly and to all ages. People dreaded mail days for that reason. Dickinson said with authentic conviction that a letter is life warrant or death warrant. Her contemporaries knew what she meant. Inevitable, death was the major experience she could not withdraw from. It was the theme of much popular literature and one she substituted for experience of her own in the outside world. Death was the topic of letters, of gossip, of day-to-day social intercourse. It was what one talked about.

But Dickinson made more than conventional use of this universal theme. For her, death was the occasion for style. She sent language to tempt it, disarm it, domesticate it, and extract thrills from it. What the painter Jasper Johns has done with the American flag, as I pointed out, is a comparably brilliant exploitation of stock material. Johns, by choosing this ever-present subject, freed himself to do with it whatever his paint could manage, and that stylistic performance is the whole excitement of his art. A similar artistic usage is apparent in Dickinson and, though surely by less sophisticated aesthetic reasoning, for the same reason. Her subject was ready to hand and included the banality of treatment exemplified by Reverend William Peabody. We note by comparison that what remains in a Dickinson poem when the subject is subtracted is precisely our concern: her linguistic performance. Here is Peabody:

> Behold the western evening light!
> It melts in deepening gloom;
> So calmly Christians sink away
> Descending to the tomb.

But the subject of death held more for Dickinson than familiarity. It was simultaneously a matter of utter novelty. For this connoisseur of agitation it was also a matter of inherent movement. As novelty, it was "that odd Fork in Being's Road" and "a wild Night and a new Road." In a world of ceaseless surprise it was the essential surprise, "stupendous" as she said in a letter. "All other Surprise is at last monotonous, but the Death of the Loved is all moments – *now*" (L-801). Her verse with her genius at lexical surprise solicited this phenomenon because it was needed. Her quick two-line movements gripped the change and novelty of death, took it as their occasion. In poem 1349, we recall, she defined the quality of the subject that allowed the drama of her words: "in going is a Drama Staying cannot confer."

Death was also her figure of not knowing, a haunting presence to which as an artist she turned repeatedly in the way Cezanne, in his late work, turned to the gray rock outcropping of Mont Sainte-Victoire with its estranging quality and opaque significance. It had an irresistible appeal for Dickinson because it was the "Sacred Ignorance" in the Sunday school parables. It put an end to conjecture, the time when "subterfuge is done" and the temporary and the eternal "Apart – intrinsic – stand" (P-664). Death was the single antidote to the great ignorance that was at the core of her problem of absent identity. "We do not think enough of the Dead as exhilarants," she wrote in a fragment, "they are not dissuaders but Lures – Keepers of that great Romance" (PF-50).

The Curse of Spontaneity

In its finality, death conferred identity, giving definition to a life as it "justified" Christ or outlined a season by its end. The lowliest acquire dignity in their moment of passing. All this was familiar thematic material for Dickinson, as here in this stanza of poem 1497:

> The hight of our portentous Neighbor
> We never know –
> Till summoned to his recognition
> By an Adieu –

In that movement into identity which she craved because of her own need, the dead have as she said "leaned into Perfectness" (P-962).

But beyond its significance to her as an emblem of completion, death meant most to her as an artist. It was the essential shock that called forth her ingenuity. She made her language grasp the absurdity of it, its "livid Surprise." That ingenuity, as I attempted to show earlier, is the cause of the persistent novelty in reading Dickinson, death being the theme upon which she played the seemingly endless variations of which language is capable. As in Stevens so often, it is the "enhancing Shadow" that enables her language of strangeness and her attempts to capture the fleeting moments that, like the seasons with their "fatal promptness," carried ever so subtly the strokes of fate. Out of that sacred ignorance of death and that generative poverty rose her ceaseless imagination. She came back and back again to play new words across its livid surprise, made the subject her principal trope, the source of her metaphors, and the emblem of her ignorance. Personified, death in her purview became some of the unique characters in our literature, including the country squire and the face of steel, a mid-nineteenth-century "Rock Drill." It was the first poverty out of which sprang her unique linguistic activity.

She could be abysmally mortuary with her poems of spiritual sustenance and her dutiful letters on faith and immortality in graveside prose. She could even verge on the ghoulish as in the poem that begins "If I may have it, when it's dead." These were conventions she shared with her contemporaries and most perhaps with the clergymen and women writers who, as Ann Douglas has written, "depicted and emphasized heaven as a continuation and glorification of the domestic sphere . . . an intricate compliment to themselves."[3] She employed death in the way people use the weather as an excuse for communicating. She was not unconscious of her preoccupation and said as much in a letter to the Norcross cousins in the early 1860s, beginning her remark with a rare reference to death in the Civil War. She then turned to her own preoccupation:

> Sorrow seems more general than it did, and not the estate of a few persons, since the war began; and if the anguish of others helped one with one's own, now would be many medicines . . . I noticed that Robert Browning had made another poem, and was astonished – till I remembered that I, myself, in my smaller way, sang off charnel steps.   (L-298)

If death, like memory, was for Dickinson a familiar realm linked always with language's preservative power, a place where parting is no more, where the loved ones that are lost reside, it was for the artist the emblem of absent knowledge that offered her the occasion not only to be epitaphic but also outrageous, witty, punning, self-dramatizing, and to display her independence. In a word, death was a summoner of style. If we attend to those death poems now with new eyes we can see the places where language as mimetic instrument or as rhetoric of consolation gives way in a characteristic Dickinson movement to an interplay of tropes. In certain poems we can see the places where this crossing from subject matter into language happens.

I discussed poem 881 as a poem of separation and loss, Dickinson's obsessive theme of victimization by ignorance, which turns into performance of style. In that poem the first location of style coincides with a location of meaning in the first line where grammar is preserved but the sense is mightily strained by the unnatural choice of an object for the verb: "I've none to tell me to but Thee." As we saw, the poem's purpose is its *style* of rendering loss—in language violations, paradox, the displacement of viewpoints, and an unexpected metaphor. Death as her great troping subject is more apparent elsewhere, and a worksheet will show us Dickinson actually at work on the style. The first line of the draft poem catches the reader with a crazy-seeming paradox compacted into four single-syllable words:

> Praise it – 'tis dead –
> It cannot glow –
> Warm this inclement Ear
> With the encomium it earned
> Since it was gathered here –
> Invest this alabaster Zest

The Curse of Spontaneity

> In the Delights of Dust –
> Remitted – since it flitted it
> In recusance august.   (P-1384)

Dickinson labored over the word "glow," trying out on her work-sheet "thrill" and "blush" to make a submerged metaphor of heat and excitement. In the word "inclement" she chose surprise against sense. But power comes with ironic wit in the bold figures for life and death as they face each other, "the Delights of Dust" against the exotic, oxymoronic "alabaster Zest." The closing emblematic figure for death is one of Dickinson's wonderfully final, utterly compact labels she seemed never to exhaust: "recusance august." Leading into that showy close is a little tour de force of internal assonance that only Marianne Moore might duplicate: "Remitted – since it flitted it," abstract and witty as jazz scat. Syntax has not suffered from the syllabic form, fitting in with an unaccustomed ease and completeness.

Death in another poem is overwhelmed at the outset by Dickinson's audacious first-line pun on "finished." Thereafter, in eight lines, death as a subject never recovers an equal footing with the style. The second stanza's absurd inversions to meet syllabic count is an added distraction. But the appropriation of vast size and time that, to rearrange and paraphrase, "enables us to infer *preciser* what we are" creates the edge of wit. Its signal is Dickinson's unnatural trick in "preciser," style overpowering death:

> There is a finished feeling
> Experienced at Graves –
> A leisure of the Future –
> A Wilderness of Size.
>
> By Death's bold Exhibition
> Preciser what we are
> And the Eternal function
> Enabled to infer.   (P-856)

The poem that begins "The Admirations – and Contempts – of time" and continues with considerable solemnity (there is none of the humor of "alabaster Zest") even so has locations of style clearly in view, drawing attention from the mortuary subject. The first one is the "Open Tomb," which follows directly upon the disarming promise of "justest." At line four, Dickinson uses a term of close and orderly calibration to define a change of immense vagueness. With "Reorganizes Estimate" the poem has made its swift movement from description into style, from rhetorical persuasion into language dance, and from conventional sentiment into wit. In the middle of the poem in a stroke of primitive humor, Dickinson puts the poem in a linguistic seesaw between what was and what is to be, the finite and the infinite, time and timelessness, the see-and-saw of "Compound Vision." The whole poem dances with style. Its subject could as well have been the science of optics. For Dickinson it was death with its void and novelty that animated the style.

> The Admirations – and Contempts – of time –
> Show justest – through an Open Tomb –
> The Dying – as it were a Hight
> Reorganizes Estimate
> And what We saw not
> We distinguish clear –
> And mostly – see not
> What We saw before –
>
> 'Tis Compound Vision –
> Light – enabling Light –
> The Finite – furnished
> With the Infinite –
> Convex – and Concave Witness –
> Back – toward Time –
> And forward –
> Toward the God of Him –   (P-906)

If calling "seesaw" a pun seems farfetched, readers may look at poem 292, a death poem that has the nerve to talk about the "steady posture" held in the "Brass arms" of death. The closing quatrain treats the soul's restlessness to fly to its fulfillment:

> If your Soul seesaw –
> Lift the Flesh door –
> The Poltroon wants Oxygen –
> Nothing more –   (P-292)

The movement of Dickinson's poetic language from its mimetic function into the dance of its own possibilities occurs in an extraordi-

nary way in the poem that begins " 'Twas warm – at first – like Us."
Aside from the devouring egotism of her style the subject corpse is
itself never depicted beyond the pronoun "it." Death is instead an
array of language analogues: "like frost upon a Glass," "The Forehead copied stone," "The busy eyes congealed like a Skater's Brook."
All the figural moments are gathered up and epitomized in a stroke of
linguistic bravado when the corpse displays its novel inertness, its
cold beyond simple cold, having "multiplied indifference." That deft
word juncture is style in the place of subject.

> 'Twas warm – at first – like Us –
> Until there crept upon
> A Chill – like frost upon a Glass –
> Till all the scene – be gone.
>
> The Forehead copied Stone –
> The Fingers grew too cold
> To ache – and like a Skater's Brook –
> The busy eyes – congealed –
>
> It straightened – that was all –
> It crowded Cold to Cold –
> It multiplied indifference –
> As Pride were all it could –
>
> And even when with Cords –
> 'Twas lowered, like a Weight –
> It made no Signal, nor demurred,
> But dropped like Adamant.   (P-519)

I started this excursion into death and Dickinson's style with a few
lines from a Donald Davie poem. As a poet he repeatedly considers
the way subjects turn into concerns of style. Perhaps this crossing
from rhetoric to play is more noticeable with the seemingly intractable subject of death. Dickinson is a pure practitioner of this. Death
was the subject the culture held out for her, but it was her special emblem of the lack of identity she suffered. For this recluse exempt from
experience it was, however trite in the literary conventions, a superb
trigger to her style. To see this and to see as well how Dickinson's
language has pulled away from actual experience, we have only to
subtract from a Dickinson death poem the Sunday school conventions. What is left is her language, urgent and self-sufficient. The
portion that is left is almost the whole shimmer of the poem.

Problem Poems: Wife and Bride

Dickinson's dissociation of language from verifiable experience created in the death poems a self-enclosed, spontaneous discourse of conspicuous style. Recognizing this linguistic reclusion will help readers to address her problem poems. Can such poems now, in the light of our observations, be made intelligible? The wife and bride poems, perhaps the most puzzling cluster in the Dickinson canon, seem to be primary examples of an art unanchored in reality. To what extent are they the inevitable texts of a programless poet? Her marriage poems are radically indefinite, even opaque. While they show urgency of consciousness and language of great force, at the same time most often they deliberately evade reality and thus evade meaning. It is in the evasions themselves that we must look for significance. "This is what I had to 'tell' you," Dickinson wrote to Bowles when she sent him the mysterious poem beginning "Title Divine – is mine! / The Wife – without the Sign!" Our task is to find what that cryptic declaration and the other problematic wife poems tell us. For in these rare combinations of linguistic power and inconclusiveness we have Dickinson's telling links to the extreme modern condition.

In earlier discussion of Dickinson's tropes, I tried to show how the habitual metonymic gesture carried her an unrecoverable distance from the origins of her figures. Murmuring thread as the metaphoric extraction for a pinetree, a plank in air for an insect, and an ice-covered road for all of the lost past were some of the examples. In each case Dickinson had employed a trope so removed from its origin that no remnant of its basis remained in evidence. The wife poems are a major example of this same habit of poetic making. Marriage was her trope and the trope became her subject, not the fact of marriage itself. That is, the *language* of marriage became poems that in turn were parables of a concealed need. The wife poems, in short, are the culmination of the Dickinson troping habit. My term was unanchored tropism. We are dealing not with carelessness here, but with a mode of writing of the greatest significance for poetic language in this country. Dickinson must be taken seriously even when she is most willfully obscure. The hard kernel of her intellect and intention will show through and we must respect it. One cutting remark gives us a glimpse of the metallic interior. Writing to her brother at the age of twenty-three, she showed her steely side. Evidently Austin had written to say their Uncle Joel Norcross had found his recent trip to Amherst dull. Dickinson replied: "So Joel didn't have a remarkable trip up here – wonder which enjoyed it the most – the pestilence, or the victims – Dont tell him what I said" (L-128). The tough intelligence shows through more fully and more benignly in poems like the one that follows, where she is concerned with the intricate process of making beauty, fate's role in this, and the precariousness of life. She was simplifying for eight lines but the thinking remained taut. Her figure is a flower but the concern of the poem, unlike the wife poems, is in view. With a primitivist wisdom, it has to do with result, coming into fulfillment, wholeness, all the things she had not attained herself in a way she could name. Here she also attends explicitly to the exigencies the world supplies to prevent identity.

> Bloom – is Result – to meet a Flower
> And casually glance
> Would cause one scarcely to suspect
> The minor Circumstance
>
> Assisting in the Bright Affair
> So intricately done
> Then offered as a Butterfly
> To the Meridian –
>
> To pack the Bud – oppose the Worm –
> Obtain it's right of Dew –
> Adjust the Heat – elude the Wind –
> Escape the prowling Bee
>
> Great Nature not to disappoint
> Awaiting Her that Day –
> To be a Flower, is profound
> Responsibility –   (P-1058)

The wife poems are concerned with life passages, with changes of status and, like the flower poem, with the acquisition of identity. There are several distinct cruxes of association for Dickinson: bridehood as a woman's normal expectation; the lurid convention of death claiming a living bride; the quasi-biblical figure of the bride of immortality; the bride of an art that bestows immortality; wifehood in a marriage to revelation and final knowledge; and wifehood as a social contract with a man. Wifehood, finally, served as an emblem for the need for status and for definition. Often in Dickinson's parabolic poems one type of wifehood status merges with another.

In "Given in Marriage unto Thee," the biblical language describing a marriage into death and immortality is contrasted with a mortal wedlock of choice, which is in turn the wedlock that "decays" with mortality. Tactfully, she omitted the second stanza from the copy she sent to Sue in the early 1860s.

> Given in Marriage unto Thee
> Oh thou Celestial Host –
> Bride of the Father and the Son
> Bride of the Holy Ghost.
>
> Other Betrothal shall dissolve –
> Wedlock of Will, decay –
> Only the Keeper of this Ring
> Conquer Mortality –   (P-817)

Dickinson's expectations of her own wedlock of will were genuine when she was a young woman. She participated in the social rites as assiduously as any of her young friends, with valentines, with invitations to gatherings, with pert notes to young men at Amherst College, and by accepting invitations to ride or to read together. At twenty-one she revealed to Sue some of her vivid thoughts about marriage and what it entailed. "How dull our lives must seem to the bride, and the plighted maiden," she wrote, "whose days are fed with gold, and who gathers pearls every evening." "But to the *wife*, Susie," she continued, "sometimes the *wife forgotten*, our lives perhaps seem dearer than all others in the world; you have seen flowers at morning, *satisfied* with the dew, and those same sweet flowers at noon with their heads bowed in anguish before the mighty sun; think you these thirsty blossoms will *now* need naught but – *dew?* No, they will cry for sunlight, and pine for the burning noon, tho' it scorches them, scathes them; they have got through with peace – they know that the man of noon, is *mightier* than the morning and their life is henceforth to him" (L-93). Several poems display active expectations in this regard, hardly the alienation or repudiation that a few readers have attributed to Dickinson in an attempt to recruit her after the fact to militant feminist positions. The bride of death moves in among the others in the sprightly, exaggeratedly cloying valentine Dickinson sent when she was twenty to a young bachelor in her father's law office. Here are lovers, damsels and hopeless swain, bride and bridegroom, set amid all the other pairings throughout nature ("The bee doth court the flower, the flower his suit receives"), including the courtship of death: "The *worm* doth woo the *mortal*, death claims a living bride" (P-1). The poet gleefully ran the gamut from death to the bee in the flower. The poem, in fact, is a simple catalogue of the types she was to return to throughout her writing. I have already noted the poem "A Wife at Daybreak – I shall be" as a counterfeit experience of the Parable of the Ten Virgins. In this poem as well the marriage is a graveyard type.

> I live with Him – I see His face –
> I go no more away
> For Visiter – or Sundown –
> Death's single privacy
>
> The Only One – forestalling Mine –
> And that – by Right that He
> Presents a Claim invisible –
> No Wedlock – granted Me – (P-463)

The wife-at-daybreak poem is a paradigm of the immortality cluster, perhaps as many as forty poems, in which Dickinson used the language of wifehood. Poem 473, from about 1862 or before, closes with a cryptic assertion of fulfillment in the figure of marriage:

> No more ashamed –
> No more to hide –
> Meek – let it be – too proud – for Pride –
> Baptized – this Day – A Bride –

The beginning of the poem shows how the habit of indefiniteness and neglect of circumstance in the language signify through absence of reality and transcendence of the soul in immortality.

> I am ashamed – I hide –
> What right have I – to be a Bride –
> So late a Dowerless Girl –
> Nowhere to hide my dazzled Face –
> No one to teach me that new Grace –
> Nor introduce – my Soul –

In a worksheet draft of the late years, about 1880 perhaps, Dickinson was still employing the language of change, coaxing out the exhilaration for her in this parable of the ascension. What she lacked in certitude of belief she supplied in extravagance of language-heightened emotion. Her words never exhausted the novelty of the conceit.

> The Thrill came slowly like a Boon for
> Centuries delayed
> It's fitness growing like the Flood
> In sumptuous Solitude –
> The desolation only missed
> While Rapture changed it's Dress
> And stood amazed before the Change
> In ravished Holiness –   (P-1495)

A different type of status change in Dickinson's wife and bride poems is more problematic for it relates at best indirectly to consciousness of her role as a poet. Twentieth-century readers, accustomed to the obsession of modern poetry with the poet's consciousness of self and of the text as poetry, seem irresistibly compelled to find a similar concern everywhere in Dickinson. It is present less than most presume. She believed that to be a poet was to be immortal. The idea may lurk here in secret reference in poem 454, which begins:

> It was given to me by the Gods –
> When I was a little Girl –

The ending suggests a claim to the exalted rank of poet. Not the figure of wifehood exactly, the joining of gold and difference are of a piece with the wife poems.

> Rich! 'Twas Myself – was rich –
> To take the name of Gold –
> And Gold to own – in solid Bars –
> The Difference – made me Bold –

Adrienne Rich's feminist view that links female creativity with an imagined male figure, a metaphor that in Dickinson's time would decorously emerge in a marriage trope, is appropriately invoked here: "I suggest that a woman's poetry about her relationship to her daemon—her own active, creative power—has in patriarchal culture used the language of heterosexual love or patriarchal theology." In the case of Dickinson, Rich refers specifically to the poems "He fumbles at your Soul" and "He put the Belt around my life." "These two poems," she says, "are about possession, and they seem to me a poet's poems—that is, they are about the poet's relationship to her own power, which is exteriorized in masculine form, much as masculine poets have invoked the female Muse."[4] Harold Bloom has suggested that the carriage and the idea of Immortality in "Because I could not stop for Death" refer to her art, "her first self-recognition, her first apprehension that the chariot belonged to her poetry."[5]

Dickinson's most powerful group of wife poems has to do with marriage to final knowledge, to revelation involving resignation in the face of the irreversible. Some pieces are ecstatic and others are dark and hopeless. To be a wife in this final understanding is, to use her phrase, to walk "within the Riddle." The condition bears on the change in status and knowledge in the little-girl poem that begins "We talked as Girls do." That elevation to maturity and understanding, to power and identity, is part of the curiously vague notion of "Degree":

> We handled Destinies, as cool –
> As we – Disposers – be –
> And God, a Quiet Party
> To our Authority –
>
> But fondest, dwelt upon Ourself
> As we eventual – be –
> When Girls to Women, softly raised
> We – occupy – Degree –

"Occupying Degree" is ambiguous here, and refers to womanhood as well as the ascension through death to immortality. In these sentiments Dickinson's poetry is as soulful as any of her contemporaries in the popular press.

But marriage to final knowledge is also the subject of poem 1756, a harrowing poem on confronting the bedrock of destiny. Dickinson, in yet another use of the wife figure, merged the metaphor of marriage with a prison sentence. The bride is condemned to live with winter knowledge after some indefinite catastrophe has interrupted her summer happiness. The poem, to which I return in Chapter 9, conveys the dissonance and audacity of a poem written yesterday. Here is a bride not of awe but of desolation.

> 'Twas here my summer paused
> What ripeness after then

> To other scene or other soul
> My sentence had begun.
>
> To winter to remove
> With winter to abide
> Go manacle your icicle
> Against your Tropic Bride

The rhetorical question of lines two and three can be unknotted and paraphrased this way: What ripening was possible after summer stopped which would enable me to live somewhere else or with another person? Bride here means to know despair fully, to marry fate, and thereafter to be inseparable from it. It is to marry loss and absence. The poem's crushing weight of desolation is carried in only thirty-five words. The first four and a half acts of *King Lear* have been compressed into fewer than three dozen words, so to speak, a feat of elemental extraction I think not to be surpassed in the work of any other poet.

Dickinson's poems, we must note, also contain depictions of actual married life. In addition to parables of such indefiniteness that they accommodate ideas of both spiritual and artistic immortality and include at the other extreme marriage to hopelessness, she imagined real wifehood in actual union. Poem 493, although it drifts in the last eight lines into vague recollection of a dream "Too beautiful – for Shape to prove," manages in the opening lines the simple sincerity of a real relationship. The lines carry a conviction that, if one did not know of Dickinson's lifelong celibacy, could be taken as the confession of a wife's affection, humility, and gratitude.

> The World – stands – solemner – to me –
> Since I was wed – to Him –
> A modesty befits the soul
> That bears another's – name –
> A doubt – if it be fair – indeed –
> To wear that perfect – pearl –
> The Man – upon the Woman – binds –
> To clasp her soul – for all –

Dickinson viewed in an authentic way some of the limitations entailed in marriage commitments and the reticence in which those frustrations are concealed. One poem is a remarkably realistic piece far removed from the gushing parables of ascension into immortality.

The Curse of Spontaneity

> She rose to His Requirement – dropt
> The Playthings of Her Life
> To take the honorable Work
> Of Woman, and of Wife –
>
> If ought She missed in Her new Day,
> Of Amplitude, or Awe –
> Or first Prospective – Or the Gold
> In using, wear away,
>
> It lay unmentioned – as the Sea
> Develope Pearl, and Weed,
> But only to Himself – be known
> The Fathoms they abide –   (P-732)

The celibate poet envisions in one poem, it seems to me, an actual life married to a minister. The view of a wife's day, surely, is naive in its homely idealism. Yet the lines create the feeling that the husband in this case has a real counterpart in the world. I find this poem exceedingly pathetic in its show of the stereotypical devotion for which this solitary figure could summon words. Although there is implied comparison in the poem with a heavenly home, it is mainly an imagining of a married life. The middle stanzas draw the domestic scene in full.

> What Mornings in our Garden – guessed –
> What Bees – for us – to hum –
> With only Birds to interrupt
> The Ripple of our Theme –
>
> And Task for Both –
> When Play be done –
> Your Problem – of the Brain –
> And mine – some foolisher effect –
> A Ruffle – or a Tune –
>
> The Afternoons – Together spent –
> And Twilight – in the Lanes –
> Some ministry to poorer lives –
> Seen poorest – thro' our gains –
>
> And then Return – and Night – and Home –
>
> And then away to You to pass –
> A new – diviner – care –
> Till Sunrise take us back to Scene –
> Transmuted – Vivider –   (P-944)

Wifehood in some of her associations meant to sustain another in adversity, to serve, endure, support. Finally, wifehood was for her both the emblem and the label for a commitment that was unbreakable. She brought to this theme and figure an urgency of language equal to that in any other portion of her writing.

> Rearrange a "Wife's" affection!
> When they dislocate my Brain!
> Amputate my freckled Bosom!
> Make me bearded like a man!

If not the poet, the poem at least has a person in mind, for the speaker at the end awaits the day when she will no longer bear her secret burden of love, showing then "Anguish – bare of anodyne" when she goes "through the Grave to thee" (P-1737).

Through the cluster of wife poems, no matter what the indicated association—actual bridehood, death, immortality, art—the single need is for identity. Each poem of the kind summons a vocabulary to define change and ascension. They are poems of passage, with the specific nature of the passage obscure, troped at an angle. In the end these poems are a practicing of death, that is, allegories of annihilation transformed into gain. They are her whistling by the graveyard, as she told Higginson in an early letter: "I sing, as the Boy does by the Burying Ground – because I am afraid" (L-261). The paradigm of the sort is the poem that begins "I'm 'wife' – I've finished that." It is indefinite even as it expresses the urgency of some passage in life. Published in the 1890 edition in the section entitled "Love," with its own title "Apocalypse" supplied by her editors, this poem about wifehood written by the Amherst recluse seems not to have shocked anyone. The editors had removed the quotation marks around *wife* and *woman*, excising the irony so that the poem reads evenly, without a slant attitude.

> I'm "wife" – I've finished that –
> That other state –
> I'm Czar – I'm "Woman" now –
> It's safer so –   (P-199)

Its terms, although indefinite in reference to any real experience, establish the importance of the change in rank. The present state of wife, czar, woman is set against girlhood, heaven opposed to earth, comfort opposed to pain. The emotional potency beneath the surface is glimpsed by the phrase "It's safer so" and by the faint suggestion that present *comfort* is not unqualified. Insistent on the change, forceful in its terms, the poem is yet vague as always in its specific import.

Death and artistic maturity as primary ideas merged behind the poet's refusal to think through the distinctions. In lines extracted from a letter to one of her Norcross cousins following the death of Elizabeth Barrett Browning in June 1861, Dickinson associates "women" with literary maturity and "Queen" as well, and then both terms with immortality. She is attempting evidently to reassure the cousin concerning some youthful sadness, but the line of her association of ideas, however confused, comes through. "Your letters are all real," she writes, "just the tangled road children walked before you, some of them to the end, and others but a little way, even as far as the fork in the road." This is conventional consolation in mortuary terms. Dickinson continues, however, with thoughts of literary rank and spiritual immortality. "That Mrs. Browning fainted, we need not read *Aurora Leigh* to know, when she lived with her English aunt; and George Sand 'must make no noise in her grandmother's bedroom.' Poor children! Women, now, queens, now! And one in the Eden of God. I guess they both forget that now, so who knows but we, little stars from the same night, stop twinkling at last?" (L-234).

The terms of the change in rank are similar to those in the poem "I'm 'wife' – I've finished that." This conjunction leads to poem 593 in which the climactic change is untypically definite, and I think that the particular change having to do with Dickinson's first reading of Barrett Browning is a major one and stirs imperceptibly behind several of the allegories of status and passage. It is a poem of setting out, of undergoing a crucial experience and being sharply conscious of it. The poem can stand as a model of these curious change and wedlock poems, for the reading of Browning can be associated with Dickinson's figurative wedlock to her. It is as crucial to our understanding of Dickinson's early poetic epiphany as Emerson's eyeball moment or his poem "The Problem." In the sixth stanza the change is compared to religious conversion and in the next stanza to a "Divine Insanity." As a result of the change, all reality is transformed. Like the wife poems, the Browning poem defines the status of revelation. It is definite in reference and thus in a rare circumstantial way establishes for us this crucial experience in Dickinson's artistic career. The poem is on the verge of hysteria in its joined urgency and ecstasy, art and sainthood. It must be presented in full.

I think I was enchanted
When first a sombre Girl –
I read that Foreign Lady –
The Dark – felt beautiful –

And whether it was noon or night –
Or only Heaven – at Noon –
For very Lunacy of Light
I had not power to tell –

The Bees – became as Butterflies –
The Butterflies – as Swans –
Approached – and spurned the narrow Grass –
And just the meanest Tunes –

That Nature murmured to herself
To keep herself in Cheer –
I took for Giants – practising –
Titanic Opera –

The Days – to Mighty Metres stept –
The Homeliest – adorned
As if unto a Jubilee
'Twere suddenly confirmed –

I could not have defined the change –
Conversion of the Mind
Like Sanctifying in the Soul –
It Witnessed – not explained –

'Twas a Divine Insanity –
The Danger to be Sane
Should I again experience –
'Tis Antidote to turn –

To Tomes of solid Witchcraft –
Magicians be asleep –
But Magic – hath an Element
Like Deity – to keep –   (P-593)

The wedding figure is directly associated with Browning in another poem, 631, and with this before us we can recognize how the merging of terms occurs: art, death, and immortality. A companion piece to "I think I was enchanted," the poem contains the line "I too – received the Sign," indicating how closely Dickinson identified her compelling need with her reading of Browning. It is a poem of decisive change, a passage to a new status. Perhaps it reflects the crucial one in Dickinson's life and lurks beneath all the other wifehood poems.

> Ourselves were wed one summer – dear –
> Your Vision – was in June –
> And when Your little Lifetime failed,
> I wearied – too – of mine –
>
> And overtaken in the Dark –
> Where You had put me down –
> By Some one carrying a Light –
> I – too – received the Sign.
>
> 'Tis true – Our Futures different lay –
> Your Cottage – faced the sun –
> While Oceans – and the North must be –
> On every side of mine
>
> 'Tis true, Your Garden led the Bloom,
> For mine – in Frosts – was sown –
> And yet, one Summer, we were Queens –
> But You – were crowned in June – (P-631)

The next to final line has one significant change in the variant version: "And yet, one Summer we were *wed.*" The crown of the last line of course refers to Browning's death and immortality. If we cast this allegory of wedding back over the wife poems, we see the persistent concern for the experience of change. In the enveloping haze of Dickinson's urgent indefiniteness and evasion of specifying, the setting-out poem on Browning is the center.

Mindful of these intense poems of oblique definition, of change that is hidden in the allegory of marriage, and set against the circumstance of this poet who herself lacked an identity and a stance in the world, we can approach the puzzling poem Dickinson sent to Bowles in 1862. It is a model of evasion, of language crafted to carry emotion without verifiable reference. "Title divine – is mine!" has combined in it all the elements that swirl about in the Dickinson charade of nomination. It has both wife figures and figures of divine immortality. It has, surely, the strangest hyperbole Dickinson was ever to concoct to measure the magnitude of the change she repeatedly made her art grasp. The phrase "Born – Bridalled – Shrouded / In a Day" means to assert that the change, whatever it was, was like living one's whole life in twenty-four hours. That is the impact she intended in the cryptic lines she sent to Bowles followed by her arch declaration: "Here's – what I had to 'tell you' – You will tell no other? Honor – is it's own pawn" (L-250). In a variant version, she emphasized the two lines in the poem by adding another: "Tri Victory." The poem is a suitable emblem for all I have said concerning her inability to step into reality with her language. It is language of enormous power striking into a world not understood, grasping for the terms of that power in a profusion of domestic, royal, and divine metaphors. The poem asserts an identity but in fact has no identity.

> Title divine – is mine!
> The Wife – without the Sign!
> Acute Degree – conferred on me –
> Empress of Calvary!
> Royal – all but the Crown!
> Betrothed – without the swoon
> God sends us Women –
> When you – hold – Garnet to Garnet –
> Gold – to Gold –
> Born – Bridalled – Shrouded –
> In a Day –
> Tri Victory –
> "My Husband" – women say –
> Stroking the Melody –
> Is *this* – the way?   (P-1072)

Wifehood, in fact, is diminished in each comparison and by the tone of condescension. Confused, the poem claims total knowledge but in its core has no knowledge at all, only hysteria. The speaker feels different from others, but there is no understanding the difference. The terms of identity are borrowed in each case from realms the poet did not know. Miracle enclosing ignorance, the poem has power to affect but not to mean, power without the sign. All the negatives—no sign, no crown, no swoon—extract the signs of life, leaving only the declaration. In this recognition can we say we "understand" the poem? It is "intelligible" by our perception of what it doesn't do in the way of *mean*.

What is common to the wife and bride poems is that they are parables finally of counterfeit identity and comprehension. They assert fulfillment and knowledge, but they are claims without a basis. The claim is all. The poem Dickinson sent Bowles holds the great pathos of this need of hers for definition. She sent her language again and again to make that identification, but it succeeded only in its own performing. This poem is the essential demonstration of that need. It constitutes a genre, I should say, of which Dickinson's work is the origin and the principal example: the poetry of incomprehension. In a broader view, Dickinson's wife poems comprise her intense but vague search for the terms of her vocation. Pathos-filled in their indefiniteness, the wife poems were her strange, spontaneous American Scholar address. She sought to claim an identity by allegory, but all she created was the allegory itself. Without the experience of marriage, without having moved away from the family homestead, what was to constitute maturity for her? She worried that problem of self and status through her work, and most conspicuously in the wife poems and with rare specificity in the Browning poems.

The terms for her search came first from her womanhood in which marriage would be a normal measure of identification. She mixed this vocabulary with that of the Bible, especially of Calvary and crown. It was her way as a woman to marshal the nearest terms to capture her surging need to name the instrument she wielded, her power, her purpose, and her achievement. Wifehood was the cultural label at hand which Dickinson deconstructed and appropriated for her own use. Women poets of the twentieth century were to do the same thing again, but with grimly conscious and sometimes bitter attitudes. We know now that it is an inherently feminine way: the reflexive perception of a woman trying to come upon herself, to discover an independent identity. Dickinson's search was almost purely feminine too, in the way she experienced the world as a vast hieroglyphic. The wife poems, then, were the poet's attempt to do for herself what she plaintively asked Higginson to help her do: "Could you tell me how to grow?" The terms "My Husband," "Wife," and "Woman," were part of a restless attempt to *name herself*, to find the sign that would stand for her, to give herself a title. But as with her titleless poems, she was not equipped by a sense of personal coherence to do the job of titling her self.

Though there is a hazy locus of meaning in the cluster of wife and bride poems involving intimations of status, philosophical comprehension, artistic maturity, and death and immortality all together, Dickinson never sorted them out. The poems make a disintegrated monument to indefiniteness and withdrawal. They are, in short, an inordinate swirl of sentiment. Emblematic, these occasionless poems concentrate the problems of her art: tropes of lost origin, language devoid of project, statement devoid of architecture. They are the strong speech of consciousness, allegories of a woman's unfocused power, the inevitable result of her existence. *In this aimlessness they are intelligible.* For in a real sense Dickinson, though she wanted to be the Bride of Revelation, was in fact the secluded Bride of Power and Inconclusiveness.

The Ownerless Gun

The key utterance of her stripped, existential condition is the notoriously vexing poem of the early 1860s that begins "My Life had stood – a Loaded Gun." This work vexes so thoroughly because it has concentrated in it the main elements of autism and opacity that I have outlined: extreme troping distance, absent referents in the exterior world, syntactic deletions, metonymic obscurity.[6] But we know now that Dickinson's mysteries of omission and difficulties of coherence have meaning for us, sometimes in a central way. A problem, we know, is a location of significance. Here in this poem it is a valuable opening of insight for the reader as well as an intuitive grasp on the poet's part of the central quality of her artistic being.

With a sensitivity to the locations of meaning in Dickinson's evasions, we are equipped to see that the poem is different from what we had imagined, and more important. It is a central expression of her circumstance. "My Life had stood – a Loaded Gun" deals essentially with the dilemma of instrument and purpose, that is, with the exercise of great, even destructive, power without coherent design. The gun in this poem, as the second stanza makes plain, is the instrument of language. Wordsworth had borne similar witness to the potency of the medium: "Words are too awful an instrument for good and evil to be trifled with: they hold above all other external powers a dominion over thoughts."[7] Dickinson's poem, with all its difficulties, is the symbol of her undefined life and the power of her language.

Three related functions create the signification of the poem: the poem's voice is language itself, the language gun has the power to kill, and language to be purposeful and not randomly destructive must be under some mature authority. I want to look at these three main elements in that order. The first has to do with the perception that language has been detached as an autonomous element and personified so that it speaks. In fact, Dickinson personified many abstractions, and the especially significant separation of instrument from user turns up elsewhere in Dickinson's writing. One of the notable instances is in the exuberant letter she wrote to her Uncle Joel in early 1850 which I quoted earlier. In it appears a perverse dissociation of action from responsibility that is as arresting as the problem of the gun poem. Midway in the letter she challenges her uncle to a duel because he has not written to her as he promised. This follows:

> Harm is one of those things that I always mean to keep clear of – but somehow my intentions and me dont chime as they ought – and people will get hit with stones that I throw at my neighbor's dogs – not only *hit – that* is the least of the whole – but they insist upon blaming *me* instead of the *stones* – and tell me their heads ache – why it is the greatest piece of folly on record. It would do to go with a story I read – one man pointed a loaded gun at a man – and it shot him so that he died – and the people threw the owner of the gun into prison – and afterwards hung him for *murder*. Only another victim to the misunderstanding of society – such things should not be permitted. (L-29)

Poem 479, written perhaps as much as a decade after the letter, similarly asserts this curious separation. Here knives are oblivious of their power to hurt, but so is the wielder.

> She dealt her pretty words like Blades –
> How glittering they shone –
> And every One unbared a Nerve
> Or wantoned with a Bone –
>
> She never deemed – she hurt –
> That – is not Steel's Affair –

She began a letter to Higginson in 1869, which I referred to earlier, with another assertion of her view of language as an autonomous actor. "A Letter always feels to me like immortality," she wrote, "because it is the mind alone without corporeal friend. Indebted in our talk to attitude and accent, there seems a spectral power in thought that walks alone" (L-330).

To see how Dickinson personified abstractions as she has in the poem "My life had stood," we may look at poem 1319 where News—that is, language—pierces like a dart. The stunning effect of unexpected news was an experience she shared with her pre-electronic contemporaries, as we saw earlier. Here News functions as the language gun does in "My life had stood."

> How News must feel when travelling
> If News have any Heart
> Alighting at the Dwelling
> 'Twill enter like a Dart!

Her variants for lines three and four employ the gun figure.

> Advancing on the Transport
> 'Twill riddle like a shot.

There are many other examples of personified abstractions. In poem 1203, memory—the past—is a creature with a face who can fire her "faded" or "rusty" ammunition without warning and destroy. A similar figure occurs in poem 1273 where memory is a closet which, awkwardly to be sure, is said to contain dust that can silence its owner. The logic of supersession in the final stanza parallels that in the final stanza of the gun poem.

> August the Dust of that Domain –
> Unchallenged – let it lie –
> You cannot supersede itself
> But it can silence you –   (P-1273)

If, finally, a burdock, as in poem 229, can stand for a political belief that has attached itself to Austin, then surely in Dickinson's economy a gun can be language.

The second of the main elements in the gun poem is the knowledge that language can destroy while it does not die itself. In the poem the speaker *speaks* for her Master and the hills echo in reply. This destructive power of language is a persistent theme. Like the Talmud, her poems declared that life and death are in the hands of the Tongue. Writing to Louise Norcross in 1880, Dickinson summarized that terrible power she had always ascribed to language: "What is it that instructs a hand lightly created, to impel shapes to eyes at a distance, which for them have the whole area of life or of death? Yet not a pencil in the street but has this awful power, though nobody arrests it. An earnest letter is or should be life-warrant or death-warrant, for what is each instant but a gun, harmless because 'unloaded,' but that touched 'goes off'?" (L-656). A well-known poem of a decade earlier, as Weisbuch noted, established the theme in a compact way:

> A Word dropped careless on a Page
> May stimulate an eye
> When folded in perpetual seam
> The Wrinkled Maker lie
>
> Infection in the sentence breeds
> We may inhale Despair
> At distances of Centuries
> From the Malaria –   (P-1261)

The two phenomena of language that Dickinson seemed most concerned with—its impact and its life beyond that of its maker—enter the poem "My life had stood." A network of significance can be established that will open into the problematic gun poem. Dickinson recorded her own experience of language that registered zero at the bone. When the news of George Eliot's death came, we know, she described her reaction to the Norcross cousins: "The look of the words as they lay in the print I shall never forget." Then she picked up her obsessive theme: "Amazing human heart, a syllable can make to quake like jostled tree" (L-710). She had worried the theme in a poem four years or so earlier, in about 1876. A message is the instrument of destruction even for a loved one if used cruelly.

> Death warrants are supposed to be
> An enginery of equity
> A merciful mistake
> A pencil in an Idol's [dainty] Hand
> A Devotee has oft [cool] consigned
> To Crucifix or Block   (P-1375)

Poem 1062 beginning "He scanned it – staggered" may be a dramatization of this moment of wounding. The maiming power of language finally was at the heart of the famous definition of poetry she gave Higginson when he visited her in 1870. "If I feel physically as if the top of my head were taken off, I know *that* is poetry. These are the only way I know it. Is there any other way" (L-342a). The figure of physical trauma is consistent with the gun image.

Language that "breathed" possessed to her mind an unquenchable "spirit" of the sort God made incarnate in Christ, and that spirit expires only if God condescends to be flesh again. In the meantime revelation continually is embodied in language. Dickinson used in at least one poem the metaphor of spirit and incarnation as twinned elements, the spirit that cannot die and the language that gives it body and can die only into revelation itself. Poetry would not be necessary if God condescended again to be made flesh instead of language. The interdependency of spirit and the instrument of its embodiment in this passage is an exact parallel to the abstruse close of the gun poem.

> A Word that breathes distinctly
> Has not the power to die
> Cohesive as the Spirit
> It may expire if He –
> "Made Flesh and dwelt among us["]
> Could condescension be
> Like this consent of Language
> This loved Philology   (P-1651)

The third element of this Dickinsonian triad is the most important. It is the search for the authority that will confer identity. It was the essence of her condition, and the central strand in the pleas she addressed to Higginson those first days of their correspondence, when she said she had no Monarch in her life, and for at least a decade afterward. She described herself as an explosive being without organization or authority. The extravagant description is a replica of the gun poem whose context I am reconstructing here.

Several poems early and late work variations on the theme of identity. How is character set in, they ask. Poem 493, one that belongs to the marriage group, speaks of the acquisition of "another's – name" through wedlock and the need to prove oneself adequate to "that mu-

nificence, that chose – / So unadorned – a Queen." The one beginning "He found my Being – set it up" is an undisguised dramatization of the act of identification. With our knowledge of Dickinson's
problem of nomination, it now moves us by a profound aptness, a
singular confession with cool decorum:

> He found my Being – set it up –
> Adjusted it to place –
> Then carved his name – upon it –
> And bade it to the East
>
> Be faithful – in his absence –
> And he would come again –
> With Equipage of Amber –
> That time – to take it Home –   (P-603)

This too is a poem of the setting in of character. Its lack in her own
self-regard, it seems, was at least a part of the reason for her reclusion
and one of the causes of the strange omissions in her poems. It is another glimpse into the center of the Dickinson mystery as it relates to
all the rest.

A brave presumptive allegory of identity achieved occurs in the
poem that begins "I heard, as if I had no Ear," its epiphanic claim
coming to us now with powerful cogency. So urgent and absolute is
the claim, however, that the consciousness that informs the poem creates great pathos, being most apparent in the slide into surreal indefiniteness. That surrealistic third stanza, dramatic but wholly abstract,
is a replay of the gun poem. (She may have sent a copy of the poem,
written perhaps about 1865 or before, to Higginson late in 1870. We
can only wonder whether or not he was persuaded, or sensed significance behind the dying-into-immortality convention.)

> I heard, as if I had no Ear
> Until a Vital Word
> Came all the way from Life to me
> And then I knew I heard.
>
> I saw, as if my Eye were on
> Another, till a Thing
> And now I know 'twas Light, because
> It fitted them, came in.
>
> I dwelt, as if Myself were out,
> My Body but within

Until a Might detected me
And set my kernel in.

And Spirit turned unto the Dust
"Old Friend, thou knowest me,"
And Time went out to tell the News
And met Eternity   (P-1039)

With this network of significances and a view of the simple but forceful elements that preoccupied Dickinson as an artist—her sense of language as an autonomous instrument of enormous power, its independent life for good or ill, and the cruel need for definition to displace the affliction of spontaneity—we come to the problematic gun poem broadly sensitive to the locations of its meanings. The poem is severely problematic precisely because it is so crucial to her. The gun is the emblem of Dickinson's undefined life and all those omissions that were the life's reflexive expression; it is the emblem of her inordinate power of language.

My Life had stood - a Loaded Gun -
In Corners - till a Day
The Owner passed - identified -
And carried Me away -

And now We roam in Sovreign Woods -
And now We hunt the Doe -
And every time I speak for Him -
The Mountains straight reply -

And do I smile, such cordial light
Upon the Valley glow -
It is as a Vesuvian face
Had let its pleasure through -

And when at Night - Our good Day done -
I guard My Master's Head -
'Tis better than the Eider-Duck's
Deep Pillow - to have shared -

To foe of His - I'm deadly foe -
None stir the second time -
On whom I lay a Yellow Eye -
Or an emphatic Thumb -

Though I than He - may longer live
He longer must - than I -

> For I have but the power to kill,
> Without – the power to die –   (P-754)

The poem is an allegory, almost pure in its self-regard, of language speaking itself. The earlier discussion of word-centeredness in Dickinson and her peculiar quality of linguistic autonomy has led inevitably to this pretended speech act of the ownerless gun. A feminist reading of the poem, despite its bias toward oppressor hunting in the culture, partly supports the interpretation. Adrienne Rich writes: "It is a central poem in understanding Emily Dickinson, and ourselves, and the condition of the woman artist, particularly in the 19th Century. It seems likely that the 19th-Century woman poet, especially, felt the medium of poetry as dangerous."[8]

But the truth of the poem is deeper than cultural behavior: it reaches beyond culture into the authentic realm of individual tragedy. It has to do with an artist's imagination fierce with purposelessness. With absolute concentration, the gun poem is a stunning figure for the essential Emily Dickinson. Its language does not regard the actual world. In this omission are all its problems, and in those problems of autogenous and intuitive self-concern we find the most revealing of all Dickinson's texts, a poem of the imagination's sheer instrumentality and its cry for a purpose.

The most difficult stanza, the final one, emphasizes the division of the elements I have outlined: the purposeful Master-Hunter with an identity about which the world organizes itself and makes itself intelligible—woods, valley, and mountains arrange themselves like Stevens' wilderness in Tennessee—and the instrument, long-lived, that can kill but cannot aim. Dickinson riddled her dilemma, substituting "art" for "power" at one stage:

> Though I than He – may longer live
> He longer must – than I –
> For I have but the power [art] to kill,
> Without – the power to die –

The language of poetry speaks here on its own behalf. This is why intelligibility suffers. It is the doubling folded-over speech of written language as against the practical speech of the world. The lines display a craftsman's skill of language but, abstract and therefore impractical, they do not feel the body of the world.

Finally, and this is what moves us most, the poem deceives itself. It claims a Master but has none. It knots up at the end in riddled desperation. The Master is never named. And so the poem remains a matter of words, an instrument capable of submission or of capture or of control of the world only if put in the right hands, but by itself without a clear idea about doing any one of these things. The poem's semiotic message for us lies, then, in its very indefiniteness. Significance rests not in what the poem says but in what it leaves out, what it cannot get into its words and therefore into consciousness. It is perhaps the most blindly forceful of all the works that reflect Dickinson's troubled freedom from experience, from meaning, and from identity.

She wrote to Higginson in the hope he could give that power meaning, show it its center and a place to stand in the world. Hers was a plea for her own fulfillment. What had all that power of language to achieve, what had it to *do* in the world? Higginson was sympathetic but finally not redeeming, only sustaining. The gun poem in its concern with purpose is the intuitive allegory of Dickinson's affliction. Elsewhere she had as ingenuously laid it out, in the early letters to Higginson, earlier still in the setting-out letter to Graves. She put it in a packet poem of about 1864 with disarming wit, the old exclusion from comprehension and the failure of identity all here not in speech but in art:

> Nature and God – I neither knew
> Yet Both so well knew me
> They startled, like Executors
> Of My identity.
>
> Yet Neither told – that I could learn –
> My Secret as secure
> As Herschel's private interest
> Or Mercury's affair –   (P-835)

With a child's simplicity in her second "Master" letter she touched yet again the void at the center of the relentless being: "God made me – Master – I didn't be myself." This was the central dilemma of her life and, more interesting by far than lost lovers, it is the drama of that life. It ramified all through her work and took its form not as autobiographical poems but in the extraordinary omissions that are the most telling aspect of her work. All those failures to organize, those inabilities to enter into experience, that turning away of her poetry from the world, all of this is gathered into that bold opening line of the perversely walled and inexplicit poem we now see as emblematic of the life: "My Life had stood – a Loaded Gun."

8 Dickinson and American Modernism

Higginson's face-to-face encounter with Emily Dickinson on the "unspeakably quiet" summer afternoon in 1870, eight years after their correspondence started, reveals an acute acting out on her part of the essential qualities embedded in the peculiarities of her writing. The ferocious need of a consciousness that had withdrawn from communal experience into an exclusive and idiosyncratic freedom is dramatically clear in her visitor's earnest account of the meeting. He was to write later: "The impression undoubtedly made on me was that of an excess of tension, and of an abnormal life. Perhaps in time I could have got beyond that somewhat overstrained relation which not my will, but her needs, had forced upon us" (L-342b). But beyond confirming our insights into some of the most problematic aspects of her writing, that visit, which Higginson called "a remarkable experience," opens the way for us to comprehend her elemental, not simply her superficial, modernism. The meeting enacts the beginnings of a new relationship between artistic consciousness and reality and stands, I venture to propose, in deeply contrastive importance in American poetry chronicles with that moment of perfect exhilaration a generation earlier when Emerson, on the wintry commons, felt himself transformed into a transparent eyeball.

Dickinson is now customarily placed in anthologies alongside Walt Whitman, Emerson's transforming heir, at the origins of modern American poetry. Nowhere, however, is there to be found evidence that Dickinson's placement is understood. The essential matter is covered over, in part concealed by the mistaking of modernist surface features for the deeper elements that mark literary change. To get to the radicals of Dickinson's modernism, a reader must penetrate two layers of conventions that impede his view: the conventional stylistic modernisms we recognize by thorough familiarity and the attitudinal conventions of the mid-nineteenth century. What is radically modern in Dickinson, then, must be extracted from beneath surface strategies which were her habit and from a body of mannered, consolatory poetry and prose that, though unique in voice, is conventional in attitude.

Nineteenth-Century Conventions

An integral part of Dickinson's concerns, yet the least original, is the attitudinal focus that confines her most emphatically to her historical time. In that stratum of her work are located the elements that grate most against our modernist predispositions: the funereal subject matter, the Sunday school consolations, the childish self-reference, and the banality of some of her themes. All around her, to be sure, in sermons, newspapers, political speeches, personal letters, and elsewhere, a dense rhetorical atmosphere nourished these conventions of insipidity even as it provided models for her efforts. Popular writing was occasionally witty and powerful as well as florid and weighted with the clichés of sensibility. Throughout Dickinson's work there are reflections of this subliterary activity. Heaven's democratic reception of the time-worn and poor shows up several times in the work, as here in poem 717 which begins "The Beggar Lad – dies early" and ends with stock lines and a mawkish image:

> The Childish Hands that teazed for Pence
> Lifted adoring – then –
> To Him whom never Ragged – Coat
> Did supplicate in vain –

Similarly, Dickinson rehearsed the story of the promised meeting in Heaven which served the century in an automatic way as consolation. Her poem beginning "'Twas a long Parting" contains the quintessential lines of facile sentiment that relied on stock response but were flaccid as poetry:

Before the Judgment Seat of God –
The last – and second time

These Fleshless Lovers met –
A Heaven in a Gaze –
A Heaven of Heavens – the Privilege
Of one another's Eyes –   (P-625)

Comparable to pop song lyrics in our own day, such derivative matter adds little to Dickinson's poetic stature, but it situates her realistically in her moment of history and at her level of literary sophistication. Whitman was equally influenced by the popular subliterary
efforts of his day.

In Dickinson's case, ritually sustaining others in grief and envisioning loved ones after death were cloying cultural habits, as was her
projected role of suppliant daisy, all devolved upon women by the
culture's division of roles according to sex. Looking after fellow
beings in the way we find in the poems and the letters was woman's
business. "Doing good," as it was called, was seen as the ruling purpose of women who were freed from the drudgery of the low and illiterate classes. Women thus fortunate accepted their identification
with "the heart," undertook the ties of female friendship, and made it
their pastime "to love others."[1]

Only when Dickinson audaciously employed her wit and candor to
penetrate these hackneyed layers to the deeper human truths did she
ascend to genuine poetic enterprise. How conscious or precise her
discriminating powers were is conjectural, for the triteness in her
work sits side by side with the cutting, raw poetic power and stunning psychological insight. We can observe that separation taking
place in particular poems like the famous one that begins "I died for
Beauty – but was scarce." In it, perhaps only barely deliberate in her
intention, Dickinson pulls her language away from the treacly fictions of her time, leaving a residue of existential clarity, hard-edged
fatalism. If we subtract, that is, the convention of joining truth and
beauty in ideal artistic coupling, what we have left in that remarkable
poem is the conviction that all is not right. The poem ends, as I noted
earlier, not at the eternal verities but with extinction. The offbeat
diction ("adjusted in the Tomb") and the off-rhymes play against
the syllabic and metrical regularity of the lines so that the nihilism at
the end is already sanctioned as it stands in wicked independence

from the conventional sentiment with which the little poem began. We witness Dickinson's modernism pulling free from the conventions that weighted her work and that must be distinguished if we are to see her essential lines of power. Scholarly work is just now beginning to discover the many links the poet had with the popular culture of her time. What will be found is that her initiative often came from these subliterary sources but that when she practiced her particular skills with a hard focus she could transcend this material.

Orthodox Modernisms

Dickinson's power derives partly from a cluster of techniques, from certain themes, and from tonal qualities that we consider modern and admire for their apparent newness. Her work is a catalogue of these modernisms, conventional to us now in their familiarity and so commonly known in her repertoire that a summary here will suffice. She possessed an intuitive knack for exploiting the capacity of language under certain distortions or tensions to arrest, illuminate, pierce, astonish. Her wonderfully engaging first lines range from the controlled audacity of flatness and understatement ("Before I got my eye put out") to marvelous lines of great syntactic pressure involving mystery, lure, expectation, and which play sophisticatedly with line-end novelty and grammatical deception.

The animated lexical selection that is the heart of her craft comprises violations sometimes of great daring. She surprised with her language and, when it was not so deliberately concocted as to be coy or patent, it brings off its risks and shocks in a modern way. A corpse in poem 287 is "This Pendulum of snow" and death's finality is in "Decades of Arrogance." Elsewhere her lexical surprises manage a careful deflation and austerity that dehumanize, objectify, as in these sciential lines about a corpse:

> The busy eyes – congealed –
> It straightened – that was all . . .
> It multiplied indifference

Dry and hard, spare in a Poundian sense, this cold language forms into an analytical instrument of great accuracy. There is also word parading of the sort we now admire as well in Marianne Moore. In

Dickinson's little known poem about a June bug, the polysyllables thump againt the single-syllable vernacular:

> From Eminence remote
> Drives ponderous perpendicular
> . . . .
> Depositing his Thunder
> He hoists abroad again –
> A Bomb upon the Ceiling
> Is an improving thing
> It keeps conjecture flourishing –   (P-1128)

Dickinson interrupted nineteenth-century poetic discourse with a vernacular so direct it seemed crude to her first public. She disarmingly called it in poem 373 "my simple speech" and "plain word." It was in fact flattened speech, a *talking* that was depoetizing and an escape from pomposity. Into her poems and particularly into those outrageous first lines came a natural breath and diction that created the illusion and the impact of real speech acts. Poems begin with the vernacular claim of intimate conversation and the casual form of mental activity:

> So I pull my Stockings off
> Wading in the Water
> For the Disobedience' Sake   (P-1201)
>
> Going to Him! Happy letter!
> Tell Him –
> Tell Him the page I didn't write   (P-494)
>
>   but as I
> Was saying to a friend –   (P-308)
>
> I'm Nobody! Who are you?
> Are you – Nobody – too?
> Then there's a pair of us!   (P-288)
>
> The Day the Heaven died –
> . . . .
> What Comfort was it Wisdom – was –   (P-965)

By the poems in the 200s, the vernacular speech is strong and assured. This naturalness is summed up in the situational poetics of the poem that, like a New England Preface to *Lyrical Ballads,* establishes her linguistic location:

> The Robin's my Criterion for Tune –
> Because I grow – where Robins do –   (P-285)

On occasion Dickinson's vernacular is so practiced at casualness that it fails by cloying. The daisy pose in her language, it is the vernacular with its power dissipated in coyness, as here in poem 663.

> *Alone –* if *Angels* are "alone" –
> *First time* they *try* the *sky!*

But where she is inelegant there is sometimes a latent power even when the subject matter is Sunday school piety. There is a sort of crazy salad, I think, in some lines about meeting in heaven:

> in Eternity –
> When farther Parted, than the Common Wo –
> [We] Look – feed upon each other's faces – so –
> In doubtful meal, if it be possible
> Their Banquet's real –   (P-296)

In democratizing poetry's language, Dickinson could choose the unexpected metaphor that is so modern in its distraction. In poem 556, working out the sustained figure of "The Brain, within its groove" and then of mental dissolution, she selects a conglomeration of terms: splinter, slit, Turnpike; trodden, blotted, shoved. The technique, willful and surreal, was a minor breakthrough and she carried it further. Vernacular cuts across more formal speech, as in this thematically conventional poem on loss of the loved one. The linguistic friction is satisfyingly modern, the syntax crazed.

> Erase the Root – no Tree –
> Thee – then – no me –
> The Heavens stripped –
> Eternity's vast pocket, picked –   (P-587)

Bold vernacular on the well-worn theme of loss provides new authenticity by informal frontal attack. This is the whole poem.

> To fill a Gap
> Insert the Thing that caused it –

Block it up
With Other – and 'twill yawn the more –
You cannot solder an Abyss
With Air.   (P-546)

Most modern, perhaps, among Dickinson's techniques is her use of
language realms as constitutive elements in analytical structure. She
makes the language medium itself objective and able to cut like a tool,
managing this in at least three ways: vernacular diction inserted in
formal language for its cross-cut effect; deploying Anglo-Saxon
abruptness against the formalities of Latinate diction (this has been
much noticed); and cleverly treating a subject with an alien lexical
set. An instance of this last, as I have noted elsewhere, is characterizing God in the language of law or commerce. Dickinson, intuitively
audacious in this, makes one language subset cut against and criticize
another level of lexical selection, making a drama of language itself as
if lexicons were themselves characters. Here is God silently measured
by cold legalisms.

I read my sentence – steadily –
Reviewed it with my eyes,
To see that I made no mistake
In it's extremest clause –
The Date, and manner, of the shame –
And then the Pious Form
That "God have mercy" on the Soul
The Jury voted Him –   (P-412)

Besides such strategies of diction choice at which she was so adept,
Dickinson employed other techniques that we call modern. As noted,
she ellided syntax (for various reasons), omitted transitions, and
dropped structural and even syntactical copulas. This habit of withholding connective material produces curiously vexatious ways we
now choose to see as modern: discontinuity of structure and story,
and remystification of phenomena that seem simple and clear, and
those extinguishings of meaning by which we experience complexity
and feel the intractable quality of existence again. Beyond this, Dickinson's habitual brevity seems modern in its glimpses and incompleteness. These are notes raised to literature, notation as authentic
response. Wayward in punctuation, the poems disregard nicety and
neglect finish. They have an aura of spontaneity and the status of

randomness which, as when we look at impressionist or action painting, we find congenial and not a counterfeiting of sensation and reality. Like Hardy, but apparently less knowingly, her poetry was revolutionary because it avoided the jeweled line. It was more a making of
the irregular line through a rough simplicity and by drastic reduction. Indeed, sometimes the print version of her manuscripts unavoidably makes a modern line disposition.

> And Life was not so
> Ample I
> Could finish – Enmity –   (P-478)

Her partial rhymes and the structural instability and shifts in poems
contribute to this impatient art.

Dickinson's rift vision, the ability to make language cut into the
disparities between concept and reality, between the expectation and
the actuality—this creation in language of cruel parallax—effects a
disruption and penetration that we also call modern. It appeals to our
suspicion of wholeness and seamless compatible meaning. This effect
is behind Harold Bloom's accurate observation that Dickinson, as
much as any modern, made the visible world a little hard to see.

The several techniques emphasized here as modern are well known
and often displayed as the true source of Dickinson's modernity. Yet
we shall see that her modernity operated at a more fundamental level
than this. For now it is clear that these several conventional modernisms, what have now become part of the technical orthodoxy of modernist verse in English, contribute to the powerful effect that is indu-
bitably of our time: the estrangement from outer reality and the
resistance of common words to definitive meaning. The estrangement
is accomplished by the compact, unsustained, raw power of language
at the surface of her clipped-off poems.

In her themes, as well, Dickinson is with the moderns. Her
language, animated by her selective cleverness, together with the
snapshot brevity of her hymn form, courted instability and change
and spotted the vulnerability of settled states. This is why sunsets
evoked some of her best imagistic effort. The spectacle of day's end
was intensely, exaggeratedly visual, it was naturally associated with
death, and it was recurrent novelty, change taking place before the

eyes. The sunset was thus a visual allegory for what most centrally engaged this poet.

Her preoccupation with change led to more desperate visions of mutability where the price of each moment of transport qualified every ecstasy, showing by her allegorical terms the furrow that threatens every glow. Unlike Emerson and Whitman, Dickinson brought into view with her strange and critical metaphors the opaque being of man, the "mysterious peninsula" as she called it, the unmanageable, excruciatingly sensitive, and needful portion that was her preoccupation.

She possessed a modernist knowledge of the mind's hidden places, what she called "That awful stranger Consciousness," terrifying to face. Equipped with her estranging language, she raised to the reader's awareness the intricate workings out of sight, careful not to "Mistake the Outside for the in" as she said. It is this interior life, in (for this recluse) the inevitable metaphor of the house, that is "haunted" and is the crucial spot where we enact our ignorance of ourselves and the world. Here is the "interior Confronting," where "Unarmed, one's a'self encounter." Now become an orthodox element of modern themes—what Irving Howe has called a modern fondness for the signs of psychic division—the interior life and the language to see it were the particular loci of Dickinson's attention. Encountering the self both dictated the strategies of her language and was the act in which her language had its circumstantial reflection.

"I felt a Funeral in my Brain" is the first coolly targeted modern interior in American poetry, and it is handled adroitly with modernist attention not to moral judgment but to judgment-free description. There is no emotional slither, to use Pound's term, or didactic assertion as in other poems such as "Bound – a trouble / And lives can bear it!" or "A Weight with Needles on the pounds," but rather psychological interiority seen minutely. The funeral-in-the-brain poem, representative of a substantial cluster of Dickinson's works on psychic distress, manifested two generations in advance the doctrine of imagism that Pound defined as the transfer of a complex of emotions in an instant of time.

It was Dickinson diving into the wreck and her devastated speaker indeed "wrecked" in the poem. Assurance of diction and line is firm. The poem has structure and lexical cohesion of a high order for Dickinson, and it is this firmness that operates so effectively against the subject matter of instability and disintegration. It is a superb performance, thoroughly modernist in its dark vision clinically portrayed.

Such language, as we shall see more fully later, made visible a new category of psychic suffering. Minutely observant, its figure of the interior funeral sustained, the poem moves with impressive directness into its surrealist transformation at the line "Then Space – began to toll." The familiar terms make new equations: Heaven is a Bell, Being an Ear, and Silence a strange Race, and the wreck itself an annihilating silence. The surreal landscape, haunted with Dickinson's sense of exclusion and ignorance, unfolds, at least to the somewhat redundant last stanza, with a sure finality of language and wholeness of vision. In its cold-blooded, unflinching way as well as in the interior location of its action, the poem is supremely modernist. From the broader view of the Dickinson canon, we see how her concern with the interior reflects an equally modern concern with intense self-consciousness extending even to self-torture and the poetry of breakdown.

The extremity of the inward vision involved not only the snowman moment but a remarkable anticipation of the Epsteinian countenances of modern horror. Dickinson's Rock Drill faces peer into the canon insistently as if the visage of the modern age were aborning in her work. Some are her irrepressible triflings with visions of the face of the end, as in the poem about drowning as the sea "Made Blue faces in my face" (P-568). But the horror comes full on in her faces more often than we realized. The proleptic Rock Drill face is in lines of cold, authentic technology:

> a Face of Steel –
> That suddenly looks into ours
> With a metallic grin –
> The Cordiality of Death –
> Who drills his Welcome in –   (P-286)

This mask of the modern horrors of destruction and fright peers into the middle of the nineteenth century elsewhere:

> She feels some ghastly Fright come up
> And stop to look at her –
> . . . .
> Salute her – with long fingers –
> Caress her freezing hair –   (P-512)

Other faces pop in unexpectedly, even irrelevantly as in this version of the poem beginning "Ah, Teneriffe!"

> clad in Your Mail of Ices –
> Eye of Granite – and Ear of Steel –   (P-666)

The protomodernist image of the durable face of technological violence, of assault masked by dehumanized visages, is related in terror to another theme of Dickinson's that is hardly depictable by such momentary frissons. That is her vision of the *absence of an end.* I find this the most frightful of all Dickinson's modernist themes because it involves the pathological extremity of her familiar images such as this, of death in life, that ends an eight-line poem of utter inertness.

> I take my living place
> As one commuted led –
> A Candidate for Morning Chance
> But dated with the Dead.   (P-1194)

The smell of nihilism rises from more than a few poems, sometimes in a complete flatness of tune where her theme is the loss that drains every gain: note the eight lines that tick off loss beginning "Finding is the first Act / The second, loss" (P-870). Associated with this theme of lost purpose and the absence of an end is a fearful corollary: the prevention of ripeness, of completion and thereby of knowledge and identity. It is the vision we saw in "What ripeness after that": that is, a life of incompletion, of ignorance, of need without assuaging. It can stand for the quintessential modernist condition—until with Dickinson we find ourselves going deeper.

Not death, then, as in Wallace Stevens' nostalgic way, but rather in the ironic way with which we are familiar since modernist psychic defense mechanisms set in with the First World War, loss is the mother of beauty in Dickinson's calculus. Hers is a modern irony. It is an attitude with which to face the final slate of reality, "the the" as Stevens called it in "The Man on the Dump" and which in Dickinson finds a painful beauty. It seeks pleasure when the oil of ideals has dried out, finds in loss the experience of the center, in ignorance the serious joy of grasping pain, "Anguish grander than Delight." If there is sorrow in losing and not knowing why, there is beauty in knowing the worst. For Dickinson the counterforce to the exclusion from comprehension is sending language to the extremity of experience. It is an existentialist joy and in the knowing is the beauty. One of Dickinson's statements of this condition is in the simple figure of a wagon. Backwoodsman, she knew that the axle turns when the grease is gone from the wheel.

> Ideals are the Fairy Oil
> With which we help the Wheel
> But when the Vital Axle turns
> The Eye rejects the Oil.   (P-983)

Dickinson's themes lacked the urban complexities that Emerson had begun to recognize and Whitman to exploit. Their sprawling activity was outside the ken of this woman of the pleasant country town. But she knew the source of some of her "news": it is the same place where another modern poet, Hart Crane, was to perform his embassy. This is a draft she discarded that attempted to chart her elemental meaning:

> The Prey of Unknown Zones –
> The Pillage of the Sea –
> The Tabernacles of the Minds
> That told the Truth to me –   (P-1409)

Particular tones in Dickinson's poetry are also part of her commonly recognized modernism. Currents of doubt and the snowman moments give certain poems a psychological desperation that was unfamiliar to much nineteenth-century poetry. The sharply discrepant tone in poems, their directness of statement, and the audacity of their attack on conventional belief and easy-going piety are elements that would have given offense in her own time and so did not appear in the first editions of her poetry in the 1890s. Her colloquial and irreverently casual heresy at times ("It's easy to invent a Life"), her deliberate inelegance in a primitive offbeat diction ("It is simple to ache in the Bone or the Rind"), and the seemingly sophisticated skepticism in offhand phrases ("Our Savior, by a Hair") combine to give a considerable portion of the poetry a discordant tone that undercuts the poetry of unquestioned assent with which her contemporaries filled the verse books of the day.

Satire and irreverence along a gamut from mild asides to bitter attack are also modernist elements that form part of our critical orthodoxy and the surfaces by which Dickinson can be labeled a modern. In the poem beginning "There's been a Death in the opposite House," she creates a gentle satire on the impersonal organization that swings into action at a death, with its ritual movements and the professional mourners who take charge. In such verse of casual irreverence, the understatement and vernacular ease effectively counterpoint the regular common meter that arranges them. Deft lexical selection provides the edge that cuts in in the modern way. Her lines on the aurora borealis, where the common expectation would be for "paint" and "tint," Dickinson slips all askew by substituting "infection" and "taint":

> The North – Tonight . . .
> Infects my simple spirit
> With Taints of Majesty   (P-290)

She deflated a generically solemn occasion by unobtrusive negation and the one unexpected word "soldered":

> I've seen a Dying Eye
> Run round and round a Room . . .
> And then – be soldered down
> Without disclosing what it be
> 'Twere blessed to have seen   (P-547)

Her language pierced theological pomposities with strokes of marvelous wit, as here with out-of-place words from the public hall set off against Resurrection.

> No crowd that has occurred
> Exhibit – I suppose
> That General Attendance
> That Resurrection – does   (P-515)

Like Hart Crane's updating of Christ on the city streets as "religious gunman" and "capped arbiter of beauty," Dickinson with the communion symbol in mind worked her own irreverent transformation more than half a century earlier.

> Sacrament, Saints partook before us –
> Patent, every drop,
> With the Brand of the Gentile Drinker
> Who indorsed the Cup –   (P-527)

Dickinson's modernist tones include the confessional one. She excelled in creating a sense of private immediacy because, by the strategy of seemingly autobiographical speech acts, she reproduced in writing the speaking voice. Archibald MacLeish has written most knowingly on the unique voice by which we identify her. It is language signifying emotional experience close at hand that impresses us. The voice, quotation marks invisible, contradicts a reader's conscious awareness of the deliberately written text. This way in which Dickinson *did* speak out to strangers produces what we take to be an immediate proximity to the mind. The flattened conversational tone depoetizes experience and gives it a confessional authenticity of the sort we are familiar with in our own time.

> To Ache is human – not polite –
> The Film upon the eye
> Mortality's Old Custom –
> Just locking up – to Die   (P-479)

Toughness of attitude and candor couched in unstudied inelegance are further tonal qualities by which twentieth-century readers have assigned Dickinson to the origins of modernism along with Whitman. The blunt tones sound frequently along her lines, as here in this bald assertion that seems to have no poetic pretensions: "Men die – externally – / It is a truth – of Blood" (P-531).

Boldly secular content and skeptical tone quite disjunct from the orderly arrangement of the hymn form make an ironic combination. The poems produce that most modern of all attitudes, the ironicalization of experience. Beyond that, the disjunction and tonal qualities together effect a modernist estrangement, dissonance, and thus a critical perspective. Her bruskness deromanticizes, as in the moon poem that begins "The Moon was but a Chin of Gold." Dickinson's daring comes out most clearly if her moon is put alongside the famous protoimagist poem on the moon by T. E. Hulme. Dickinson's lines have in their more compact shape a greater bravado. It is part of what she shares with poets who followed her.

> like a Head – a Guillotine
> Slide carelessly away –
>
> like a Stemless Flower –
> Upheld in rolling Air –   (P-629)

The best summing up of these tonal qualities we now see as a modern set is in that phrase *the ironicalization of experience*. The tonal undercutting, the evasion of stock sincerity, the protective irreverence and throwaway understatement, thus making the hymn form play a different tune: all these effects, even if there were behind them no perspective of mind much more fundamental, would withal make Dickinson a modern. Neither sophisticated nor sustained, hers was a poetic cunning working by stealth of language and subversion of form to create surprise by strangeness. Out of these strategies came a disordering of experience, a new confession of our precarious status.

But we must now be concerned with what is left once these layers of modernist strategies and then the nineteenth-century poetic conventions are subtracted. In this way we shall arrive not only at Dickinson's unique role in the modernist poetry shift but at the extreme limit of American modernism itself.

Higginson's Visit

"The world has been painted; most modern activity is getting rid of the paint to get at the world itself," Wallace Stevens wrote in a letter.[2] Beneath the conventional modernisms of Dickinson one can spy that unvarnished world itself. It lies in the radicals of her writing and her existence. The condition is nothing less than the disaster of Babel. Thomas Wentworth Higginson witnessed the dramatization of that essential modernist ordeal.

Higginson came to Amherst on August 16, 1870. It was a pleasant town, he said in a letter to his wife that evening, unspeakably quiet in the summer afternoon. On his arrival he sent a note to the poet at the Dickinson homestead, just down Main Street from the Amherst House where he had accommodations, asking if he might call. She replied, "I will be at Home and glad." He described the visit repeatedly, first in the note to his wife, then in his diary, again to his wife the next day as he rode in the cars north to White River Junction, once more in the postscript of a letter to his sisters four days later, and again twenty years afterward in his article on Dickinson for the *Atlantic Monthly* in 1891.[3] His is surely the best account of the poet face to face we have, made in the early instances while the visit was fresh in his mind, not sentimentalized as are accounts by other people over the years or, as in the case of Sue's affectionate obituary for Dickinson, stylized and protective.

He was let in by the housekeeper and shown to the parlor, which was "dark and cool and stiffish," with "a few books and engravings and an open piano." Having received his card upstairs, Dickinson made her famous entrance with two daylilies in her hands, saying as she gave them to him, "These are my introduction." What struck Higginson was her childlike demeanor, a step like a child's, he wrote, her gesture with the lilies "a sort of childlike way," and her manner "thoroughly ingenuous and simple." She was nervous and said in a breathless voice, "Forgive me if I am frightened; I never see strangers and hardly know what I say."

This woman, now almost forty, who had withdrawn completely from the world outside her father's house, began to talk and, to Higginson's wonderment, talked "thenceforward continuously—and deferentially—sometimes stopping to ask me to talk instead of her—but readily recommencing." What came of this nervous deluge of talk was the essential circumstance of her life that we must not miss. She lived so thoroughly in her own mind that she had a curious ignorance of how others managed their lives. These are her patronizing words as Higginson recalled them for his wife that evening: "How do most people live without any thoughts. There are many people in the world (you must have noticed them in the street). How do they live. How do they get strength to put on their clothes in the morning." This life in the consciousness was of an intensity, it seems from her remarks, in inverse ratio to her reclusion and her lack of exterior stimuli. "I find ecstasy in living," she said to Higginson in that dark parlor with the drapery drawn over the windows, "the mere sense of living is joy enough." What he observed, surely, is an autogenous intensity almost totally self-induced. The impression made on him, he recalled years later in the *Atlantic Monthly* article, "was that of an excess of tension, and of an abnormal life."

With the acuteness of a mind that had turned away from the world to live in its own activity, she was exerting in her life precisely what we recognize in the body of poetry and the language of her poems: a disabling freedom. She was utterly the maker of her life without any obligating pressure from without. Higginson tried to find openings in this self-absorption and found there were none. "I asked if she never felt want of employment, never going off the place and never seeing any visitor." She replied, "I never thought of conceiving that I could ever have the slightest approach to such a want in all future time," and then, in an afterthought that measures for us the compounded energy of this auto-consciousness, she added, "I feel that I have not expressed myself strongly enough."

Her needs were of a magnitude to match the closed-in, concentrated power, and it was this desire, removed like her poems from a natural traffic with the exterior world, that she might have structured into manageable priorities. Activated constantly but without avenues to satisfaction outside the words in her mind, it was this reflexive ardor that brought Higginson to write in 1891 of "that somewhat overstrained relation which not my will, but her needs, had forced upon us." The night after his first conversation with her in 1870 he acutely summarized his reactions in what is the most telling account of the force field she created. Higginson had felt himself endangered by the strength of the interior vortex that the absent world had created in this woman. He wrote: "I never was with any one who drained my nerve power so much. Without touching her, she drew from me. I am glad not to live near her."

With this knowledge of the woman who wrote about the weight and space of time better than most, who had for years stopped seeing any strangers face to face and now was to meet the famous Higginson, literary arbiter and Civil War hero, we can appreciate with stunning comprehension the most laser-charged twenty-four hours perhaps in American literary history. Higginson arrived in Amherst at two in the afternoon on August 16. That was a Tuesday. Dickinson expected him to come on Monday, the day before. We begin at last adequately to imagine her state of mind in the intervening day's time as she waited.

Dickinson was a text of enormous interest to Higginson but, removed as she was from the world with which he was familiar, she had no settled self he could discern. She seemed a force to him on the verge of flight or dispersion. This figure living always at the moment before the self's disintegration is, in a word, the emblematic figure of the epimodern consciousness: a self with no coherence or stability but of unutterable power of consciousness and need. Union of desire with the world's responses was not a possibility for her. As Higginson's accounts attest and as her poems make manifest, she mixed in talk of puddings along with ideas and books and poetry. The puddings were like comets; she couldn't tell time by the clock until she was fifteen; she remembered Major Hunt had told her once that her dog understood gravity. It was the hodgepodge we are familiar with in the poems. For Higginson she was the mystery of incipient disintegration wrapped in the enigma of quirky genius. Here is another of his summings up: "She was much too enigmatical a being for me to solve in an hour's interview, and an instinct told me that the slightest attempt at direct cross-examination would make her withdraw into her shell; I could only sit still and watch, as one does in the woods; I must name my bird without a gun, as recommended by Emerson." We must name what is radically modern—call it postmodernist I think—in this enigmatic artist witnessed through Higginson's eyes as he listened and did not interrogate.

Radical Modernism

Dickinson's definition of poetry which she gave Higginson in that monologue looks very different to us now if we hold it in the light of their interview. Poetry, she thought, takes its definition from explosive personal, even idiosyncratic, sensory response. Intensity is the element she emphasized exclusively. In her stark sensationalist definition, which we now can see is characteristic, what she leaves out is most significant: a sense of structure and complexity, of links to the world of experience, of a philosophical gravity and coherence. She valued the intensity and was oblivious to coherence. Her definition then, by its emphasis and its absences, by its narrow aspiration and forfeited wholeness, is the essential Dickinson as artist. This is, once again, what she said:

> If I read a book [and] it makes my whole body so cold no fire ever can warm me I know *that* is poetry. If I feel physically as if the top of my head were taken off, I know *that* is poetry. These are the only way I know it. Is there any other way.   (L-342a)

The words mirror the negations we have seen: the ferocious imagination with no conceptual center; the disdain for the actual world and its complex structure; the unconcern for architectural craft and philosophical coherence; in a phrase, the affliction of spontaneity. It is a definition of poetry of unalloyed power, and with all its absences it has, we see, all the pathos of power without a project.

Sue designated in another way the concurrence of force and incoherence in some lines in Dickinson's obituary. Her descriptive words add up to the adjective *impatient.* Her sister-in-law, she wrote, was "quick as the electric spark in her intuitions and analyses, she seized the kernel instantly, almost impatient of the fewest words." Sue's description will come to be more significant than we have perceived before if our understanding adequately grows of this particular Dickinsonian strain of American modernism. For Dickinson's life and work are examples of the inevitable but not necessarily objectionable pathos of modernism in pure form. She existed in purposelessness but was possessed simultaneously of a self-enclosed concentration of consciousness and language that made an energy center of unappeasable need.

Irving Howe once ventured this summary of modernism: "a dismissal of absolutes, a perception of historical impasse, a fondness for the signs of psychic division, a contempt for received cultural norms, an impatience with customary literary decorums, an underlying doubt as to the coherence of the human enterprise."[4] If his catalogue shares a common element, it is the doubt of coherence. But radical modernism is not basically to be found in a theme or philosophical attitude, as Howe supposes, but rather in a mode or the lack of a mode of apprehending experience; that is, in the way the world is arranged by words, in short, an *idiom.*

Dickinson's radical endomodernism is found in her stroboscopic idiom which, lacking a structure of foreknowledge, effectively negated any totality of intent. Thus are produced the special problematics of her work: the lost referents, the sporadic incoherence and indeterminate meaning, the lack of self-definition, the lost viewpoint.

With these particular circumstances of linguistic derangement, we are inside the modern dilemma. The orthodox view of two principal modernisms will not capture Dickinson's peculiarity, her power, or her significance. She can be catalogued as neither a traditionalist nor a schismatic. She is not the Eliot type who seeks to preserve the orderliness of the past despite a degrading present, attempting to hold to continuity under the direst of difficulties and when the turning back for values seems a sharp break with the present. Nor is she a schismatic like Gertrude Stein who celebrates discontinuity, freeing the tribe from the constraints of the past, rejecting what was oppressive. Dickinson is something else entirely: fitful where others are purposefully in revolt, disjoining where others are synthesizing, cutting apart where others are accumulating, radically metonymical where others are metaphoric. Not traditionalist or schismatic, her idiom is artistically pathogenic, deconstructive, hyperconscious.

The concept of a "catastrophe of consciousness," to borrow Bloom's term, turns us in a useful direction. The phenomenon whose trace we seek is the poet's fall into intense consciousness and thus into language, the world's absence, the enigma of being. "No Drug for Consciousness – can be," Dickinson wrote with a doomed prescience (P-786). But her fall was not only into language and consciousness but also into metaphysical ignorance. This concatenation explains why in her poems meaning gets sacrificed to presence. The subject has been absorbed so that what the poem is about is subjectivity. For Dickinson, then, at the modernist extremity, the Single Hound not only accompanied her but dogged her. Consciousness, as the poems declare, is both a triumph and an anguish. This heightening of reflexive thought is coincident with diminishment of the organizing ability of the mind. With this origin, Dickinson's language possesses a menacing force that is new in American poetry. Where her startling figures couple most shockingly they reflect most evidently the burden of consciousness. By this intense action, the exterior world is irretrievably transformed into the linguistic strategies of the mind. Thus preoccupied with itself, the consciousness, to use Lukács' term, finds itself unavoidably suffering a transcendental homelessness, the self terrifying and constant, intense without a cause, heightened feeling with no content.

If we seek a field theory that connects her existence and her art it is this: her artful selection along the plane of lexical choice and her lack of sustained structure on the plane of combination exactly reflect the phenomenon of intensity without a cause. It is vertical linguistic power without cumulative direction. The result is triumphantly rewarding: because normatively descriptive reference and order are suspended, there is created a negative condition in which a radically unconventional, unmediated way of looking is possible, even to the point of uncovering deep, random, primordial layers of reality heretofore hidden by conceptual coherence.

Dickinson is baffled in the way we sometimes now perceive as postmodern, but she is restively artful. Rather than enacting the choice of a human attitude, her poems speak and speak in the absence of a stance. There was the enormous need, and this without a purposeful bearing is the Dickinson extremity of the modern dilemma. Language begins only with the void, Maurice Blanchot has said. Plenitude and certitude do not speak. Dickinson, possessed of a quenchless capacity for signification, is a paradigmatic creature of the void with a will to words that removes her twice over from the world.

At a stroke, Dickinson brilliantly extracted the apt metonymical emblem of the essential modern condition: her intrusive housefly. As Emerson's eyeball moment is the touchstone of the nineteenth-century New England epiphanic idealism, Dickinson's fly marks the fall into disorder. Her poem "I heard a Fly buzz – when I died" is the central allegory of ignorance, the failure of the vision. Whereas Emerson in perfect exhilaration could say he became a transparent eyeball, Dickinson's speaker at the end of her nihilistic poem says "I could not see to see." The fly takes the place of the savior, irreverence and doubt have taken the place of revelation. Her fly, then, "With Blue – uncertain stumbling Buzz," is incomprehension, derangement itself. It is noise breaking the silence, not the world's true speech but, externalized, the buzz of ceaseless consciousness. It is Yeats's long-legged fly on the surface of the mind, but utterly sterile. It is to become one of Camus' flies of corruption.

If Hart Crane believed there was a coherence beneath the disordered surface of the world, there was for Dickinson beneath the incoherent surface incoherence. By the time of T. S. Eliot's "Ash-Wednesday," the modern angel of spirit had turned into something like her fly of incomprehension:

> these wings are no longer wings to fly
> But merely vans to beat the air . . .

Similar obscurities were caught up in that fly of Dickinson's. "You see I cannot see – your lifetime – I must guess," she wrote in poem 253. The fly had displaced vision. It can stand for us as an emblem of the final modernity.

Brother to that fateful, despiritualized fly, the needful modern consciousness resorts to words and words and words. As Stevens' man on the dump is to realize, and Lacan later, the void between desire and its fulfillment can only be filled by the language for that desire: "One sits and beats an old tin can, lard pail." Dickinson's compulsive and scattered monologue, her abhorrence of silent pauses in that draining interview with Higginson, dramatizes the condition. The more the world receded before her protective rush of words, the more words were needed to make their self-sufficient world. "I never see strangers and hardly know what I say," she told him. In that condition of signifying frenzy, the functional nature of language was destroyed. There is our glimpse of the origin of a poetry of a neuropathically intense sort. Language with Dickinson begins to break off its old kinship with the complicated exterior world and enters into a lonely sovereignty, to use Michel Foucault's words in a new reference, from which it reappears in its separated state as one kind of modern literature. Reality becomes impervious and what is put in its place, in reclusion from the world and existing with willful freedom like Dickinson herself, is the poetic construction that is nondiscourse. The world then is only a remoteness that haunts the house of art.

This dissociation is at the heart of an important area of powerful modernist literature. The hyperconsciousness, the word compulsion, and the absence of a cohering philosophy have combined, as they did in Dickinson, to exist in an autogenous and destructive state without authority and with only sporadic reference to experience. What happened, as we learn from Higginson's notes, was enacted in that darkened parlor closed against the August sunlight. It was the breakup of a privileged point of perception, the breakup of conceptual coherence, and the reflexive resort to language itself for the mind's activity. The language of consciousness, then, incapable of the wholeness of narrative description, is simply instrument. It is at the service of whim with no coherent belief, the spectacle of power without a purpose. In a word, the contemporary poet of this sort stands a loaded gun.

Dickinson's poetry thus signaled the end of anecdotal verse, just as visual art beginning with cubism ended for more than a half century the dominance of anecdotal painting. Dickinson's poetic canon existed in pieces, reflecting quite apart from the question of her conscious intention a world and a perception without an axis. In its makeup, her poetic world doubles the modern world without redeeming it. All the fragments came to attention randomly as they rushed through the vortex of Dickinson's own unranked sensations and word-making compulsion. In this disordered vortex, as the poetry of Dickinson demonstrates to us by the significance of its *wholelessness*, the perpetual erasure of impressions takes place, the constant displacement, and refusal to order that constitute the main disposition of late modernist poetry in America.

Dickinson is our first great modern, then, with her failure to regard the copula in form, in thought, in reference, in process. The parts without the connections: as she was in her person, her poems are constantly astounded as they inspect the space between the pieces. "The mere sense of living," she told Higginson, "is joy enough."

It was a devastating combination, this power of language and consciousness enfolding incomprehension. The result was an agitated inconclusiveness. Lacking rule, there was no end in sight by which to assign either identity or purpose. There was, as I suggested earlier, only an interminable aftermath. Both the fragmented canon and the individual poems with their character of notation, unfinishedness, and spontaneous sensation enact a disconcerting anxiety. And so, in a radical way, as one of the essential precursors, Dickinson suffered with a pure, transparent terror the eschatological anxiety of the moderns. Paradise within, as she said in a fragment, is invariably out to callers. As with her failure to title the poems in her packets, in her mind there was no finality. Instead, there was an excited sense of no ending, no election, no triumphant goal.

Dickinson seems to have sought evidence in vain that an end existed that audited and explained the terrible equation of ecstasy and terror, delight and its price. Her anxiety over the missing end is modern in the most profound way: beneath all merely literary strategies, it is the anxiety of existing spontaneously.

In her prose fragments, thus, there are the darkest moments Dickinson knew and some of the darkest in modern American literature, entered with a chilling extremity at the very beginning of the tradition. "It is essential to the sanity of mankind," she wrote, "that each one should think the other crazy – a condition with which the Cynicism of Human nature so cordially complies, one could wish it were a concurrence more noble" (PF-87). To overarch these destructive moments she had no artifice of eternity. For her, in the essentially modern way, the end was elusive. Her imagination dwelt in the aftermath that distinguishes her from all others. It is an aftermath which, by its nature, is eternally anticlimatic and, most devastatingly, always open-ended.

Under the curse of spontaneity, the Dickinson modernism is profoundly distinct from Stevens' or Frost's. Each of these later poets, obsessively aware of the chaos of the exterior world, asserts again and again the ability of art to order or at least to resist that chaos. The statements of this mildly stoic, idealized, aesthetic modernism in "The Idea of Order at Key West" and "Anecdote of the Jar" and in Frost's "The Pasture" and his famous dictum that poetry provides a momentary stay against confusion, a clarification of life, are of a different order entirely from the Dickinson strain of modernism. Her original language was not in celebration of aesthetic order no matter how momentary, but in unconscious acknowledgment of a sense of aftermath and no ending. Her poetry was not a stay against confusion but confusion itself.

If, as I have said elsewhere, Emerson's disconnected poem "The Poet," incorporating some earlier manuscript verse entitled "The Discontented Poet," is the first modern American poem in form and attitude, then Dickinson's dresser full of unpublished poems that, in photographic fashion, repeatedly glimpse the failure of ripeness and identity are the most extreme of all its corollaries.

She is the first figure of Babel in American poetry as she inaugurated, without a deliberately subversive intention but from the autogeny of her condition, a new experience of language and things. I am willing to speculate that while the Civil War is largely absent from her writing, it may be present but unseen behind the tension, the fragmentation, the anxiety, and the lack of purpose. But whether or not this can be demonstrated, it is clear that Dickinson's work is not, as Richard Howard attractively stated, "the most relentless epic of identity in our literature." Rather, it is the most powerful reflection of dispossession and failed identity in our literature. Compared to her, the older contemporaries Emerson and Whitman, modern as they were in formal loosening, were pillars of coherence and purpose in an age already entering upon a terminal state. The extraordinary dispersal of the speaking persona in her poems is evidence of this vastly novel phenomenon. It involves the early separation and dominance of written texts, for an actual or simulated voice, as in Emerson's lectures or Whitman's monologues, could not endure atomized as this of Dickinson's that evades us in the words on paper.

The shift was not, as some would have it, her conscious revolt against a traditional reasonableness in poetry—against narrative, magnitude, and clarity of reference—for she seems not to have had enough interest in traditional modes to overthrow them. Her poetry was a headstrong assertion that came as close as it was possible to come to Emerson's idea of the New World's artistic Berserkir or terrible Druid, who would come out of unhandselled nature to destroy the old. So pervasive now in art is this lack of a project that we assume it to be the natural state of much post-Victorian and earlier twentieth-century verse. Because we currently accept this lack of a design, in fact find grand projects embarrassing and verisimilitude trite, we go soberly searching for hidden patterns that we then call visions, world views, tendencies of consciousness. We no longer expect art, nor should we, to justify the ways of God to man. Eliot's label "dissociated sensibility" was more far reaching than we have supposed: it is a shadow of this larger disorderliness of which Dickinson was the extreme.

We now find this lack of a point of view in combination with intense consciousness and striking verbal power our own: no optimistic illusions, no blinking the dark side of human existence; instead, acutely self-conscious, seeking the courage to be and perhaps a moderate bliss; in loneliness the desire for wholeness. Dickinson did indeed break through the deadening concept of the unity of personality and, before Pound, Joyce, Eliot, and many others were to diagnose the condition with conviction later, began the unholy dispersal of self, belief, and perception.

Syllable was her sign for poetry speech, *sound* her sign for the unintelligible exterior world and the mystery of God. If the poet is not God, she wrote in poem 632, "they will differ - if they do - / As Syllable from Sound." I had long thought that by this she meant art as a momentary stay against unintelligibility, or the making intelligible what is only sound, a precursion to "The Idea of Order at Key West." But the truth I see now is that her syllable is only that, powerful but with no *ordering* of syllables, no belief that binds them. Instead, she selected syllables of great power that stun, of momentary insight but finally of a combined meaninglessness as vast and dazzling as the sounding world itself. This incoherence, then, is the deepest modern dilemma, and it is why, perhaps without our knowing it before, her work speaks more directly to the twentieth century than the forgotten works of her contemporaries.

American poetic modernism, broadly speaking, involves one feature that above all distinguishes it from modern British poetry, the other poetry in this common language: its impatience. Extreme in ambition, American poetry is sometimes extreme in mode. Sentence structure is wrenched; poems proceed not by syntax but by clots of imagery and metaphor. Sometimes willfully formless, it is independent, highly self-conscious, and often ruminating on aesthetic problems to the exclusion of reality. But most of all, it is impatient of orderly expression, of rationality and communication, and thus it is blind to history and the lock and chain of time. Dickinson's clipped-off verbs, for instance, are her way, nervous and eccentric, of evading time, even if the evasion costs the price of grammatical clarity. She took her utterance out of tense and thus out of time. Difficult, roughened, impeded, ellided, jam-packed, mystifyingly abstract, her language after 1860 waited for a later age to reinvent it so as to be free of the mundane, to bypass history all over again, to make syllables without priorities to order them. Such impatient, flawed language was the product of the now lost similitude that had once existed between experience and language.

Dickinson's art reified in writing those terrifying qualities she acted out in her extraordinary meeting with Higginson in the closed-in house in the little country town. Ironically, considering her lack of worldliness, the language became deeply appropriate to later realities in America, carrying the dilemma into American literature, with no sense anywhere of an ending that would confer identity. Highly charged and at the same time dispersed by untargeted need and by ignorance, impatient of understanding, an unsortable vortex of sensation, it fixed the incomprehension of the world in a stumbling, buzzing, obliterating fly.

Without design but instinctive, hers was the profoundest sort of critique of the human condition in a new language in this country. The stroboscopic art would come to be, when the times caught up with its febrile language, one of the indigenous forms of art. Whether it still has a future will be a question for my final chapter.

9 Art After the Fall

Several important consequences follow from this structural dispersion of Dickinson's, the more significant for being concealed from our view beneath the familiar modernist elements of style. The sense of loss and indefiniteness, of no ending, and of condemnation in the language of violence are all concentrated in the wife metaphor of her poem that begins "Twas here my summer paused." The final three lines seal the chilling imperative.

> With winter to abide
> Go manacle your icicle
> Against your Tropic Bride

This is fundamentally Art after the Fall. The poem's drama is not in the idea but in the roughened language enacting the archetypal Fall from comprehension and then the poet's fall from the decorum of the literary tradition into aboriginal language and intense consciousness. That fall of man and art in America into the intimate experience of loss and condemnation takes place in Dickinson's poems. In them the aftermath is the condition of the consciousness, the state not only of feeling but of knowledge. Her art signals the threshold of a literary modernity in which we still find ourselves so completely immersed we do not notice in her lines their curse of centerlessness, their language of idiosyncratic authority, their separation from any active project outside of victimization by the denial of comprehension.

In this constant aftermath, as I illustrated earlier, grace is a lost condition. The state rather is the one in the letter Dickinson sent to Graves where, even so young as they all were, she and Austin and

Graves seem already to be living afterward, after youth's closeness and love, after the ideal April. Into this post-April world come the long shadows as presentiments of loss: "A shade upon the mind there passes." Dickinson's poetry then shows slants of light and long shadows that prefigure death. Several poems fix that loss as an instant's crisis and then, in that familiar time of a painful aftermath, "God forbid I look behind – / Since that appalling Day!" The extreme moments of dejection in the aftermath find the Dickinson speaker exempt from exaltation as the stones.

Unique in America before Edwin Arlington Robinson, this poetry is haunted by eclipsed visions of paradise. In Dickinson the vision calls up curious spatial and luminous figures. That lost April of youth's dream is a period of no change, of "perpetual Noon." Similar figures of a possible world recur where existence is whole, a seamless existence without—in her repeated tropes—crease, gash, stain, or furrow, without break or loss. Everything that is undimmed and loved is, in her dominant mode of the aftermath, as she says in the poignant fragment on lost childhood, "parts of a closed world." It is all that became impossible when ripeness was aborted.

"Mysterious human heart," Dickinson wrote on a scrap of paper, "whose one mistake in Eden has cost it all its Calm to come" (PF-39). That condition of disinheritance seems to be a silent assumption partially framing this otherwise dispersed body of poetry. As with other nineteenth-century writers but perhaps most like Hardy whose provincial directness she shares, the breakdown of the received faith was an experience of the utmost consequence. If hers was not so final as a complete abandonment of belief, it was a profound indefiniteness toward faith. Thus life at its darkest for her was a painful and repeated travail to no clear, compensating end. She wrote to Sue in 1885, a year before her own death, "Emerging from an Abyss, and re-entering it – that is Life, is it not, Dear?" Out of such a perceived exclusion from design, then, came her pervasive consciousness of aftermath and the alienation from authority. And out of this poverty, as we have observed, the poetry sprang, taking on its strangely unconscious character of art after the fall. Suffering sporadic desperation, it made sharp assaults on the old assurances. Doubt and ignorance were its way of perception. If another summer is to come, she meant to say in a few cramped lines that serve as the companion piece to "'Twas here my summer paused," nature withholds the knowledge of it.

> If other Summers be
> Nature's imposing negative
> Nulls opportunity – (P-1673)

The absence of knowledge comes to the surface in Dickinson as a pervasive undersong. "The Future," she wrote, "never . . . will . . . Reveal . . . a syllable Of His Profound to Come" (P-672). The desperation sounded in a line in Poem 378: "I saw no Way – The Heavens were stitched." In the harshest moments of all, she parodied prayer with unconcealed bitterness:

> We apologize to thee
> For thine own Duplicity.   (P-1461)

Dickinson's stance, the dominant temper of her verse, has a negative ground. Without authority to confer identity, the consciousness within her poems almost always takes a passive role withdrawn from experience, and it is living mainly in psychic activity, *response* to assault or crisis. Existence is in the interstice created by the fall from comprehension, that is, in the interval between knowing and only hoping. It is a perpetual exile from a visionary assurance. Dickinson had no artifice of eternity to construct an eschatology. In the modern way, but with a concentration of address in her brief lines and an immediacy on the nerve ends, the form of the end was elusive. Nothing conferred meaning and therefore there was nothing by which to organize her art. Dickinson is the supreme poet of this accursed limbo and, at the same time, the first in our literature.

In the face of psychic death and afterness, the course of nature is a mystery, however moving and beautiful. "Summer's soft assemblies," she writes on one occasion, in their death are "Estranged, however intimate" (P-1330). Similarly, a crucial portion of one's own existence resonant with mystery, the self that has suffered the fall from understanding, is the "part of us" that "is a not familiar peninsula" (PF-2).

Only the tissue of remembrance and the shaky hope of a continuous consciousness held the pieces of thought together. "Were Departure Separation," she wrote on a scrap, "there would be neither Nature nor Art, for there would be no World" (PF-52). Life precariously held in this predicament of lost belief presented life's actual summer, not a perfect season but "this of Our's, diversified / With Prospect, and with Frost" (P-930). Most consequential of all and the preoccupation of Dickinson's ur-modern work, the exclusion from comprehension in this postlapsarian art highlighted an existential self-absorption in which redeeming identity came only with a possible Resurrection where each consciousness suffered its own sentence utterly alone:

> Solemnity – prevail –
> It's Individual Doom
> Possess each separate Consciousness –
> August – Absorbed – Numb –   (P-515)

Dickinson's predicament in having no authority outside her own nerve ends centrifugally dispersed her art and made it unmanageable, but the same predicament was the impetus of her writing. Immediate response to existence under the shadow of ignorance created that familiar American individual, cut loose from history, facing the Fall. Naiveté amid death and ignorance is a characteristic stance of this modern precursor, but the predilection for the stark view is there in what Dickinson called with precise intuition "An instinct for the Hoar, the Bald – / Lapland's – necessity" (P-525). In blindness and loss there was a desperate kind of modernist beauty.

> faithful be
> To Thyself
> And Mystery –
> All the rest is Perjury –   (P-1768)

Out of this straitened condition so alien to the verse of her contemporaries, Dickinson created her allegories of ignorance. Hers is a canon of severe individuality in this respect. When the systems of belief failed her she did not turn outward to things but rather to her words and allegories. It is a remarkable primitive inwardness, the more powerful for being undistractedly exclusive. Her language looked for night coming on, invited change, sought the process of nature's shifting for which there is no reasoning. From the conceptual void came such stark poems as "Four Trees – upon a solitary acre" in which Dickinson is as explicit as it is possible to be on the absence of discernible purpose. In a bitter parable as tight as possible in construction, nothing wasted on lamentation, she wrote the epitaph for hope. It is a proto-modern perspective, Dickinsonian in its concentration. Like others of hers of comparable darkness, it was not published until the twentieth century:

> And this of all my Hopes
> This, is the silent end
> Bountiful colored, my Morning rose
> Early and sere, it's end
>
> Never Bud from a Stem
> Stepped with so gay a Foot
> Never a Worm so confident
> Bored at so brave a Root   (P-913)

Given an art that courted motion and the life after crisis, Dickinson emerged quite fortuitously as the sovereign poet of altered states. Cut off from any philosophical design, her language in an uncanny way could detect change and shifting conditions where they are least expected. It is language that is belief-bereft, saying incessantly and with great pressure, as in poem 462, "But – the Instead." The Instead involved for Dickinson, adrift but intensely conscious in the fall from knowledge, the inversion of normal expectations as they scarred the psyche to the verge of madness:

> a Day as huge
> As Yesterdays in pairs,
> Unrolled it's horror in my face –
> Until it blocked my eyes –   (P-410)

It involved the perversion of nature's routine:

> Sunset at Night – is natural –
> But Sunset on the Dawn
> Reverses Nature – Master –
> So Midnight's – due – at Noon.   (P-415)

When frost the deadly changer comes, "whatsoever Mouth he kissed – / Is as it had not been" (P-391).

Death is the chief bringer of change, her Emperor of Ice-Cream, and this is why it formed a main proposition for Dickinson. "Come slowly, Eden" is the same concern, minutely experienced in this function-specific language, but seeking alteration into ecstasy. Sunsets, breakdown, death: all were alterings and Dickinson with her language of glimpse and cut was able to deconstruct the states subsumed by abstract labels. "Crisis is...," "Death is...," "Hope is...." Her definition language with its unexpected diction and tortuous syntax occupies the hymn form of tradition, enhancing the vision of discrepancy and alteration in the language itself. Dickinson selected her words along that vertical axis to provoke sightings of changed states. This poetry of alteration is fundamentally against heroisms; it is against what is stable. By such subversion it is more the language of the victim, the seeker, the compromiser, the person caught in ignorance, "the only Kangaroo among the Beauty." It is thus the specialized instrument of a deconstructive modernism.[1]

How does one account for what F. O. Matthiessen called "the bare fact that from the half century that separates the births of Whitman and Robinson only three poets were able to create work comparable to that of poets from our earlier and later history"?[2] He referred to Henry Timrod, Sidney Lanier, and Emily Dickinson. My answer is that the program of poetry was lost, and the losing of the program is enacted in Dickinson's poetry. The period saw the crisis of literature in America in which, without the authority of shared basic assumptions, there was no way, responsibly and at a level above the banal and self-delusive, to respond to the accelerating novelty of a world where a common philosophical center did not hold. Only the isolated small-town poet, possessed of a strict genius, embodied in an unsophisticated, phenomenological way this dire time in our literature. Dickinson, in her own vast vacuum of life after the fall, created an idiom for the epoch that was beginning because, let us say it, she did not know enough to be daunted.

She stood, as I have observed, at the place where genius and ignorance meet. In the perspective of that ignorance, she saw *man deposed*. That denuded pageant, as she called it, was all of her concern, the focus of her ignorance. Man's defeat was more important, she said, "Than least vitality." Fate was in command, dominion had to have room; ignorance in this woman became the impetus of her words. She confronted, then, "these problems of the dust" that terrify. Her territory was the one that, since Poe, and with an immediacy unimpeded by any system of belief, had not presented itself so starkly to any of her contemporaries. It held "the suggestion sinister / Things are not what they are" (P-1451).

Facing this profoundly sensed alteration, she fortuitously possessed the language to make visible the rifts in the old doctrines. Hers was an idiom of change that turned in the smooth seat of hymnal belief, and by that unnatural discrepancy she expressed as no one else could the deep spiritual discrepancy that opened into the twentieth century. Withdrawn from society's distractions, intense, with her state of personal diffusion, she stood in a fateful way as a language maker on the scene in which others were oblivious to the changed circumstances. Amy Lowell recognized the exception. In her lecture on "The New Manner in Modern Poetry" to the Boston Round Table Club in 1915, she said poetry in America was inert at the end of the Civil War, "inert, that is, save for one still, small voice. One little voice which was the precursor of the modern day."[3] Narrow concentration and linguistic spontaneity that released power without belief: these constitute her language of submerged anxiety, of a fragile sanity, the spectacular word displays with hysteria beneath the surface. In short, the idiom produced by this poet who had withdrawn from the world was to come inadvertently to be a language that described that world. We thus, as Eliot was to say of Milton's language, which he called after Butler a Babylonish dialect, "find grace in its deformity."

Dickinson's poetry, like Sophocles' tragedy, works at the boundary between human limitation and the divine, affirming not transcendence but the disjunct world. Allen Tate's thesis is correct: fate placed Dickinson at the exhausted end of the old theological dispensation in New England and with strong, distorted language and undistracted by a life in society she was uniquely situated to give voice not only to her own dilemma but also to the age that was descending. For her it was, however painful and incoherent, a perfect literary moment. Her anxieties, her powers, and her limitations coincided by chance with the onset of the times that were to come. She had made the language of personal disintegration. It was ready to hand, then, for a later age disillusioned in faith and lacking firm values. Whereas her contemporaries repeated the assurances of an earlier age, Dickinson suffered the throes of an imagination of incomparable force, unformed, performing at the hinge of the age as America passed into the modern era. With profound symbolic appropriateness, her surprising words of a personal void and acute consciousness grated within the orderly boundaries of the old hymn and the Sunday school verities.

Art on the Dump, "Stanza my Stone"

Dickinson of all American poets over the past hundred years illustrates earliest and most clearly the passage of poetry into an irreversible crisis. Joyce, consciously, accomplished the same distinction in prose a half century later. It remains for the discussion in the next and final chapter to say if she is to be held responsible for pulling her particular strain of literature into a dead end. She seems in any event to have been the first to confront the question of the *materials* of poetry in a decentered world. Eliot, we recall, explicitly posed the problem for his age in 1923 in *The Dial*, discovering in the use of myth in *Ulysses* a way of "ordering, of giving a shape and a significance to the immense panorama of futility and anarchy which is contemporary history." Joyce's mode (and his own as well), he believed, was "a step toward making the modern world possible in art." Dickinson well before this faced the question of how poetry is to be made in a haunted, ignorant world. In her dilemma, in an oblique way, rests the real significance of the Civil War in her poems: in it were met the death and disorder of the larger world. Whatever the proximate reason, the result is clear to us now from our present perspective of the character of her verse: she prefigured, perhaps even precipitated by the end of the century when, with some editorial anxieties, her poetry was published, the condition of poetry in crisis, of poetry like experimental music, "A fine – estranging creature."

"Modern poetry," Paul deMan has reminded us, "is described by Yeats as the conscious expression of a conflict within the function of language as representation and within the conception of language as the act of the autonomous self."[4] In Dickinson's case, the expression of precisely this conflict seems to have been unconscious, mainly the inevitable reflection of an autogenous self withdrawn from the world. Thus her personal situation, like Eliot's that was transformed by his poetry into a cultural emblem, served as one of the places where American poetry entered the modern era. Her texts display the three main aspects of the modern poetry dilemma: the question of the material of poetry (its realm and subject matter), the crisis over the conceptual tissue of poetry (its perspective and coherence), and the crisis over its function, that is, the great modern question of the relationship of language and artistic imagination to reality. In Dickinson's work, each of these crucial questions is acted out in a direct, unsophisticated, and therefore almost pure form. We can look at them in order.

A basic question defines the crisis in poetry concerning its subject matter: How is poetry possible in the modern world of cities and commerce, disorder instead of harmony? Poets after Keats and Arnold, W. J. Bate has said, for want of adequate subjects in the world and in the long shadows of Milton and Shakespeare, turned to poetry and poetry making as their subject. With man's fall from nature into language, from presence into difference and therefore into the acute consciousness of death, the instructive, consolatory, and celebratory functions of poetry ended. In their place arose the obsessive dilemma we have recognized in Dickinson: the powerful *will to signify* but without adequately noble subjects for that language of consciousness to engage. Stevens' "The Man on the Dump" is the modern text that holds the crucial conditions of this irrepressible will with its irrepressible need, its outlet in language and the absence of a commensurate subject. There one sits and beats an old tin can for that which one believes. Just at this point, the hard truth of the isolate self and of self-doubt intrudes with the essential modernist question that Dickinson, hymn after hymn, implicitly posed long before.

> Could it after all
> Be merely oneself, as superior as the ear
> To a crow's voice? Did the nightingale torture the ear,
> Pack the heart and scratch the mind? And does the ear
> Solace itself in peevish birds? Is it peace,
> Is it a philosopher's honeymoon, one finds
> On the dump? Is it to sit among mattresses of the dead,
> Bottles, pots, shoes and grass and murmur *aptest eve:*
> Is it to hear the blatter of grackles and say
> *Invisible priest;* is it to eject, to pull
> The day to pieces and cry *stanza my stone?*

Where are the tuneful subjects? Departed from pristine, whole simplicity, as Stevens' sight turned in his poem from the brilliant bowl of carnations to the imperfect that is our paradise, Dickinson's flawed words and stubborn sounds made art out of the ashheap of hopes, the wreck of the assaulted psyche. Harmony and comprehension were not the material and the purpose, but rather death and ignorance. They were, as I observed, the sacred poverty out of which her verbal imagination leapt and leapt again and again. We thus can see that the fragmentation of the Dickinson poetic canon—the brevity, the scraps, the impacted language, the intensity without development, the failure of wholeness—is the visible wrestling of her imaginative power with the problem of art without belief, without grace, without assent.

The second crisis, deeper than the first, is the absence of a conceptual agenda. Without an inhering—not necessarily conscious—design that establishes perception, which in turn binds poetry into a body so that it has a measurable relationship to an extralinguistic reality, poetry is willfully self-concerned, rambunctious in its logocentrism. This is demonstrably the case with Dickinson's extraordinary work. Modern poetry of this sort concerns itself with its inner workings, with the linguistic processes by which it constructs its exclusive character. Dickinson's language likewise is concerned with its interior strategies. It is a dangerous moment when the meaning goes out of things and life stands straight and punctual, and yet no signal comes. That is the moment of poetry without belief, the blatter of grackles, the buzzing uncertain fly. So in Dickinson, as in much later poetry, there are no radical similitudes, no representation, no organization beneath the self-promoting language. The defective mirror displays the disconnected images of a defective reality. Behind the language is—nothing but the language power. The scraps of Dickinson's verse, with all those absences of finality, constitute the visible sign of one kind of verse that was to emerge at the limits of modernism in America.

The third crisis forced art into its modern extremity. It is the result of the doubt about what poetry is to be about, and what it can possibly do with no conceptual coherence, no project. The reality that comes into view in Dickinson's unarrangeable verse is the art language that she took into her reclusion. The outward drama of this occurred when she met Higginson in that first interview. She disengaged poetry from the complicated network of exterior existence, making the art self-conscious, private, momentary. It was a major breakup of the language of American literature. Her words had begun to lose resemblance to events and even to the things outside her window. The result was that her language released itself from the strict architecture of syntax, from the architecture of thought, and thus from the architecture of reality. It was an ungodly freedom. The ultimate result of the withdrawal was the enactment of an essential character of modern poetry: the opening of the breach between reality and the imagination.

Out of this disjunction that has served for decades as part of the essential subject matter of modern American poetry came the ironicalizing of reality through language disparity. Art, some of it, no longer has a way to possess or even to name speechless green or social nature. It does not seek to transform that exterior world. It is satisfied with fragmentation. It calls the world into question because it has abandoned it.

The special modernity signaled by the problematics of Dickinson's verse can be related to the vague outline of a poetics. It is not a long step at all from the idea of art split off from the world to Dickinson's intuitive, accurate sense that her poetry was only haunted by reality, and to our discovery that the poetry is haunted in a way that made the absence of the world its most singular feature.

This compounded problem of art's realm and art's function is expressed in American poetry by a host of peculiarly American excesses. The extremes include stylistic and grammatical indulgence as well as tonal and metaphysical intemperateness. D. H. Lawrence called it, in Whitman's case, "chuff chuff." There are other examples.

> Passage indeed O soul to primal thought,
> Not lands and seas alone, thy own clear freshness,
> The young maturity of brood and bloom,
> To realms of budding bibles.   (Whitman)

> To be certain . . . certain . . .
> (Amid aerial flowers) . . . time for arrangements—
> Drifted on
> To the final estrangement   (Pound)

> Why then Ile fit you. Hieronymo's mad againe.
> Datta. Dayadhvam. Damyata.
>   Shantih shantih shantih   (Eliot)

There is a similar compulsion almost everywhere one looks in the poetry that representational clarity and rhetorical persuasion should yield to the spontaneous interplay of tropes. This curse of anarchy has created a pervasive colloquial uncertainty with no conviction that reality, the foul rag-and-bone shop of the heart, can be encompassed by any system of justice. Instead, what we are so numbingly familiar with in some American poetry is toughness, sloppy expression, and the absence of sequential or sophisticated thought. They are qualities prefigured in that "kind of a Cockney, dressed in jaunty clothes," the foppish, unmatured, even crude but showy unheroic bee by which Dickinson identified herself in the letter to Graves. Disorderly spontaneity, evasion of tradition or of a complicated project: this is irreverence made into an art of diminished ambition. The devastating combination that drives so much brilliant, difficult, opaque, affective contemporary poetry is this same nexus: power of consciousness and of language made unruly by purposelessness.

Dickinson's stunning intuitive performance of these crises of power and authority is "My Life had stood – a loaded Gun." But her April is a sign as well of the modern dilemma. Dickinson never left off venting the hyperconsciousness that was so conspicuous in the middle years of her poetry writing. Six years before her death, when from the available evidence she was not writing much at all, she was making poetry out of death and ignorance. Even then, and in the modern way we now understand, she was making poetry in the wasteland. Lines glowing with their irrepressible will to make syllables, to signify the ecstasy the imagination could know but experience could not supply, went down in pencil on a scrap of wrapping paper. Our knowledge of her syllabic counts and her contorted syntax enables us to make out the fifth line here, which is meant to say "only the desolation was missed."

> The Thrill came slowly like a Boon for
> Centuries delayed
> It's fitness growing like the Flood
> In sumptuous solitude –
> The desolation only missed
> While Rapture changed it's dress
> And stood amazed before the Change
> In ravished Holiness –   (P-1495)

Dickinson, Emerson, Whitman

Establishing discontinuities is a difficult task, but Dickinson, we see, played a role in one of the most profound shifts in American culture. Within the space of twenty-five years, between 1837 when Emerson delivered his American Scholar address and 1862 when Dickinson was swept by the fire of her creative writing, the dominant culture in the increasingly industrial northeast evidently ceased to organize its experiences as it had and began to think and to represent its essential experiences in a new way. The shift was more complicated than that, for while Emerson moved the artistic consciousness in a sweeping dynamic toward a new prosaic flexibility and absorption, Dickinson was inaugurating an exclusive, reductive, proseless language that actually established the opposite extreme to Emerson and his follower Walt Whitman. We have, indeed, as I have outlined in *Emerson and Literary Change*, the poles here of synthesis and separation in American poetic art.

The conventional wisdom is that two of these central figures, Emerson and Dickinson, the one in fact exceptionally conscious of his aesthetic revolution and the other not at all, are to be seen as partners in the same philosophical enterprise. Harold Bloom's proposition in *Wallace Stevens: The Poems of Our Climate* is perhaps the most forcefully stated. He sees them both as figures in an Emersonian dynamic of power and idealized transformation. Yet clearly, on the more consequential level at which we are looking, in the knowledge of where the major meanings reside, we see how contrary these two imaginative forces are and how they represent even to our own day the opposing perimeters of American poetic activity.[5] Emerson and Dickinson are different in consciousness, in craft, and in language. Dickinson is so different and so unconventional and wayward at the levels out of sight, that she is really a major but undefined and contrary language force in America.

The fundamental arrangements of experience and of expectation of the three major poets at the language divide are established by the central metaphors each chose as an emblem. Emerson's and Whitman's, while differing in the degree of earthiness, are ultimately related. Emerson's is the eyeball moment. His conversion process, by which experience is transformed into truth by the infinite capacity of man and of Man-Becoming, is the act by which all events are made intelligible in the large scheme of man's divinity. It is a momentous and affirmative figure, this making the world transparent, for in it man stands at the center of all the circles, the world concentric with him and, most idealistic, each part of that world a reciprocal extension of that divine man. All flowing yet unified, all parts linked and mutually generative, Emerson's belief that the poet made this revelation intelligible and turned the world to glass is at one extreme of the activity of American poetry.

Whitman's figure of the poet as manly autochthon is of a piece with Emerson's poet-hero, though more forthright, more body-conscious. Both arrange their world in a unity, all things sprung from the same ground, all experience a celebration of this divine and democratic cohesion, poetry itself a song to union. Whitman's poems filled Emerson's absorptive, lyrical, prose-essay form with American images—decking his song as he says in "Lilacs"—in a tallying chant. And so we have with Emerson and with Whitman a half-generation after him—in the transparent eyeball and authochthonous poet-hero—comparable figures of an intelligible and exhilarating world. In Dickinson the figure is fundamentally opposed, the haunted-house arranging experience of a different order. In this ghostly iconography are all the mysterious, terrifying, unintelligible experiences Emerson and Whitman left out. Her poet, neither earthy hero nor transported mystic, is instead "Some pale Reporter, from the awful doors." Her knowledge is of ignorance, fear, and crisis, met not in communal experience but in solitude. "All the Earth strove common round," she wrote in her anti-Emersonianism, "Without Delight, or Beam." She dwelt as she said in possibility but by interposing her words in place of the familiar she managed, though quite undeliberately, to make the visible hard to see. Contrary to Emerson, there is the experience in her poetry of both a seeing and an unseeing. Dickinson's is not Emerson's eyeball moment, but its opposite. Where his poems and essays convey perceived clarity and idealistic conviction, hers spring, in significant part indefinite and occluded, out of ignorance and pain. Not epic synthesis or celebration and certainly not Concord platonism, Dickinson's poems are haunted by all that they do not understand or have lost. Side by side, their epiphanic statements are profound opposites. First Emerson:

My head bathed by the blithe air and uplifted into infinite space – all mean egotism vanishes, I become a transparent eyeball; I am nothing; I see all; the currents of the Universal Being circulate through me; I am part or parcel of God.

Now Dickinson:

Tis a dangerous moment for any one when the meaning goes out of things and Life stands straight – and punctual – and yet no signal comes.

Incompatible assumptions underlie their main poetic metaphors of the world changed to glass and the house of specters. For Dickinson the past exists in the present as a haunting sense of loss. What makes nature and art haunted, as she implied to Higginson, is that both preserve witness of what has departed through loss or death or appears in the mysterious cyclical resumption of life and the process that leads to death again. The fullness of summer for Dickinson is haunted by the inevitability of its ending. This fierce consciousness of the past, while not foreign to Emerson, was always of far less import to him than the possibility of the future. His art looked to the future and Man-Becoming, as did Whitman's after him, with a deliberate transcending of the limitations of fate. Dickinson, in acute contrast, repeatedly figured fate in her work. She wrote in poem 926 of patience as an insect's futile effort among infinite forces: " 'Scaping one – against the other / Fruitlesser to fling." She sang her steady undertheme of fate and the absence of choice, emphasizing the tragic inevitability of certain experiences.

> How Complicate
> The Discipline of Man –
> Compelling Him to Choose Himself
> His Preappointed Pain   (P-910)

When her speaker says in poem 1549 "My Wars are laid away in Books," this surrogate faces the world with a good deal less sanguineness than did Emerson. Dickinson's assumption about the ever-present threat of trial, psychic immobility, loss, and death is not his.

Dickinson did not seek to abolish time and space as did Emerson, but accepted them as the barriers against which consciousness strove. Hers were more the assumptions of Hardy with his unblinking sight of time's limitations than of Emerson in his characteristic exhilaration, as in "The Over-Soul": "not a valve, not a wall, not an intersection is there anywhere in nature, but one blood rolls uninterruptedly ... through all men." Dickinson recognized singularity, disjunction, doubt, and the abyss, with only faint promise of cosmic solutions of spirit. If Emerson was immersed in the bath of idealism to the point of disembodiment—the egoless eyeball moment—Dickinson drew back into acute consciousness and the pain of the aftermath. She wrote of emotional partitions more fearsome than walls:

> A Cobweb – wove in Adamant –
> A Battlement – of Straw –
>
> A limit like the Vail
> Unto the Lady's face –
> But every Mesh – a Citadel –
> And Dragons – in the Crease –   (P-398)

Their languages were fundamentally different in form and capacity. Bloom sees the two poets as versions of the same mentality, but their languages signify the opposite. Emerson's clarifies and liberates, sweeps particulars in and absorbs, makes large synthetic designs, but Dickinson's, as I have been at pains to demonstrate, resists clarity, excludes rather than accumulates, carves out instead of combining. With an aesthetics of its own, her language became both an instrument and a form for atomizing reality, the idiom a cutting tool, a separator, a dispersal instrument rather than one of broad inclusiveness. Hers could incise and discriminate with unfamiliar minuteness: "Crumbling is not an instant's Act ... Delapidation's processes are organized Decays." Her poem "Further in Summer than the Birds" is a powerful exercise of incursion. Its language addresses a moment of seamless continuity—the fullness of summer—and inserts an alien lexicon—Antiquest, spectral Canticle, Druidic Difference—to find the very moment of change when summer turns to fall. She is not celebrating the change but calibrating it, dissecting it, placing it in no system. In the starkest modernist way, the poem is an analysis without an explanation. In this same momentary power of perception, lacking a conceptual frame as a way of comprehending, lie the terrible separation and ignorance that mark a considerable amount of modern and postmodern verse. Like Epstein's Rock Drill sculpture, this Dickinsonian idiom speaks fear without understanding, force without purpose, art without redemptive intention.

Dickinson cut and dispersed where Emerson and then Whitman embraced and unified. In her work is our first glimpse of the decomposing, nontranscendent strain in American poetry, the other extreme from the epic builders. If Whitman arched the landscape in his windy lines, she distinguished, dissected, got beneath labels in her tight lines. In the end, she represents one of the two basic language visions, one of the two primary idioms of American poetry. The long-lived Emerson idiom, elaborated by a host of followers beginning with Whitman, is cumulative and metaphoric. Dickinson's, out of personal need, experiential limitation, and primitivist power, carves out, takes the moment, is metonymic. Hers is the other great idiom of American poetry.

If Emerson's is the constructive vein in American poetry, with a platonic program and conversational architecture and connective tissue, hers is the destructive vein. Out of an idiom afflicted by spontaneity, set in motion without authority or self-definition, grew the dilemma in American poetry of dissociation and audacity without a project. While urban life decisively influenced, even brought about, modern forms of disjunction and pathological temper, Dickinson's idiom had the simpler ideas of a nineteenth-century rural background and came out of personal withdrawal, incoherence, and the exclusion from comprehension. The two poetries form a curious parallel with remote and different origins. Both languages make the modern world visible.

Even the speaker of Dickinson's verse is appropriately dispersed. Unlike the heroic Adamic voice that speaks in Emerson's essays and in *Leaves of Grass*, Dickinson's voice is broken up, variable, unsure, latently hysterical, frenetically inconsistent. The fragmented tones indicate opposed needs and fears; what binds them together is the metonymic language and the force of its surprise. The disintegration of the voice itself is part of the acute consciousness in the language that lacks a conceptual center.

Such an idiom necessarily catalyzes an intelligence different from that of Emerson and Whitman and her other contemporaries. This new linguistic intelligence enabled Dickinson to do what the language of Emerson and Whitman was not equipped to do but which the modern age had an especial need for: to find art and wit in the inner as well as the exterior wasteland. Her aphoristic brilliance was the equal of Emerson's; yet where his clipped adages are testaments of idealized conversion, hers remind about what is taken away, the deprivation that accompanies prosperity. This Dickinson idiom took for its natural territory what Emerson's and Whitman's idiom could not see. Dickinson mapped it in eight words:

> Winter under cultivation
> Is as arable as Spring.   (P-1707)

Here was a constitutive modernism uniquely creating art after the Fall, which meant, as we have seen in the modern way, art as part of the ash heap.

The Dickinson Strain

Dickinson went her own intuitive way, necessarily in profound contrast to Emerson's highly conscious, articulated but expansive prosaicising and to Whitman's aggressively prosaic, synthesizing poetry with what D. H. Lawrence called a superhuman allness. Alien from their ways, extreme in her disjunctive form and incoherent thought, she was precursive of another line in the major modern and postmodern American poets. That strain involves elements of both form and attitude. Formlessness would be a more exact term, for she inaugurated the literary era when the controlled, silent, projective significance of formal unity would break up irreparably, and when this mutilation of the whole would reflect, perhaps in some cases even bring about, the great modern syndrome of anxiety. The fixation continues to dominate in fiction writers, such as John Hawkes, whose declared poetics sounds like a current communiqué from the modernist extremity. Everything for me "is dangerous," he said for the record, "everything is tentative, nothing is certain. I think the writing of fiction involves enormous anxiety and enormous risk. And I want fiction always to situate us in the psychic and literal spot where life is most difficult, most dangerous, most beautiful."[6] This was Dickinson's ground a century earlier. In an uncanny way, the characteristics of her verse that reflected her own disintegration became emblematic and peculiarly expressive of these particular postmodern preoccupations and anxieties.

T. S. Eliot in mid-career arrived at an attitudinal indecision and formal incompleteness that was also the opposite of Emerson's heroic dramatization of Man-Becoming, was identical rather to Dickinson's acute but centerless consciousness. The voice in *Ash-Wednesday*, that crucial text of his evolving concerns, is the inversion of the Emerson voice of the great essays where man is at the center of the world's experiences, assimilating them, synthesizing them, turning them to moral truth. Here is Eliot's Man-Doubting, man debilitated:

> Because I do not hope to know again
> The infirm glory of the positive hour
> Because I do not think
> Because I know I shall not know
> The one veritable transitory power
> Because I cannot drink
> There, where trees flower and springs flow,
> for there is nothing again

Seven decades after Dickinson's own audacious linguistic trials at the experience of psychic death and ignorance, this is once again the sound of exhaustion and the exclusion from comprehension. Winters said of Eliot in 1937 what he could also have said of Dickinson, if he had concerned himself with the significance of the peculiarities of her poetic oeuvre and of what she was demonstrably incapable of doing: "his career since [he abandoned Laforguian irony] has been largely a career of what one might call psychic impressionism, a formless curiosity concerning queer feelings which are related to odds and ends of more or less profound thought."[7]

Before Pound, whose work evolved from his early translations into an art of ellipsis, of the sophisticated composing of pieces and glimpses held loosely together by a vaguely epic voice, Dickinson had out of natural necessity adopted an aesthetic of fragments for which the intense but indefinite poetic consciousness presiding over the poems served as the psychological vortex, what I ealier talked about as the microchristus role. Pound exploited the fragmentation that he rationalized as an updated mode of classical abstraction, like making planes out of soft human contours as the sculptors Epstein and Gaudier-Brzeska did. It was a way of handling the multitudinousness rushing into the metropolitan consciousness that in turn resembled London in its diversity and lack of form. Dickinson's was certainly not a metropolitan consciousness, but her idiosyncratic arrangement of experience into fragments with no heirarchical order was the innocent prefiguring of much that Pound did. The *Cantos* have the same problem of self-characterization and therefore, like Dickinson's work, the same absence of closure.

Because she had withdrawn from the world, living almost exclusively in the hyperconsciousness, she widened by quantum dimension the gulf between the active artistic consciousness and exterior reality. This difference between syllable and sound was a prefiguring of the dilemma of the separatist imagination that constitutes the fixed concern of Wallace Stevens. His poetry is an elegant, many-textured inquiry into the moment when the forming mind faces the natural world, the silence between the woman's song and the sea. Dickinson's work is an intuitive expression of that same rift at its most astonishing as well as most terrifying. Her poetry taken together hymns the failure at last of finding the idea of order at Key West. Hers was the Blue Peninsula, mysterious and beautiful. Into that difficult space between the language and the reality, for both poets, came the moments when ignorance was supreme, the fictive orders defeated by reality, the Emperor of Ice-Cream the fit suitor for her Tropic Bride. When the consciousness, word-charged and acute and needful, was excluded not only from comprehension but from art as well, the banging on the lard pail began. Then there was no way to make the world over into an order, no way to stanza the stone, sound bereft of syllable.

So basic was her situation as an artist of penetrating speech but lacking the harsher discipline of the outer world, she anticipated still other moderns and postmoderns. Hart Crane felt the bond between them, their shared need to find an order that always evaded. His supercharged and arbitrarily signifying language followed on with the problem of art on the dump and the corruption on the American ideal of cultural innocence. His contorted language, similar to hers in its logocentric intensity and discplacement of the fallen world, discharged in what he called "illogical impingements," and thereby displayed strains and needs comparable to the ones she had confronted in the freedom of her eccentric privacy. Indeed, that Dickinson was partly a symbolist precursor is made most apparent when we consider her work alongside Crane's. Both poets sought in their overburdened language fired by an acute consciousness to make language reify what, in Dickinson's phrase, was "Out of Plumb of Speech."

This was the audacity that appealed to Crane and where he sensed their shared preoccupation. It was the realm of sensation inside speech, inside consciousness—"Before Decision – stooped to Speech" as Dickinson phrased it in poem 643—that each sought to bring to speech. In the attempt, both hunted the instinctive, primary sensations of the symbolist mode and manifested similarly mystic assumptions concerning the relationship of root language and psychic experience. Crane, in his fond sonnet to Dickinson, limned their common goal.

> The harvest you descried and understand
> Needs more than wit to gather, love to bind.
> Some reconcilement of remotest mind –
>
> Leaves Ormus rubyless, and Ophir chill.

Theirs was a parochial faith that language would make the embassy from deep-drowned realms, decipher, as Crane said in his Melville poem, "The portent wound in corridors of shells." It was a case for both of them where language took the place of understanding.

She shared with William Carlos Williams, as she did with Crane, a faith in language's grasp and, at the same time, displacement of everything outside of language itself. In Williams, the word-centeredness shows in his constant concern for the freeing of the artist's imagination. The preoccupation is mirrored in all those images of fragile or momentary beauty—the girl, the flower, the dance—that are violated by blockages in the culture or self-induced. Both poets, a hundred years apart but alike in their limitations of range intensified by their enormous needs of consciousness, sought to induce a meaning from the accumulation of pieces. Williams, though he aspired to an epic sweep and coherence, attained mainly a voice in search of epic. Winters, with a sure eye for the primitivist character in American poetry, said of Williams what can, as we have abundantly seen, surely be said of Dickinson: "he is wholly incapable of coherent thought . . . His experience is disconnected and fragmentary."[8]

These major modernists share with Dickinson the dazzling attempt in language to get at primary wisdom, but the wisdom she sought evaded her to the end. Only the language weapon remained and the need of her acute consciousness. Improvisation, then, the loss of conceptual centering, a sharp sense of the separation of the artist's language from the reality she doesn't understand, the loss of any purpose except to interrupt the unspeaking All, the sense that material for poetry has ceased to exist (leaving old mattresses on a dump for aptest eve), the fragmentation—all these elements came, one way or another but mainly in the absences, to the surface of Dickinson's writing, as if the world of the later, most extreme moderns had first existed in her psyche, in its ignorance and need. She had no epic aspiration as did Pound, Eliot, Crane, and Williams, or Dwight and Barlow before her. The centerlessness in Dickinson was of a purity that stops one's breath, as I think it did Higginson's. He wrote her in 1869 to say: "Sometimes I take out your letters & verses, dear friend, and when I feel their strange power, it is not strange that I find it hard to write & that long months pass. I have the greatest desire to see you ... but ... you only enshroud yourself in this fiery mist & I cannot reach you" (L-330a). There was no scheme he could grasp in this intense woman who had rejected the world. In fact, she replied to his letter with this disarming but accurate self-assessment: "When a little Girl I remember hearing that remarkable passage and preferring the 'Power,' not knowing at the time that 'Kingdom' and 'Glory' were included" (L-330).

The poets I have mentioned, precursor and moderns alike, are poets of expressive need and lost purpose, of the crisis of poetry on the dump. Robert Lowell, in some of his late work, is perhaps the epitome among the Americans. It is not simply that Lowell had deepened as a confessional poet who, like Dickinson, felt himself in the role of microchristus, the individual sufferer of the time's pain and the personal ground of all the religious doubt and need. It is rather Lowell's increasing sense of lost purpose, the recognition, in unguarded and then in the most conscious moments, of his inability to find coherence not only outside art but in the art itself. There was, as with the other poets but here more baldly stated, only a language instrument without a conceptual frame, the power of a hyperconsciousness and scorching words without a redeeming vision of the world or the self. In the modern way, all were sustained in part by the fiction that language in a certain order still had a function, and perhaps with good fortune the ability to call up a purpose and a truth.

The most plaintive cry sounds in Lowell's final poetry where, out of desperation, he equates his poems with snapshots. Any epic sense or synthesis is gone. The imagined whole of which he dreams as an artist is impossible to achieve. What is left is what Dickinson managed with such elan in her terrible ignorance and planlessness: the giving of a moment's attention and a moment's language to—well—moments. What for her was an intuitive instance of what poetry could accomplish in reclusion was in Lowell's case, and with fine analytical power, an instance of what poetry can hope to be in an age of barbiturates and breakdown. Here, in Lowell's language, is Dickinson's terror of the piecemeal, acute consciousness in a postmodern plaint. From *Day By Day* (the book's title signals the lack of project), the poem "Epilogue" stops us cold with its identical dilemma.

> I hear the noise of my own voice:
> *The painter's vision is not a lens,*
> *it trembles to caress the light.*
> But sometimes everything I write
> with the threadbare art of my eye
> seems a snapshot,
> lurid, rapid, garish, grouped,
> heightened from life,
> yet paralyzed by fact.
> All's misalliance.

The poem shows with sharp explicitness the Dickinson syndrome. We see each of the principal elements of the dilemma in Dickinson's expression more than a century before: the absence of a project, the impossibility of wholeness, the inevitable turning with the power of language to separate moments, heightening each in a gaudy way, setting the words to swallow reality as snapshots do, making an art that takes the world apart into moments that have no coherence or redemption. The poem's genesis is the modern dilemma of acute desire, an irrepressible language consciousness, and the exclusion from comprehension. "Epilogue" is Lowell watching himself banging the lard pail on the ash heap. The first person there, because she had no alternative, was Emily Dickinson.

Beyond Lowell's orderly expression of inability, the same disjoining limitation allied with power has informed other recent poetry in an extreme way. We see this language of separation becoming autistic discourse with a vengeance. It takes the form of linguistic scat, the natural development it seems of preoccupation with words and lack of a metaphysics. Denise Levertov has called it "the poetry of linguistic impulse," and absorption in language itself involves "the ap-

parent distortion of experience in . . . a poem for the sake of verbal effects."[9] It is a kind of jazz sketching with words. James Tate and perhaps John Ashbery most conspicuously have willfully created disjunction in a language of aborted idea and compulsive speech which
in Dickinson was the crystallization of a fierce primitivism. These
lines begin Tate's poem "Heatstroke," a performance of the exhaustion of meaning, a hammering on the lard pail:

> I always have many flowers –
> My neighbor gives them to me.
> I seem not to have the strength
> to go on with my confession.
>
> That beautiful woman is a Chilean:
> she is a fickle woman, an intelligent
> good woman, very beautiful. That is
> the trouble: I never have the correct
>
> time. You see the sense this is making,
> the old Presidential Palace? Always
> she is tending the garden with loving
> excellence – in one motion, everything
>
> at stake for that instant. Some star
> fell down on her and so what.

The title "Heatstroke" is wonderfully indicative of the poem's combined passion and enervation. Tate's poem "The Human Eraser"
speaks similarly of lost meaning in tender but pathological language.
It is Dickinson's hysteria in quiet, segmental pretended speech.

> My one minute stands up and salutes
> a monument of strangled grass.
> The flow of stone says forget it,
> there's no life here, only a detached
>
> headache; but it has its own idea
> of the cold and expensive smile.
> It is soft with words and comes back
> emblazoned in white on the sky,
>
> a terrible message that has stopped
> searching for the perfect night . . .

Surely the inescapable curse of spontaneity is on these lines. Tate's
poems are self-consciously language-centered and intent on sporadic

beauty. The language is contorted by the violation of selectional rules of diction and by unreal tropes cut off from the world we see, all arranged in a deceptively familiar, overly simple, syntax. There is, in a brilliantly cool mode, a willful repudiation of a signifying web that can engage the world outside the words, and thus there is no meaning in the signs. The words have turned away from the world into a negating discourse in an extreme exercise of the freedom we can call Dickinsonian.

What began as personal deprivation for Dickinson, with her unique intersection of power and reclusion, has in the late moderns become the shared destruction of representation, authority, development, wholeness; what remains are the shreds of intense consciousness. It is an anxious activity.

10 A New Intelligence

The special significance of Dickinson's decentered language is that it activated a new intelligence that reverberates in the poetry of our own day. Causative links from words to thought, words to seeing, seem to be as mysterious as they are actual and strong. "The meaning of a book," Merleau-Ponty wrote, "is given, in the first instance, not so much by its ideas as by a systematic and unexpected variation of the modes of language, of narrative, or of existing literary forms. This accent, this particular modulation of speech—if the expression is successful—is assimilated little by little by the reader, and it gives him access to a thought to which he was until then indifferent or even opposed."[1] Altering this formulation to take account of Dickinson's unique texts with their unsystematic modes of language, we gain a further insight into the process by which forms of language begin to affect forms of perception. Gertrude Stein possessed a comparable view of how expressive forms relate to perception when she observed that World War I could only be understood as a cubist phenomenon.

The absence of the cumulative wholeness of prose in Dickinson's poetry, its lack of connections and an accomplished identity, do not add up to a language of compliance toward the world. With all the impediments to precise meaning, hers is not a language consonant in disposition to an open, lucid world. The obscurities and omissions force us under the surface. We discover there, with Dickinson's language as a plow, disquieting events that are radically modernist.

We know with reluctant certitude today that language is not our docile servant but that we submit to the concealed demands of its arrangements and frame our understanding by its patterns or lack of patterns. In a literary context, this suggests that how a culture regards itself and how its poets' languages speak are related. In short, what is seen and what is said are connected. Different words incite different kinds of sight and understanding. When the man in Frost's "The Most of It" cries out plaintively that he wants original response, original love, from the green grove where he stands alone, the speech is such that whatever is heard or comes the next moment into view is the answer. In the event, a buck draws near the man and its "answer" to his language is the very construct of the cry: the buck passes with no sound except the inhuman one of a horny hoof on stone. The buck is simply a creature, but the man's cry for original love has made the buck a response and thus the sign of nature's indifference and apartness.

Similarly, Dickinson's language with its habitual surprises and disjunctions is a peculiar aesthetic system that breeds a disposition toward the world, activating, that is a new intelligence.

Rift Vision

Dickinson's language defines and disconnects. It disperses perception rather than integrating it and making complex fields of experience visible in a transparency of words. In this sense the idiom is a new way of making history by reflecting incoherence. Unlike melodic music, which seems to be the harmonious and resonant language of the human central nervous system, her language meets our inherent need for dissonance, derangement, and liberation. Dickinson thus provided an idiom by which to see piece by piece, like photography, two of the obsessively explored areas of a later time: life in the psyche and life in the city.

I have described the special field of her language as restless motion and alteration. She came incessantly to attempt, as she did in the poem about the transformation wrought in her by Barrett Browning's poetry, to *define and calibrate the change*, making infinitesimal as well as colossal difference visible. Invisible, silent changes within, perhaps to madness when "The first Day's Night had come," were part of the altering that occupied the vision of her language. She remains the supreme poet, as I have said, of the altered or altering state.

This ability is the more impressive because it is checked by no conceptual concern. It is isolated alteration, saying what a thing is as against nothing but what it was a moment before.

The primary moment that presented itself to her restless, glimpsing language was the moment of instability: the instability of happiness or rapture, the unstable elements of composure or satiety because "the Thief ingredient accompanies all Sweetness." Mindful of this condition, the language acts out in Dickinson's concentrated way how conscious consciousness could grow. Her defective word strings, because they force language into the rift of difference, activate an intelligence characterized by its incising power. The main elements of this language, discrepant in tone, unsettling in its violation of expectations and in its candor, promoting insights set off by its opaqueness and mystery, add up to a rift vision.

She excavated with language beneath the labels—Pain has; Hope is; Exultation is; Faith is—and found a modern fact, the rift between the ideal and the actual, between figure and fact, the fall from wholeness and purpose, all the stages of sensation blurred by labels. This is the language of a new curiosity, and with it Dickinson's imagination flies to widen the gap between words and things, words and dogma. She idealized seamlessness but the ground of her language was what roiled beneath, unsettling, specific, slightly terrifying under the surface. Her language, to borrow words from Stevens, knew there was that difference between "the" and "an."

Her subject, then, is the *structure of difference*, and this in the end is the rooted meaning of *modern*. Language forces the labels up, and the moments open, establishing disjunction. Her language is a differential calculus dealing with the rate of change of variable functions, and thus it is a language of modernism. It bends the eye to altered, unfamiliar sight. She put the idea under great compression in poem 571 which, its eye aslant, "notes delight / As difficult / As Stalactite."

This is language that is an instrument of new perception. It is outspoken, threatening, capable of cutting through momentarily to unvarnished reality. It is capable of causing "A vulgar grimace in the Flesh." More self-conscious than was ordinary, her words defeat the delusions of facile labels. It is archeology performed not on experience but on the terms of experience, a language of excavation:

"Crumbling is not an instant's act." In an elemental way, the defective grammar helped to deconstruct perception and consciousness, finding in this way, even though it could not sustain an analysis, exact instants of intelligence even in the most evasive states of existence.

The parallactic technique that produces the estrangement, instability, and aftervision discovers the world we think of as peculiarly twentieth-century. This view is a function of the character of her texts which together form a metalanguage that is momentary, a cameralike instrument of seeing anew. It shows up the disparity between communal sentimentality and individually felt sensation; it explores the rift between faith and urgent needs, able to make, as in the famous bird, snake, and butterfly poems (the butterfly "parts Himself"), a stunning *otherness*. It is a whole language of discrepant life, discovering the pervasive absences in modern existence: the loss of a spiritual core and the living in the condition of aftermath. In that wasted environment buzzes the hyperconsciousness that is synonymous with Dickinson. And in this acute consciousness are acted out the twin crises that afflict modern poetry: the crisis of art in the wasteland and the withdrawal of language from the structure of reality.

Her language opened up the very wounds it then entered to explore, as in the calculating of pain in "There is a pain – so utter." The words enter into differences, as between various griefs, with a hard edge and a sharp eye for how people wear their pain. The poem beginning "I measure every Grief I meet" uncharacteristically goes on for forty lines, but throughout it is characteristically acute, like analytical cubism before a table or a face, taking apart a generalization. The basic modern dilemma is a loss of wholeness that cannot, it seems, ever be filled, and this is the territory of Dickinson.

Facing difference, the language seeks definition as momentary sustenance, as in "It was not Death, for I stood up." The rift exists between the sign of a thing and the thing itself, as in poem 633: "When Bells stop ringing – Church – begins." It opens up strange sight, as in the grave there is "Another way – to see – " (P-627). Dickinson did not "take the Tale for true" characteristically, but talked about the swindle (P-476). The definition poems are an explicit part of this language penetration into difference, seeking finer states of loneliness, doubt, exhilaration, and defeat. Her technique of parallax consists of holding two things together and seeing difference, as in comparisons like these: a bird and a piece of down, autumn color and blood, death and taking leave for a trip, death and sleep. It was a matter of seeing comparatively. Heaven, seen in this rift vision, may be disappointing.

> Some morning of Chagrin –
> The waking in a Gnat's – embrace –
> Our Giant – further on –   (P-534)

Difference intensifies consciousness. This prospect of hers was proleptically modern, for harmony did not induce it but rather, as Williams came to know, dissonance and the induction of hyperconsciousness, holding what is in the mind against what is outside it and actual. The Dickinson question, the kind her language incessantly posed, was always this: "Was Dying as He thought – or different" (P-622).

The Dickinson language was itself the perceiving of discrepant events, the disassembling of familiar categories. Withdrawn like her from the experiential world, it existed in a perpetual interstice. The poet is fully aware of this existence. The poem beginning "Civilization – spurns – the Leopard!" is an exemplary allegory of being estranged. Again and again the language entered the interval between the abstract and the individual saying "To Ache is human – not polite." Between the convention and the private nerve is the revealing interstitial word.

The idiom inevitably opened a rift in the seamless event of Me. In the poem that begins "Me from Myself – to banish," her words consider the extinguishing of consciousness as a way to peace, the "Abdication – / Me – of Me." This is the language of the psychic life of the modern: isolated, problematic, the mental event cut loose from any context that would make it intelligible. The poem is the drama without the plot, the pain without the cause, the existential phenomenon simply of self-destructive psychic energy. That "most Arduous of Journeys" is made by Dickinson's language with instinctive penetration. At its destination in the psyche it found those modern bugaboos: restlessness, lack of identity, mystery. The riveting qualities of her opening lines all are of a piece with the unfamiliar world seen. It was a composite strategy that included her use of an exotic topography—Naples, volcanoes, hissing Corals—to expose the hidden destructive forces in the psyche. "A still – Volcano – Life": for all his power of drama and accumulation of terror, Poe never broke out of his unified aesthetic vision to show the randomness of the self-consuming mind. His psyches, as in "The Raven," consume themselves in orderly fashion.

Dickinson's language opens with alarming ease onto estates of astonishment. The horses' heads at the end of "Because I could not stop" are the unexcelled example. The idiom has a remarkable vision for the alluring fantasies of the psyche, "The Myrrhs, and Mochas, of the Mind" which "Are it's iniquity" (P-1537). Her language began to see the complexity of the modern psyche but especially its reposeless, identityless activity. It was a language of dark disquiet, most so when she began poems with the mysterious, unreferring "It." So the poems inaugurated immediate awareness of the absent, the yearned-for, the terrifyingly undefinable.

Though there is no city in Dickinson's work, her language of the incoherent psyche is inevitably the language of the modern city. Whitman had seen the city as the emblem of vitality and democracy. The analogy of the modern city and the modern mind, however, developed in a later generation of poets who knew both the dehumanization of massed mechanized living and the anxious psyche that had lost its idealism. Hart Crane, for all his visionary striving, equated the mind with the city's darkest passages. The equation is in his phrase in the tunnel section of *The Bridge*, the "interborough fissures of the mind." For the poets beginning with Baudelaire and then Pound and Eliot, the city was the patternless construct that held the conglomerate, incoherent, sometimes raging and destructive experience of the modern age. The city was Pound's and Eliot's vortex of experience, a concrete ragbag into which to put the modern experience, Spinoza, and the smell of cooking. Dickinson's language was one of the modern city's idioms coming into being. Like the city, it was activity without content, a process without a design. It fragmented experience, allowed the viewer to enter but gave him no order of perception. It held countless delights but showed no arrangement, offered surprises but no principle of selection. The stroller was on his own. Dickinson's piecemeal vision, had the city not emerged in its own haphazard way, would have invented it. Hers was a language waiting for a subject. Her anarchic aesthetic, in a fortuitous way that originated in her private makeup and problems, would be a ragbag aesthetic of the modern mind, the modern city its emblem.

My point is not that she is the major influence in this aesthetic of fragments but that the change in language form—disintegration, absences, incoherence—occurred in her work in paradigmatic fashion. The language mirrored a reality not yet born. It was a sort of x-ray vision that had scanned the future and, to the extent it made centerlessness visible, even familiar, it helped to bring that future about.

The Publishing History

The publishing history of Dickinson's poetry testifies to the inherent modernism of its language and the impact of its deranged corpus. By a process of natural selection, it seems, the poems generally of conventional themes and less threatening language and candor predominated in the first editions that appeared in the 1890s. Editions with new poems and a noticeably stronger strain of contorted language and perverse sensibility—the problematic poems, that is—began with the aptly titled *The Single Hound* in 1914 and continued in a sporadic, sometimes misrepresenting, way by editors of varying scrupulousness and purpose. The volumes of both new and previously published poems that came out in 1929 and in 1945 contain the modernist temper and difficulty in the most concentrated grouping.

Inescapably, the spotty succession of editions, the hit-or-miss selection of poems, and the arbitrary attempts to make categories of the poems reflect, indeed reenact, the poet's own lack of an agenda. The most sensitive and skillful of the editors were unable to make a unified body or a smooth progression, whether thematic or stylistic, certainly not chronological because of the absence of reliable dating of the manuscripts. The texts were fragmented individually and as a canon, arbitrary in their focuses, start-and-stop in their attention, bright capsules shuffled in together. But by 1924, when Conrad Aiken, in his preface to a selection of the poems, placed her among the finest poets in the language, the disorder that stemmed from the poet's lack of a design was acceptable, even fashionable.

A list of the editions graphically shows the scattered sequence that, as surface contours visibly express deep earth stresses out of sight, reflects not only the unfortunate division between the inheritors and holders of the manuscripts themselves but much more significantly the poet's irremediable disorder.

1890   *Poems of Emily Dickinson.* Edited by Mable Loomis Todd and T. W. Higginson. Boston: Roberts Brothers.

1891   *Poems by Emily Dickinson,* Second Series. Edited by T. W. Higginson and Mable Loomis Todd. Boston: Roberts Brothers.

1896   *Poems by Emily Dickinson,* Third Series. Edited by Mabel Loomis Todd. Boston: Roberts Brothers.

1894   *Letters of Emily Dickinson.* Edited by Mabel Loomis Todd. 2 vols. Boston: Roberts Brothers.

1914   *The Single Hound.* Edited by Martha Dickinson Bianchi. Boston: Little, Brown.

1924   *The Complete Poems of Emily Dickinson.* Edited by Martha Dickinson Bianchi and Alfred Leete Hampson. Boston: Little, Brown.

1924   *The Life and Letters of Emily Dickinson.* By Martha Dickinson Bianchi. Boston: Houghton Mifflin.

1929   *Further Poems of Emily Dickinson.* Edited by Martha Dickinson Bianchi and Alfred Leete Hampson. Boston: Little, Brown.

1930   *The Poems of Emily Dickinson.* Edited by Martha Dickinson Bianchi and Alfred Leete Hampson. Boston: Little, Brown.

1931   *Letters of Emily Dickinson.* New and enlarged edition. Edited by Mabel Loomis Todd. New York: Harper.

1932   *Emily Dickinson Face to Face: Unpublished Letters with Notes and Reminiscences.* By Martha Dickinson Bianchi. Boston: Houghton Mifflin.

1935   *Unpublished Poems of Emily Dickinson.* Edited by Martha Dickinson Bianchi and Alfred Leete Hampson. Boston: Little, Brown.

1937   *Poems by Emily Dickinson.* Edited by Martha Dickinson Bianchi and Alfred Leete Hampson. Boston: Little, Brown.

1945   *Bolts of Melody.* Edited by Mabel Loomis Todd and Millicent Todd Bingham. New York: Harper.

Higginson's article on Dickinson in the *Atlantic Monthly* of October 1891, written to draw attention to the appearance of the second series of poems published that year, indicates not by sophisticated prescience, but because he knows what his readers will find troublesome, certain aspects that were to become elements of modernist poetry: "defiance of form," "irregularities," and "obscurity." The poems that appeared in the three decades after *The Single Hound* in 1914 were more troublesome and thus more in vogue because of their problematic, contorted language and obscure reference. By then, poetic taste had caught up with the poems' clipped, irrelevant stanzaic form, lack of an overall design, their discrepant tone, and their unfinishedness. Amy Lowell had signaled that eventual acceptance in 1916 when, in her talk "American Poets of Today," she fondly called Dickinson "a true pagan" and applauded her exactness of diction and image, her "unrelated" mode of writing, her description by brief, telling strokes.[2] There were exceptions, of course, to the acceptance, indirectly but noticeably in some intrusions by editors, including those of the *Atlantic Monthly*. An example will show how even a twentieth-century editor could turn a fine pictorial moment, one with crucial relevance to adjacent images, into a Sunday school banality. The editor changed "Hemlocks" to "hundred" and then, eliminating the serenely durable aspect of nature Dickinson had intended, he changed "Where" to "When." Dickinson's superior lines endure, but not because she was around to tell her modern editor what was right. In eight lines she grasps the sterility of death. The poem begins "Doom is the House without the Door" and, in her words, ends this way:

> 'Tis varied by the Dream
> Of what they do outside –
> Where Squirrels play – and Berries die –
> And Hemlocks – bow – to God –   (P-475)

Dickinson's timely voice was most apparent in *Further Poems* of 1929 and *Bolts of Melody* in 1945. By the end of the new century's third decade readers had ears and eyes and, yes, stomachs for poems that were difficult, grating, irreverent, grave. The audience was new and the poems matched their impatient and skeptical consciousness. Why this happened is made clear in the editors' introductions to these two exemplary volumes that intruded into the poetic territory of Eliot, Pound, Crane, Stevens, and Williams. The apologia by the poet's niece Martha Dickinson Bianchi and Alfred Hampson in the 1929 book of new poems points up some of the qualities that had by then become not only acceptable but obligatory: "irreverence," "lack of studio finish," a "stark need to know" by a poet who "could not be made to have faith." They went on with a modernist catalogue of candor and compaction: "She pretends nothing . . . It is all laid down without a superfluous gesture." A reader finds "flat fact," "sheer simplicity," and that momentariness and instant penetration the editors described as "her spontaneity in words [that] pried under accepted usage or set fire to it." The problems of the poems in the 1890s—their roughly torn roots with earth still clinging to them—were now virtues to be displayed.

Similarly, *Bolts of Melody* sixteen years later, edited by Millicent Bingham and her mother Mabel Loomis Todd, is virtually an anthology of the modern Dickinson poems of the sort that were appearing at the time in the *Atlantic Monthly* and *Saturday Review*. Mrs. Bingham in her introduction said of the 650 hitherto unpublished poems—the bitter lawsuit brought by the poet's sister Lavinia against Mrs. Todd had prevented their earlier printing—that they were "groupings." By this normally innocuous, now heroic word associated with the brave struggles of modern confusion, she meant the difficulties as evidence of poetic seriousness and genius: several confused texts, some scraps, irregular punctuation and the disregard of linear form in the manuscripts, the obscurity of idea.

Clenched language driven by huge ambition had become one of the expressions of American poetic impatience for primary truths. Dickinson was in the forefront with an unlikely historical precedence and a spinster's country image that made the verse bizarre in a pleasingly decadent but primitivist way. Eliot and Pound of the high modernist manner seem not to have had a thing to say about her work. The correctors of taste, as Eliot called himself and his followers, had excluded her for her primitivism, I suppose, because it was not deliberate, and certainly for her lack of a historical sense and complicated allusion, though of this latter she had plenty. Yet all the while she played the Cockney bee, out of place and crossed by the contrary pulls of April's paradox, part of what became the high decadence of the poet excluded by a materialist society.

Winters admired her for the wrong reason. What he liked was her ability to draw back from irrational Romantic dissolution in spirit, denying the mystical trance, and to stand on her two feet, to feel the iron of her essential human reason.[3] But the truth of the matter, as we have seen, is not that she recognized limits and, except for the life-beyond-death poems that Winters called fraudulent, drew back, but rather that she was the hated chaos itself. She was the very designlessness that Winters abhorred. He was fooled because she said in certain lines, elsewhere contradicted, what he believed to be "the necessary moral adjustments" to that boundary.

> Our feet were almost come
> To that odd Fork in Being's Road,
> Eternity – by Term –
>
> Our pace took sudden awe –
> Our feet – reluctant – led –   (P-615)

Winters discovered in this woman of surpassing linguistic power, as other critics have, what he wanted to find in the first place. In the profusion of pieces it is easy.

More appropriate is the view of Dickinson as a greatly endowed poet whose equally great mental difficulties and strengths thrust from her, as Roland Barthes would say, a style as a closed personal process, not an intention but a necessity, a product of the carnal structure. That style erupted as the language of loss, incoherence, failed sequence. If we read her work aright and find some of the signs of her uniqueness—where she stood outside and free of any tradition—we see, not unlike the case of Eliot, the origins in a private life of what was to become one of the public forces in American poetry. The Dickinson idiom, like the web that Valéry's spider builds, waited for the age which would be its mirroring ground and for which it would become an articulating voice.

A Feminist Intelligence

Dickinson's aggressive, self-perceiving style activated as well a radically feminist intelligence. The medium possessed new scanning capabilities and, instinctively and audaciously, an x-ray penetration. It made, to use Wyndham Lewis' words for a later literary time, new eyes for women.

Her idiom perceived the minute activity beneath exteriors, the intensity and change, the unexpected, all she meant by "denuded Pageant." It discovered the individual psyche as the world's vortex, the person as sufferer, reactor, sensor, with what she called the depths in every consciousness from which we cannot rescue ourselves. It discriminated between two kinds of ripenings, the peach from the outside and the chestnut maturing within (P-332). This was a radical female awareness, a "tropismic" level of intelligence, as Josephine Donovan calls the special regard, an awareness of the inner mind.[4] The language is predisposed to the inward and hidden. In Dickinson, it sees things differently by violating the rules, seeing the intricate workings inside.

What is accomplished is the recovery of the inward sensations of life by assaulting the automatic, the habitually perceived, the prose perception. Her metonymic extractions found the utter novelty of the self's existence. It was a language that enabled Dickinson's hyperconscious speaker to say with simple conviction and accuracy. "I felt my life with both my hands."

The self-deprecating moments, the passivity and docility, all the attitudes that are now among the conventional targets of feminist critical orthodoxies are in Dickinson, but they are obvious and require no more than a note here in passing. Facile description in the poems evokes feminist finger pointing, but it is superficial Dickinson: "one so shy – so ignorant" (P-50); "She bent her docile sails" (P-52). Her speaker in several poems measures herself by a male lover's acceptance, as in poem 968: "I shall be perfect in his sight." Such dependent imagining turns up elsewhere: the poem beginning "My worthiness is all my Doubt – His Merit – all my fear" is feminist allegory. It avoids a story or circumstance, as is characteristic of Dickinson, but displays the parabolic roles of passive reliance and masculine demand and dominance. This is insignificant insight, however, as is the observation that one of the "golden thread" letters when she was almost twenty (April 1850) showing her self-consciousness as a gifted poet is adjacent to another letter describing her mother's illness and her own absorption in "culinary arts," as if domestic obligations were hateful distractions from what mattered most to her. There are several letters confined to female epistolary conventions. Of the letters to the Norcross cousins, Dickinson seems to have undertaken the earliest as part of the rite of the older sister edifying the younger, "poets" together, but the correspondence evolved before long into the custom of remarking mainly, if not exclusively, sickness, death, and faith.[5]

Dickinson's breakthrough into a new feminist vision was accomplished rather by her technique of verbal disconnection with its rift penetration, dissonant mode, and shock of recognition. In the hidden interior she raised to visibility the concealed contradictions, disjunctions, ironies. She found latent terror and hysteria, the psychic plunderers of happiness, the countervailing price of joy, the cost of hope. In doing this, she made a new category of female existence, the classification of life as *mutilation*. The discrepant tropes (rind, gimblet, panther) forced a separation of experience by incursions into the minute actuality of "the soul in pain" and the experiences that "Mangle daintier." The poem (244) shocks one way or another nine instances in a row. It is language with the scanning ability to perceive the hurt that is the precursor to bliss. By the later years, and one would give much to be able to determine more precisely when the deepening occurred, she could send the language diving into the wreck: "The Ruin was within / Oh cunning wreck that told no tale / And let no Witness in" (P-1123).

Her violative language had an eye for experiences that crosscut, contradicted: "She – was mute from transport – / I – from agony" (P-27). It is strained, hysteroid language: "I held my spirit to the Glass, / To prove it possibler" (P-351). The hallucinatory excursions surveyed in protosurrealist language were an element of the new. In the end, it was the pitch of the words—ironic, understated sometimes, grisly, offbeat ("I am alive – I guess")—that Robert Lowell, Plath, Sexton, Rich, and others were to reproduce: a language excruciatingly precise in adversity.

Identity and the psychic alteration that shows its achievement became central elements in the scrutinizing ability of this inherently feminine Dickinson idiom. Surely certain aspirations in her poems, especially the "vision of latitudes unknown," are a transposing of her intense need for identity and, beyond that, fame. Outside recognition is a latent plea in the ideal-contemplating poems, the thought of the Blue Peninsula of fulfillment; they are in part her metaphorical handling of her poet's life and need. But the more incising angle of a woman's vision begins just as early, in a poem dated about 1858, "To fight aloud, is very brave." It is basic to the wife poems. In the urgent grasp for identity that her verses exhibit, the wife poems hold the paradigmatic cultural label she appropriated for her own definition of identity. Wife, Woman, Queen gathered up the ideas of maturity, identity, literary fame, and, finally, the ultimate state of immortality.

Though her insistent language of identity activated feminine awareness in a later time (she is regularly referred to now as the "foremother" of women writers), there was the childlike voice that showed simultaneously the Dickinson who was very much a part of her era, taking up the self-demeaning female role. We cringe for the artist but know that remarks such as those to Bowles when he was in Europe are an inescapable part of the uneven expression of this poetic force called Dickinson. The lines to Bowles in 1862, the year she was writing dozens of her most forceful poems, show us the reverse side of the modernist edge on which we have focused. They slavishly take up the convention of sincerity enclosed in innocence: "I dont know how many will be glad to see you, because I never saw your whole friends, but I have heard, that in large Cities – noted persons chose you." The wife poems, and in particular the gun poem, are the urgent search for identity, that pursuit of the needful feminine intelligence raised to impressive concentration.

Part of the audacious feminist intelligence that drove the Dickinson idiom emerged as sarcasm directed toward the stereotype. In "Title Divine – is Mine," the poet condescends toward the conventional role of wife as subservient, cooing. In the letter to Graves she associated herself with the chickens who "crow and whisper." In both cases, obliquely but recognizably, carried there by the probing edge of her language, she is beginning to descend into the lives of women. When her speaker's voice came out directly, as it did in the P-508 worksheet, her language stark with feeling, it pierced the surface, exploded an outrageous pun on "Ceded," and cut away the "half unconscious Queen" with impunity: "I'm ceded – I've stopped being Their's," the female voice announces:

> The name They dropped upon my face
> With water, in the country church
> Is finished using, now,
> And They can put it with my Dolls.

Dickinson's disorderly but penetrating force had begun to create new categories for observing a woman's life. It found a range of troubled being that was peculiarly female in its terms because of the intrinsic nature of her tropes. The inner territory, "the Precinct raw" as she called it in a late scrap, was made visible by the new retina her language provided. It saw with stark clarity the killing aspects of women's lives: division of self, assault, breakdown, life diminished, life in the aftermath.

It disclosed how a self under stress could separate into parts, one a mask of composure and the other the disintegration within. Her language accomplished this in compressed paradox junctures of the sort the phrase "this sufferer polite" suggests in the irreverent poem 388. She perceived the separation in poems where psychic trauma lies out of sight behind a charade, as in the riddling poem "I breathed enough to take the Trick." In that hard-faced poem the careful, impersonal understatement changes life subtly, linguistically, and unannounced into inanimate machine: "How numb the Bellows feels!"

Her words perceived pain with a clarity that transformed it into beauty. "Delight," she wrote in a brief mid-career aesthetic of adversity, "becomes pictorial – / When viewed through Pain" (P-572). Delight as difficult as stalactite formed with unsurpassed compactness in oxymoronic pairs like "easy torment" and "ghastly holiday" where pain becomes a reprieve because it is more tolerable than the alternative state. The same frictional technique operates in phrases like "suffocate – with easy wo" (P-312). Language cuts across itself and in the process creates this category of pain that is masked and mixed inseparably from its beauty and joy. The poet accomplished the compound by cutting the stereotype straight through with its denial, that is, with psychic reality.

There is an accurate eye in her language also for illness cut through by wit, leading to the desperate swagger we know more recently from Sylvia Plath. Dickinson had done it a century earlier in the homely plaint of the woman's life, "Dont put up my Thread and Needle." Emotional instability dramatized through the intimate confessional tone we have come to know from the tradition of women's poetry in our century is already in Dickinson's language by her early thirties:

> take the Balance
> That tips so frequent, now,
> It takes me all the while to poise –
> And then – it doesn't stay –   (P-576)

The language perceives subtle breakdown because the terms of disconnection—seams coming apart, balls of yarn unraveling—portray the undoing more terrifyingly for being slow and soft. More starkly, the disintegration brought on by psychic suffering, that pure Dickinson category, is the unswerving focus in "I felt a Funeral in my Brain." The poem offers a cold new intelligence of pain minutely observed, sustained, surreal. The wreck lies submerged in the brilliantly maintained metaphor of a floor collapsed by overload.

Mutilation, the self violated by a lover or by fate, Eros that wounds – these are categories of existence as well for which Dickinson's language had a uniquely sensitive grain. Her constructions give as they take away, in the plundering manner Poulet noted a long time ago: "It is simple . . . But." This is the characteristic takeaway motion of her language. It engages the reader rather than offending because it sings before it jolts. The mutilation comes with the implications that cling as the meaning's afterglow. Here her lines propose characteristically that maturation comes within, disclosed only by tribulation. The image of ripening is the heart of wit:

> A Process in the Bur –
> Which Teeth of Frosts – alone disclose –
> In still October Air –   (P-332)

Dickinson joins opposites with surgical wit when she writes of "a Bliss like Murder" or asserts "We love the Wound / The Dirk Commemorate." Inverted in the way we are beginning to see is a woman's perspective, the violence is inside the images, "The mob within the heart" and the emblematic figure of the territory of Dickinson's idiom: "a hurricane / In a congenial ground" (P-1745).

The state of being used or assaulted is plotted by this language of inward plundering. In poem 603 the passive speaker is used, then labeled, the willing submission tainted subtly by the dehumanizing quality of her mechanic language: "He found my Being – set it up – / Adjusted it to place." Another poem conceals the terror of the assault in a disarmingly soft phrase at the opening: "He fumbles at your Soul." Erotic voyeurism in Dickinson is nonthreatening when the roles are played by the bee and the buttercup or the lily. But elsewhere there is a brutality of language barely coated by stock garden images anticipating the mode of Plath and Rich, who could have written lines in the poem that begins "I tend my flowers for thee." The tropes that follow abruptly stop us with their brutal suggestiveness.

> My Fuchsia's Coral Seams
> Rip – while the Sower – dreams –
>
> Geraniums – tint – and spot –
> Low Daisies – dot –

A New Intelligence

> My Cactus – splits her Beard
> To show her throat –   (P-339)

Finally published in 1929, the poem is a compounding of Eros and laceration that a much later generation of poets, without perhaps having read Dickinson, adopted as their special stratagem to open a new view of their own lives.

This frightful experience and others are held in the acute consciousness to which Dickinson's language gives voice. The single hound pursues. The time of aftermath is when it heels most urgently. The idiom has an eye for "Pain's Successor" and, in an instinctively artful way, for the anticlimactic moments: an eye for the dull, the stunned but minutely sensing intelligence of afterward. Words threaten as softly as this: "There is a Languor of the Life." Life after life's meaning has finished, after "Existence . . . stopped," becomes experience seen anew in flat rhythms and tropes of hollowness.

Dickinson's art enters moments of turning that inaugurate these stretches of aftermath. Crisis in her language can thus be the fullest sort of blooming, after which there is in the entire universe only the fact of the consciousness surviving. Those crises, in her high-resolution film, can be superbly malevolent. The poem that begins " 'Twas like a Maelstrom, with a notch" locates the threshold of madness with a fidelity other idioms necessarily concede. This is Dickinson's territory, the congenial ground of her language. The poem studies the nightmarish state that is like a maelstrom, like a fiend's paws, like the dungeon before the gibbet. The category her language has made here involves a profoundly feminine intelligence of terror and reprieve.

A final category her language newly surveyed and made visitable was not simply death-in-life when the psyche folds up but, by Dickinsonian wit and sensational acceleration, the death that occurs again and again. Comparing this repeated annihilation to trees that have been struck by lightning or by blight, whose leaves show the damage, Dickinson writes of a further category when "We – who have the Souls – / Die oftener – Not so vitally" (P-314).

The deaths she could not for long leave out of her poetry were metaphors for loss of self. Certainly her speaker rehearsed her own death, as for example in the strange poem beginning "They wont frown always – some sweet Day" where death is troped as "the Ice that filled the lisping full." But her language was most innovatively perceptive in disclosing what later women poets with a new approach have taken as their own territory: the pain of accommodating to a diminished life as well as the new perceptions that come with scrutiny of what Dickinson called with maximum control the "Demurer Circuit." It was, from her remarkably prescient, even postmodernist, angle "the narrow Round." Or this new event: "the slow exchange of Hope – / For something passiver." Or this category of resignation: "Content / Too Steep for looking up."

Suicide

Perhaps the most conspicuous province of the radical feminist intelligence is self-destruction. Dickinson surveyed that realm of final option with a language that, for the first time in American poetry, looked at suicide directly, held its facets to the light of an acute consciousness, and with a keenness unparalleled until recently gave voice to the exhilaration of getting close to death. Her imagining of dying arrested readers with its simple, unflinching, audacious observation. "'Tis Dying – I am doing," she wrote in poem 692 in her regular syllabic count, "but I'm not afraid to know." The subject, as I said earlier, was really a matter of style for her, but in its modern feminist aspect it seems an even more powerful stimulant. If suicide for Dickinson was not an actual possibility or even a philosophical conjecture, she made it in her pretended speeches a crucial trope for a withdrawn life.

> When One has given up One's life
> The parting with the rest
> Feels easy.   (P-853)

So many of Dickinson's poems skirt the subject of suicide or suggest it or face it straight on that we know, even as we cannot fully understand why and only partially understand how, that the matter held profound significance for her and for her work. She called it "my Right of Frost" (P-640) and meant by it the choosing of "Death's privilege." Elective death in her artfully tangential diction is the constant alternative by which, simply put in the terms of commerce, "One might depart at option / From enterprise below!" (P-54). Suicide is as well, in the poem that begins "Unto like Story – Trouble has enticed me," the most alluring of propositions: it beckons, an "Etruscan invitation."

To be sure, our interpretation of the suicide theme must take account of Christian doctrine in Dickinson's work and take care to subtract it from particular poems before judging their special viewpoint. There was in Dickinson's era, especially before the Civil War as I noted, a pervasive literary death nostalgia, not much elevated above Sunday school cant. Early, she wrote with all the dead weight of clichés:

> I wait thy far, fantastic bells –
> Announcing me in other dells –
> Unto the different dawn!   (P-24)

Her speaker in an allegorical poem from the middle years stands in ritual fashion before death's door to ask after a friend who died. And death also meant in this hoary convention a freedom at last for the weary, as in the last stanza of "A prison gets to be a friend."

But the poet's momentary meditations on self-termination are as direct and compact as they are on any other subject, rarely indulging in extended lugubriousness. The poem "Going to Heaven!" with the lines "I'm glad I don't believe it / For it w'd stop my breath – " is of this clipped sort even as the alarming implication intrudes. She means stopping the breath quite precisely here, and that single word "stop" alerts us to think again on the suicidal possibilities in the apparently unreflective opening lines: "Because I could not stop for death (that is, end my life myself) he kindly stopped for me." But just as often her speaker contemplates in her quick way the impossibility of self-destruction. Contemplating a gnat's blind self-battering, the persona contrasts her own inability to do the same:

> Nor like Himself – the Art
> Upon the Window Pane
> To gad my little Being out –
> And not begin – again –   (P-612)

Dickinson recognized elsewhere in her verse the impossibility of the act, for she called the self

> that Repealless thing –
> A Being – impotent to end –
> When once it has begun –   (P-565)

The letters do not, I think, support any theory of Dickinson's propensities to suicide. Yet in one passage there is an offhand implication when she writes as simply as possible that the pain of parting can be forestalled by death: "Parting is one of the exactions of a Mortal Life. It is bleak – like Dying, but occurs more times. To escape the former, some invite the last" (L-399).

Ellipsis conceals the nub of poem 384, but the argument addressed to the reader once again is unmistakable, a tight circle. Your soul is as free as the eagle to escape the body's torture, except that the body's mind is the soul's captor, and thus enemy. The soul remains captive because consciousness depends upon the captivity, and consciousness knows (this is true Dickinson) that the soul's "liberty" involves its own death. That enduring Dickinson wisdom reappears in this last stanza, where we realize that the first line ends with a full stop and the second line, crammed into six syllables, stands for "The alternative of dying" and provides the subject of the two-line predicate that follows:

> No drug for Consciousness – can be –
> Alternative to die
> Is Nature's only Pharmacy
> For Being's Malady.   (P-786)

The subject lured even as it baffled. Her dilemma takes form explicitly in the fragment where she wrote "it is amazing that the fascination of our predicament [exclusion from comprehension in the face of death] does not entice us more" (PF-70). Her earliest poem on suicide as a serious alternative seems to be the one beginning "My Wheel is in the dark!" Evidently the metaphorical wheel is the heart, the interior paddle wheel driven by the blood's current. Such strangely acute awareness of mortality leads into the ambiguous but suggestive declaration: "My foot is on the Tide! / An unfrequented road." Suicide surely is the implied possibility held out in the early poem that begins "I hav'nt told my garden yet" and ends with the disclosure that "within the Riddle / One will walk today."

Suicide poems and obliquely suggestive ones make a considerable list. Sometimes the first lines tell the story:

> Just lost, when I was saved!
> At last, to be identified!
> If I'm lost – now –

I breathed enough to take the Trick
What if I say I shall not wait!
I read my sentence – steadily –
Good Morning – Midnight –
'Twas just this time, last year, I died
A Wife – at Daybreak I shall be –
The Manner of its Death
To put this World down, like a Bundle –
I had no Cause to be awake –
This Chasm, Sweet, upon my life
Escape is such a thankful Word

Interior lines in other poems like this one appear partly frantic with death's titillation:

'Tis an instant's play.
'Tis a fond Ambush –
Just to make Bliss
Earn her own surprise!

But – should the play
Prove piercing earnest –
Should the glee – glaze –
In Death's – stiff – stare –

Would not the fun
Look too expensive!   (P-338)

There is thus in Dickinson's idiom of acute consciousness the origin of an extreme feminine vision. Faithful to the interior experience, her language saw the raw precinct with a new clarity and generative candor. It was a language that possessed impatience and strenuousness, a penetrating edge and violence. Dickinson devised its grammar out of her provincial directness, out of her cells. Its vision opened on an interior wasteland cut through by exaltation. The idiom made art—however limited it was by its impulses and its lack of a project—out of deprivation and anxiety. It was not a system but an art of momentary wounds and plundering and estrangement. To borrow some of Stevens' phrasing, it was "an alteration of words that was a change of nature . . . The countrymen were changed and each constant thing. Their dark-colored words had redescribed the citrons."

An Irregular Perception

But Dickinson's language is an irregular instrument of perception and, therefore, of knowledge. To be sure, it performs with brilliance as an expression of the probing consciousness: with concentration, aggressiveness, and the shock of recognition. Daring in its violation of normal selectional rules, it catches motion and establishes the immediacy of a voice. It enlists one lexical realm to speak against another, thus making the language dramatic in itself as it speaks itself. It exercises astonishing control over destructive emotional content, possesses a capacity for honesty and psychological accuracy and, above all of these, displays an elemental wisdom.

The idiom shows us how attentive consciousness can be. It creates by the derangement of sense a vision that reaches to the absence at the core of the mind. She sent her language into the breach sometimes by a route of negative perception. But her short word arcs make no reconciliation, provide no answers, only rarely consolations. Their severing of the connections of discourse and the patterning lines of more conventional syntax reveals not growth but the pillaging of life. The language has no duration, so that it labels with glittering strokes but builds no edifice of conviction. In a word, it is divorced from what Pound called the prose tradition in verse which he said is part of the desired "centaur," the cross between the thinking, word-arranging, clarifying faculties of prose and the energizing, sentient, musical faculties of poetry.[6] Conscious in the extreme of itself, this proseless language insists on the discrepancy between itself and representational language that mirrors a densely layered reality, cuts the familiar labels apart, and carves up the accustomed surfaces. Dickinson used it not to join but to distinguish, to pick out discrete instances of private sensation: a certain slant of light, the long shadow in the grass, the distance the single will sees in the look of things. Her language opened up the moment between the instant when something is about to happen and the instant when it has, that is, the snap of time that requires no architecture in an art to signify it. Her language abhorred the expired imagination but had no taste for lingering.

With such virtues of incision and shock and the analytical estrangement that the monitoring of disintegration made possible, she made diving into the wreck possible. Hers was a language of curiosity that flew to the gap between need and destiny. When the mind speaks, it simultaneously knows in the same way as it speaks. As Dickinson wrote, so she disposed of the world. Her language discovers much that is terrifying, sometimes sublimely terrifying, in our knowledge.

But for all its arresting local strategies, this remarkable poetry language is without a binding capability. With no presiding hypothesis, it lacked the ability to see the multitude of facts that in turn induce an appropriately capacious architectural form. The poetry could not enter the complicated world. Highly personal, it drew on no authority outside its immediate ends. An instrument of glimpses, it seems to make the intense inner event separable from the universal. Bound in irrelation except for their common idiom, the 1775 brief poems written through all those years face one another closed and independent, subject to no other family claims or the check of a comprehensible philosophy.

Dickinson had the one strict hymn form in which to crowd her language and thus only one eye motion. The narrow beam from that constant stylistic eye saw its own narrow world. It was peculiarly without larger expectations because it was without a broad organizing capacity. Experience thus aggregates but does not coalesce. This, I would say, is why no editor to this day has arranged her poetry in its own best order. The poems, in the final evaluation and for all their power, are, one by one, one-dimensional, a poetry of incorrigible exclusion.

Terminal Modernism

Limited to a vision of restlessness and pieces, with intense power that flashes and stops, the Dickinson idiom is a cloistered language for postmodern poets, and particularly for the women poets whose lives it discovered. It can serve superbly for moments of a style, for instants of highlight, but it cannot be a model for a body of work or a body of knowledge.

This poetry of single sharp impressions is a treacherous code because its impressions are isolated points, single eye movements, no more than fitful in their duration or range of coverage. Without healing its cut or recuperating its bleakness, her language gives us a world that glitters and affrights. Brilliant in momentary effect, it nourishes itself, the attention excited by the lexical frisson that trips an instant of terror or blindness.

As in photography, I suggested earlier, reality is appropriated by pieces. Each of these languages at the threshold of the modern era changed our perceptions. Each separated the expressive medium from the reality that was its ostensible subject and became the subject itself. In that process the world became disjunct and a piecemeal reality. Dickinson's poems do not invoke a full world. Instead, they are the vast hoard of a traveler's snapshots without an itinerary of the trip or a map showing the destination. The momentariness, the language flashes, signal the unique qualities in the Dickinson idiom that, for all its arresting power and audacity, render it a hazard for later poets.

1. *The language has a limited capacity for ordinary observations.* It cuts apart, distinguishes, intensifies, but does not trace the self coming to terms with reality, rarely resolves a truly complex event. Withdrawn from social experience, it tends to locate itself in the aftermath, possessing no sense of an ending, only the postlapsarian drift and incomprehension we have noted. The axis of its vision, to use Emerson's phrase, is really not coincident with the axis of things, and so the world appears not transparent but opaque. Narrative and the other discursive capabilities of language are unattempted, and so the possible buttressing by a proximate prosaic world of experience is missing.

Because this kind of poetry often does not look at the actual world, its limitations for a postmodern poet in the world have to be severe. The Dickinson idiom rigorously evades meaning. Instead, as we have seen, there is frustration in the poems, an obscure agitation that often does not break through into consciousness: the poems are troubled by knowledge for which there is no adequate structure to perceive it. The result is an art of strictly limited perception facing complexities it may not address. Like early computer chips of sixteen functions, Dickinson poems are unequipped to handle the information on structures that function sixteen to the fourth power.

The idiom seems inappropriate for those times when we ask for entry into experience and a clarification of it, perhaps even a synthesis of it that will suffice. The Dickinson idiom in its pure form, without prose capacity, makes much of the world impenetrable. It is a language that, by withdrawing from the world into its own performance, into sensational figures and souvenirs, is a way of refusing the world.

2. *It is a style incapable of consolidation, brilliantly doomed to ignorance.* It is linguistically pathogenic, a language of failed maturity.

Dickinson's buzzing fly of incomprehension is its emblem. The poet who would use this narrow, evasive idiom today must do as Dickinson did: "Deprived of other Banquet," one of her poems says, "I entertained Myself."

The semiology of the Dickinson texts establishes the significance of this self-possessing. The poems, superb realizations of a few elements, drift in a systemless indetermination, animated by a spontaneity that makes them an influence for only momentary effects. The poetry seeks no resolving chord, registers mostly diversity and dissonance. Hers is a fundamental modernism comparable in centrality to the language by which Joyce created a crisis of literature a half century later. H. G. Wells wrote to Joyce in 1928 regarding *Finnegans Wake* and its lack of "a big unifying and concentrating process . . . a *progress*": "You began with a system of values in stark opposition to reality. Your mental existence is obsessed by a monstrous system of contradictions . . . What is the result? Vast riddles." An art without progress: this describes the poetry of Dickinson. Wells's world, our world in part, is not a world that Dickinson's idiom will enter, take up, unify. Much earlier than Joyce but with his urgency of consciousness, instinctive in expression, Dickinson created an idiom characterized by purposelessness and irrepressible speech. Not Stevens' art as order or Frost's art as a stay against confusion, it is the idiolect of that confusion: existence in purposelessness and language.

A further significance is now to be seen as equally central: the acts of omission and evasion are the profoundest reflexive self-reading of the Dickinson texts by themselves. The poems, so to speak, see their own incoherence, the blind alley they have made with such elan. It is situated in the contortion of the language wedged into the hymn form that left no space for clarity, meaning, progress. What, indeed, what ripeness after then?

3. *Dickinson's spontaneity, self-assaulting and self-doubting, is the destructive strain in American modernism.* Beside the conventionally recognized modernisms by which we make our age roughly intelligible, Dickinson's is now seen to be another, the autogenetic. For all its genius—and it is unsurpassed in its way—it is an idiom of subjectlessness, one that holds no dialogue with history and thus has no location in it, cannot see time or duration, and borders finally on that most inviting but distracting of final resorts, a retreat from reason.

Some contemporary poets, I think especially women poets, are like Dickinson embarking again in the same freedom of intense and sporadic power with its artistic and perceptual limitation. In that case the poet takes on the terrible and narrowing office of becoming her own authority. This condition in fact already has become, in some current work, a sober self-dramatizing state in which solemnity prevails, its individual doom "Possess each separate Consciousness – / August – Absorbed – Numb."

Dickinson activated at long distance some of these aspects of the contemporary woman poet's intelligence. She made diving into the wreck a communal vocation. In that freedom of withdrawal and artful whim, with the dispersed way in which the words flash and the links between things are unattended, a world is constituted with a similar disorder and incoherence. After the initial activating and the recurrent exhilaration, the Dickinson language must then prove to be a medium of terminal daring. Because it achieves no experiential breadth and holds no dialogue with history, it has no time of its own. Like Dickinson's emblematic fly, the poems are active and bright but uncertain, and just there is the potential strain of disintegration. Wordsworth, more alarmed than we need be, called that language without inherent thought a "counter-spirit" that does not feed but unremittingly and noiselessly works to derange, to subvert, to vitiate, and to dissolve.[7]

The old system of positivities was transformed in this woman's work, and in a far different and contrary way from that of the great builders Emerson and Whitman. Where they swam in the world with their absorptive styles, she did not resign herself silently to the bewildering contingency, but kept writing and thereby allowed her soul to defend itself.

She was, then, a participant in the great language change that led into modern and postmodern poetry in America. It was not so much a shift in theme or idea at first but, in the way I have proposed, a shift in language that helped to bring about the changes in perception.

Dickinson is one of the writers who over the last hundred years, like Joyce, pulled literature into a crisis in which language ceased to think or represent but instead performed its own existence. That change, as vexing as it was inevitable in her case, is all the burden of her remarkable gun poem. Whoever would take up the Dickinson idiom must heed the caveat in the question she posed in poem 1656:

A New Intelligence

What Buccaneer would ride without a surety from the wind or a schedule of the tide?

But it is this woman of the finless mind who devised one of the idioms for the chartless modern venture. Speech without design, signifying without purpose: here is the root of modernism. That force of poetic destruction, that self-garrisoned individual of acute consciousness, without identity and looking for a Master, the unique bodiless body of work, the instinctive formlessness of her thought, her hidden revolution in American poetry that began the menacing ascendance of consciousness—all this fearful ordeal of art is represented in the proper name Emily Dickinson.

NOTES

INDEX OF FIRST LINES

INDEX

Notes

1. The Crucial Experience

1. Texts of poems, with the Johnson numbering adopted, are from *The Poems of Emily Dickinson*, ed. Thomas H. Johnson, 3 vols. (Cambridge: The Belknap Press of Harvard University Press, 1958).

2. *The Sense of An Ending* (New York: Oxford Univerity Press, 1967), pp. 44-45.

3. *In Defense of Reason* (New York: William Morrow, 1947), p. 289.

4. This phrase and another noted later are quoted in J. Hillis Miller, "The Geneva School," *Modern French Criticism*, ed. John K. Simon (Chicago: University of Chicago Press, 1972), p. 284.

5. The Johnson numbering of the letters is adopted from *The Letters of Emily Dickinson*, ed. Thomas H. Johnson, 3 vols. (Cambridge: The Belknap Press of Harvard University Press, 1958). The abbreviation PF designates prose fragments printed in *Letters*, vol. 3.

6. *After Great Pain* (Cambridge: Harvard University Press, 1971), p. 292.

7. For a discussion of this characteristic shift, see my essay "Emily Dickinson: The Poetics of Doubt," *Emerson Society Quarterly*, 60 (Summer 1970), pp. 86-93.

8. *In Defense of Reason*, p. 293.

2. Strangely Abstracted Images

1. This passage and those that follow are from the chapter entitled "The Private World: Poems of Emily Dickinson," in *Poetry and Experience* (Boston: Houghton Mifflin, 1961).

Notes

2. *Literary Essays of Ezra Pound* (London: Faber and Faber, 1954), pp. 151, 154.

3. *Critical Essays* (Evanston: Northwestern University Press, 1972), p. 157.

4. *Le Point de départ* (Paris: Plon, 1964), p. 40, translation from Sarah N. Lawall, *Critics of Consciousness* (Cambridge: Harvard University Press, 1968), p. 83.

3. The Puzzling Idiom

1. See Lois A. Cuddy, "The Latin Imprint on Emily Dickinson's Poetry: Theory and Practice," *American Literature*, 50 (March 1978), 74–84, for some terms in Latin grammar that designate but cannot, it seems to me, account for Dickinson's waywardness.

2. For a fine discussion of Dickinson's inveterate indefiniteness, specifically her use of indeterminate metaphors, see Roland Hagenbüchle, "Precision and Indeterminacy in the Poetry of Emily Dickinson," *ESQ*, 20 (1974), 33–56.

3. Hagenbüchle, pp. 36, 38, 41.

4. (New Haven: Yale University Press, 1975), p. 29.

4. How Dickinson Wrote

1. "Emily Dickinson's Notation," *Emily Dickinson: A Collection of Critical Essays*, ed. Richard B. Sewall (Englewood Cliffs: Prentice-Hall, 1963), p. 79.

2. A facsimile edition of the packets, edited by Ralph Franklin, was published by Harvard University Press in 1980.

3. See Ann Douglas, "Heaven Our Home," in David E. Stannard, ed., *Death in America* (Philadelphia: University of Pennsylvania Press, 1975), p. 63. See also my chapter on the hymn in *The Art of Emily Dickinson's Early Poetry* (Cambridge: Harvard University Press, 1966).

4. *The Complete Works of Ralph Waldo Emerson*, VIII (Boston: Houghton Mifflin, 1904), 46.

5. Disabling Freedom

1. Quoted in Richard B. Sewall, *The Life of Emily Dickinson* (New York: Farrar, Straus and Giroux, 1974), p. 26.

2. "Vesuvius at Home: The Power of Emily Dickinson," *Parnassus*, 5(Fall-Winter 1976), 51–52.

3. Elizabeth F. Perlmutter, "Hide and Seek: Emily Dickinson's Use of the Existential Sentence," *Language and Style*, 10 (Spring 1977), 110.

4. Louis A. Renza, "The Veto of the Imagination: A Theory of Autobiography," *New Literary History*, 9 (Autumn 1977), 13.

5. William Packard, "Craft Interview with Anne Sexton," *New York Quarterly*, 1 (Summer 1970), p. 11.

6. *Poems*, I, xxviii.

6. A Finless Mind

1. Jay Leyda, *The Years and Hours of Emily Dickinson*, II (New Haven: Yale University Press, 1960), 58.

2. *Illuminations* (New York: Schocken, 1976), p. 203.

3. *The Puritan Origins of the American Self*, p. 112.

4. See *Victorian Poetry and Poetics*, ed. Walter E. Houghton and G. Robert Stange (Boston: Houghton Mifflin, 1959) p. 470.

5. *The Life of Emily Dickinson*, 205.

7. The Curse of Spontaneity

1. *Thomas Hardy and British Poetry* (New York: Oxford University Press, 1972), p. vii.

2. *The Poems of Robert Frost* (New York: Random House, 1946), pp. xix–xxi.

3. Stannard, *Death in America*, p. 55.

4. "Vesuvius at Home," pp. 62, 57.

5. *A Map of Misreading* (New York: Oxford University Press, 1975), p. 186.

6. The fullest discussion of the poem is in Robert Weisbuch, *Emily Dickinson's Poetry* (Chicago: University of Chicago Press, 1975), pp. 25–39. In the end his reading is overrationalized. When he says the poem repudiates the act of "making a thing of one's human self in order to gain power" (p. 38), he is too philosophical and too literal in reading the poem.

7. "Essay Upon Epitaphs, III," *The Prose Works of William Wordsworth*, ed. W. J. B. Owen and Jane W. Smyser (Oxford: The Clarendon Press, 1974), II, 84.

8. "Vesuvius at Home," 66.

Notes

8. Dickinson and American Modernism

1. See Nancy F. Cott, *The Bonds of Womanhood* (New Haven: Yale University Press, 1977), pp. 23, 164–169.
2. *Letters of Wallace Stevens*, ed. Holly Stevens (New York: Knopf, 1966), p. 402.
3. Vol. LXVIII (October 1891), 452–454.
4. *New York Times Book Review*, November 19, 1978, p. 54.

9. Art After the Fall

1. Cultural shifts may have contributed. "After the French Revolution it was in the nature of 'nature' to change. Suddenly in the late eighteenth century to look about was to see alteration, accelerated speed, and flux." Carl Woodring, "Nature and Art in the Nineteenth Century," *PMLA*, 92 (March 1977), 193.
2. *The Oxford Book of American Verse* (New York: Oxford University Press, 1950), p. xxi.
3. See Klaus Lubbers, *Emily Dickinson: The Critical Revolution* (Ann Arbor: University of Michigan Press, 1968), p. 111.
4. *Blindness and Insight* (New York: Oxford University Press, 1971), p. 171.
5. Besides Bloom's, the studies that ally Emerson and Dickinson most closely include Albert Gelpi's *Emily Dickinson: The Mind of the Poet* and Hyatt Waggoner's *American Poets from the Puritans to the Present*.
6. *New York Times Book Review*, April 1, 1979, p. 31.
7. *In Defense of Reason*, p. 101.
8. *In Defense of Reason*, p. 93.
9. *Naked Poetry*, ed. Stephen Berg and Robert Mezey (Indianapolis: Bobbs-Merrill, 1969), p. 145.

10. A New Intelligence

1. *The Prose of the World* (Evanston: Northwestern University Press, 1973), p. xiii.
2. Lubbers, pp. 111–113.
3. *In Defense of Reason*, p. 288.
4. See the discussion in Annette Kolodny, "Some Notes on Defining a 'Feminist Literary Criticism,' " *Critical Inquiry*, 2 (Autumn 1975), 78.
5. On some women's epistolary habits in the nineteenth cen-

tury, see the ground-breaking essay by William R. Taylor and Christopher Lasch, " 'Two Kindred Spirits': Sorority and Family in New England, 1839–1846," *New England Quarterly*, 36 (1963), 25–41, and subsequent elaborations such as that by Carroll Smith-Rosenberg, "The Female World of Love and Ritual," *Signs*, 1 (Autumn 1975), 1–29.

6. "The Serious Artist," *Literary Essays of Ezra Pound*, p. 52.

7. "Essay Upon Epitaphs, III," *The Prose Works of William Wordsworth*, II, 85.

Index of First Lines

Poem numbers from the variorum edition appear in parentheses.

Index of First Lines

Index of First Lines

Index of First Lines

310

Index

Index

Christian background, 18, 157, 167–169, 288; circumference, 27, 35, 60, 105, 116, 181; change as theme, 226–227; compactness, 37, 51; composition, 94–98; conceptual mysteries, 182–187; consolation, 176–179; death as subject, 4, 13, 127–129, 130, 149, 162, 187–194; devouring language, 130–137; doubt and dejection, 160–170; ellipsis, 39, 43–51, 102; exclusion from comprehension, 170–175, 245–252; feminist intelligence, 280–287; first-person voice, 125–126, 127; field of reference, 146; final lines, 94; first lines, 89–94; fly emblem, 7, 239, 244, 294, 295; fragmentation, 105–112; grammar of absence, 137; grammatical defects, 52–54; gun allegory, 1, 209–218; hymn form, 4, 98–104, 160; hyperbole, 112; idiom of defects, 75; inflections dropped, 52–54; inward vision, 227–228; irregular perception, 291–292; lack of architectural design, 134, 139, 105–112; lack of ars poetica, 5, 140, 184; lack of capacity, 293; lack of coherence, 111, 243; lack of development, 37, 83, 184–185; lack of identifiable speaker, 57–58, 136, 183–184; lack of magnitude, 138–139; lack of narrative, 138; lack of order of perception, 3, 139–140, 153, 184, 291–292; lack of outside reference, 5, 38, 115, 119–125, 183; lack of pronoun referents, 54–55; lack of titles, 185; memory, 154–155; metaphor and metonym, 58–74; metrics, 101–102; microchristus, 149, 167; nihilism, 229; obscurity, 29, 30–31, 58–74, 97; obstacles as revelations, 5; omissions, 5–6, 20; paired lines, 85–86; parallelisms, 85; photography as analogy, 106, 133, 292–293; poetics, 14, 36, 153, 236; polysyllables, 86–89; popular literature as background, 220; primer for reading, 74–80; printing misrepresents, 2–3, 82; publication history, 50, 276–280; puritanism, 70–71, 117, 167, 170; revision, 89–90, 94–97; rift vision, 271–276; style more insistent than meaning, 131–133,

187–194; stylistic difficulties, summary, 134–135; synecdoche, 20–21; syntax, 39–51, 77–80, 102–104, 123–124; technical mysteries solved, 137–142; transposition, 41; tonal qualities, 230–233; unfinishedness, 105, 110, 135, 181–182; visitations as motif, 14–18; violation of selectional rules, 39, 51–52, 55–57, 127; vernacular, 223–225; wife and bride poems, 4, 195–209; withdrawal, 114–119; women poets foreshadowed, 6, 280–287, 290

Dickinson, Emily Norcross, 178–179
Dickinson, Gilbert, 150, 162
Dickinson, Lavinia, 40
Dickinson, Susan Gilbert, 37, 47, 63, 88, 94, 99, 109, 114, 160, 162, 164, 177, 197, 234, 237, 246
Dickinson, (William) Austin, 37, 40, 106, 147, 156, 195, 245
Donovan, Josephine, 281
Douglas, Ann, 190
Dwight, Timothy, 266

Eliot, George, 159, 212
Eliot, T. S., 112, 148, 171, 237, 239, 243, 251, 252, 255, 263, 266, 275, 278, 279, 280
Emerson, Ralph Waldo, 7, 56, 79, 99, 152, 159, 161, 167, 171–172, 176, 204, 219, 227, 230, 239, 242, 243; the fundamental difference, 257–262, 295
Epstein, Jacob, 190, 228, 260, 263
Existentialist criticism, 34–35
Expressive fallacy, 125

Foucault, Michel, 240
Frost, Robert, 106, 183, 185, 187, 241, 242, 271, 294

Gaudier-Brzeska, Henri, 263
Gombrick, Ernst, 36
Gorgias, 176
Graves, John, 3, 145–149, 151, 158, 170, 177, 217, 245–246, 256, 283
Griswold, Rufus, *The Female Poets of America*, 75

Hagenbüchle, Roland, 64
Halleck, Fitz-Greene, 152

Index